A DECLARATION

of

★ ★ ★

INDEPENDENTS

★ ★ ★

A DECLARATION

of

★★★

INDEPENDENTS

★★★

HOW WE CAN BREAK *the*
TWO-PARTY STRANGLEHOLD *and*
RESTORE *the* AMERICAN DREAM

GREG ORMAN

GREENLEAF
BOOK GROUP PRESS

Published by Greenleaf Book Group Press
Austin, Texas
www.gbgpress.com

Distributed by Greenleaf Book Group

For ordering information or special discounts for bulk purchases, please contact Greenleaf Book Group at PO Box 91869, Austin, TX 78709, 512.891.6100.

Design and composition by Greenleaf Book Group and Kim Lance
Cover design by Greenleaf Book Group and Kim Lance
Cover image: Thinkstock/iStock Collection/orderfinishedart

Cataloging-in-Publication data is available.

Print ISBN: 978-1-62634-332-0

eBook ISBN: 978-1-62634-333-7

Part of the Tree Neutral® program, which offsets the number of trees consumed in the production and printing of this book by taking proactive steps, such as planting trees in direct proportion to the number of trees used: www.treeneutral.com

TreeNeutral

Printed in the United States of America on acid-free paper

16 17 18 19 20 21   10 9 8 7 6 5 4 3 2 1

First Edition

For my daughter, Imogen,
who inspires me every day.

CONTENTS

Reclaiming Our Birthright

—— ★ ★ ★ ——

AT THE DAWN OF the 1960s, President John F. Kennedy dared this nation to commit itself to exploring the moon. Asking his fellow citizens to meet this huge challenge, JFK invoked the inspirational words of one of the earliest American political leaders, William Bradford. A Pilgrim and an immigrant, Bradford served as governor of what is now Massachusetts. Speaking in 1630 of the founding of the Plymouth Bay Colony, he declared that all great challenges are accompanied with great difficulties, and both must be "overcome with answerable courage."

We choose to undertake such awesome efforts as conquering space, Kennedy said, "not because they are easy, but because they are hard." Americans of Kennedy's generation were stirred by the president's boldness. And their representatives in Congress—of both political parties—led the way in accepting the president's call.

That wouldn't happen today. Despite scientific advancements that the early astronauts could only dream of, our broken politics won't allow such unity of purpose.

In the twenty-first century, official Washington bickers over how to make nineteenth-century modes of transportation safe. After the May 12, 2015, Amtrak derailment in Philadelphia, the victims' bodies were not yet removed from the wreckage when congressional Republicans began whittling Amtrak's budget. At the same time, Democrats accused Republicans of killing Americans in their zeal for spending cuts.

"You have no idea—no idea—what caused this accident [so] don't use this tragedy that way!" Idaho Republican Representative Mike Simpson admonished New York Democratic Representative Steve Israel. "It was beneath you,"[1] Simpson said, to use the Amtrak tragedy to make a political point.

Actually, no matter what Simpson and Israel might say, most of what passes for discourse in our nation's capital these days is beneath the men and women who represent us in Washington. Nor is what's happening in Congress intended to help the country. It's political theater meant to persuade voters back home that their representatives are "fighting the good fight" on some hot button partisan issue, or highlighting the virtues of one party over the other. It leads nowhere. In placing the interests of their respective parties ahead of the interests of our country, our elected officials have descended into political tribalism and put our country at risk.

This must change. Put plainly, our elected officials are not independent-minded enough. And independence from the party line, from the special interests that control both major political parties through campaign cash, and from extremists who control each party's primary process—that's what this country needs to move forward.

Together, Republicans and Democrats form a ruling duopoly that keeps itself in power by protecting the status quo. Although the two political parties are forever at each other's throats, they really work in tandem to divide the electorate along partisan lines and distract it from the failings of the ruling elite in Washington. They've spent their time and treasure convincing Americans that we are far more different and divided than we actually are. They keep this creaky, corrupt system operational by encouraging Americans to be unhappy with each other. And we are unhappy—with them.

Americans are getting wise to the duopoly's collusion. According to data compiled by Emory University political scientist Alan Abramowitz, a stunning number of Americans now think our politics is rigged. In 1964, the percentage of U.S. voters who agreed with the statement that "government is run by a few big interests looking out for themselves" was 29 percent. In 2012, it was 79 percent.[2]

Poll after poll has found similar levels of dissatisfaction.

Another survey, done in 2014 by EMC Research, asked whether the nation's political leaders "are more interested in protecting their power and privilege than doing what is right for the American people." Eighty-five percent of Americans agreed that the political leaders were in it for themselves.

Two-thirds of the survey's respondents felt that they had "no say" in government.

"People like to say that the country is more divided than ever," said Patrick H. Caddell, the pollster and political analyst who designed the survey. "But in fact the country is united about one thing: that the political class does not represent them and the system is rigged against them."

This problem isn't going to fix itself: A lack of confidence in the two parties is felt acutely by the Millennial Generation. In a 2014 Pew Research Center poll, half of millennials said they identified with neither party.[3] Little wonder: Fully 53 percent of them believe that it's "unlikely" that Social Security will even exist for them when they turn retirement age.[4]

We need to pull back the curtain on a duopoly that divides our country to divert attention from its failure and neglect or our nation's best days will be behind us.

If we don't start facing our country's difficult challenges head-on, our standard of living, our status in the world, and the very existence of the middle class in America are at risk. As a result, we could become the first generation of Americans to leave our children and grandchildren a country that is in worse shape than the one we inherited. The obligation to leave a better country for future generations is the sacred social contract at the foundation of the American Idea.

We cannot stand idly by and allow the ruling elite in Washington to walk us down that path.

It is why I ran for the U.S. Senate in 2014, it is why I am writing this book, and it is why I believe we need to cast off the yoke of partisanship and declare our independence.

I'm not the first person to decry the evils of political parties and call for an insurgency of Independents. Many of our founding fathers— George Washington, John Adams, and James Madison among them— were concerned about the potential detrimental effects that political parties could have on America.

Our elected representatives aren't all bad people. If you apply the familiar test about whether they are people you'd like to have a beer with, many would pass. Most of them initially pursued politics with idealistic intentions. Once in office, however, they became corrupted by the money and power of Washington, D.C., and they grew obsessed with staying in office. Federal judges are appointed for life. Members of Congress behave as though they are, too.

As for the citizens of this nation, too few of us vote. But for those of us who do, too many of us numbly pull the lever for candidates we barely know, based mostly on whether they have a "D" or an "R" after their names. In many cases, what little information we do have about the candidates comes from biased media sources and cynically negative campaign ads that play to our fears and our basest emotions.

We can, and must, do better.

Twenty-five years after John Kennedy's death, Texas businessman H. Ross Perot suggested that his fellow Americans were neglecting their obligations as U.S. citizens. Even while basking in the benefits of a free and prosperous society, Perot said, the people of this great nation were shirking the civic duty that made it all possible. "We're like the inheritors of great wealth in this country," he told an interviewer in 1988. "We've forgotten all the sacrifices that the people who've gone before us made to give us this wonderful life that we have. We accept it, we take it for granted; we think it's our birthright. The facts are, it's precious, it's fragile—it can disappear."[5]

I was a college student in 1988, and that sentiment spoke to me. Three years later, just before Perot mounted an Independent presidential campaign against incumbent Republican president George H. W. Bush and Democratic nominee Bill Clinton, I chose Perot's quote to accompany my photograph in my college yearbook.

At the time Perot ran for president, it had already become a cliché to say that U.S. politics was stalemated by hyper-partisanship. Today, gridlock is even more an established fact of American public life. All of us are paying the price for it. Partisanship inhibits government's ability to perform the basic functions of legislating and governing, whether it's building highways or providing medical care for military veterans. These are duties that voters once expected elected officials to address routinely, in a bipartisan, competent way. Unfortunately, officeholders can no longer succeed at the most fundamental tasks of their jobs, let alone tackle difficult structural problems such as social immobility, decaying inner cities, growing gaps between rich and poor, mismanaged entitlement programs, stagnant wages, and disparities in educational levels by ethnic group and between the U.S. and the rest of the developed world. They have lost sight of the reasons they took office in the first place. They are invested in partisanship, not principle—gamesmanship, not statesmanship.

When is the last time you heard of elected officials who cast votes they knew would cost them their jobs on Capitol Hill?

When is the last time a member of the executive branch—or the judiciary, for that matter—resigned over principle?

The ruling members of our political class treat public service as a lifetime benefit. In the occasional instance when a member of Congress is defeated for reelection—a rarity because of how Republicans and Democrats collude to rig elections to favor the two major parties—they salve their pride by remaining in the capital and getting rich by lobbying their former colleagues. It's the same for those working in the executive branch. Cashing in on a White House stint is a primary perk these days of working for a president. Whether it's modifying a position on a bill with an eye toward feathering their own nest after they leave Congress or accepting campaign cash from a special interest in exchange for a vote on a bill, it's corrupt and it infects our society.

One former presidential advisor, former Labor secretary Robert Reich, doesn't hesitate to call this Washington lobbying by its rightful name: legalized bribery. "What's the real difference between me bribing a customs agent so that I can bring a banned substance into the country or me contributing money to a senator and then cajoling him into making the substance legal for import?" asked Reich, who is now a professor at the University of California at Berkeley. "Frankly, I don't see much difference. A bribe is a bribe. People authorized only to act in the public interest may not use their office for private gain. Period."[6]

Not surprisingly, Congress objectively fails at its most basic duty: producing a rational federal budget. In their zeal for reelection, Republicans and Democrats run the same annual scam on the American people. This con job consists of spending more than they are willing to ask the citizenry to pay for, with each side again playing its assigned role. Democrats scream like newborns at any suggestion that government services and entitlement programs be reformed; Republicans who claim to be fiscal conservatives sign pledges to cut taxes irrespective of how much must be borrowed from future generations. The obvious result is annual budget deficits that balloon the national debt. The debt now stands at $18.7 trillion, three times as much as when George W. Bush took office in 2001. That figure represents $152,000 for every American household, with no end of red ink in sight.

None of this is inevitable. All of it can be fixed.

Yes, America is currently ruled by an increasingly liberal Democratic Party and an increasingly conservative Republican Party. According to a survey done by Washington political magazine *National Journal*, 2014 was the fifth straight year that the most liberal Senate Republican was more conservative than the most conservative Senate Democrat.[7] The inverse was true as well. In the House of Representatives, the same dynamic has been true for years. Only two House Democrats were more conservative than any Republican, and only two Republicans more liberal than any Democrat. And yes, the Electoral College map for the presidential election looks like a sea of Republican "red" states in the South and rural Midwest offset by dependable Democratic "blue" states on both the East Coast and the West Coast, leaving a dwindling pool of battleground states scattered like lonely purple islands through the country. That may seem like a permanent, unchangeable state of affairs—two armies dug in to fight an unending war. But this nation has been here before, and we pulled ourselves out of it. Here is how *The Wall Street Journal*'s Washington bureau chief Gerald F. Seib described the state of American politics:[8]

> The country is narrowly divided between Democrats and Republicans, with a bright line separating red states and blue states. Rapid technological change is sowing economic unease. A wave of immigration adds to the unsettled feeling. Anger rises

over income inequality, which is discussed in popular books. Put
it all together and the result is a rising tide of populist sentiment.

Seib was actually recounting U.S. politics in the last part of the nineteenth century and the early part of the twentieth. It's an eerily accurate
portrait of American politics today, with the same perils—and the same
promise.

Over a century ago, "populist sentiment" helped bring down the
curtain on the era of political stalemate that gripped America from the
late 1880s to the end of the First World War. That reform happened
because of the efforts of a Populist Party that arose out of the Democrats' grassroots and a Progressive Party that emerged from the ranks of
disaffected Republicans. In other words, it happened because independent Americans came together, cast aside the ruling duopoly, and made
it happen. The voters forced the two major parties to adapt. The ensuing era of cooperation produced constitutional amendments authoriz-
ing a federal income tax, direct election of U.S. senators, and women's
suffrage. Legislatively, the two parties banded together to create the
Federal Reserve, a system of national parks, and uniform standards for
food safety.

By the end of the twentieth century, however, Congress could no
longer summon the political will to address our growing national problems. This is what Ross Perot was attempting to facilitate with his Independent presidential bid in 1992 and his Reform Party reprise in 1996.
His failure wasn't due to any misdiagnosis of the political malady facing
this country. Perot blunted his own momentum in 1992 by dropping out
of the race with a confusing explanation and then reentering after the
battle lines between Bush and Clinton had already solidified. In 1996, he
never gained enough momentum and was excluded from the presidential debates. But in 1992 nearly one in five voters pulled the lever for an

Independent—a clear indication that Americans were willing to turn to nonpartisan solutions for our profound problems.

Twenty years after Perot last ran, America's civic life is in worse shape than ever. The demand for an alternative to our two-party system is growing, particularly among an increasing number of Americans who want to cast aside partisan labels, get things done, and make government work for them.

In short, voters want a real alternative to the ruling duopoly and the establishment forces that control both major parties. They want a real choice to the Washington politicians who have treated public service as a platform for personal gain. They want true Independents. Absent genuine Independents on the ballot, they'll gravitate to any candidate willing to challenge the status quo. Make no mistake: It is exceedingly difficult to win U.S. political office as an Independent. I walked that path in 2014 in my home state of Kansas. Yet it's never been more important for Independents to run—and for independent-minded citizens to back them.

Americans hate what is going on in Washington and they are beginning to respond accordingly. Congress's popularity remains at shockingly low levels: The Gallup Poll reports that only 15 percent of Americans approve of the job Congress is doing, while 80 percent disapprove.[9] The majority of Americans understand intuitively that the real divide isn't between Democrats and Republicans, but between the Washington elite and the rest of America.

Despite the desire for fundamental change in Washington, a culture of lies, deception, and negative campaigning has made American voters skeptical of any genuine alternative to the two-party paradigm. This was a lesson I learned after *The Washington Post* columnist George Will visited me at my campaign headquarters in Shawnee, Kansas, in late September of 2014, six weeks before Election Day. By then, Republicans had agreed on a story line in their efforts to help my opponent, incumbent

Pat Roberts, win reelection to a fourth six-year term in the Senate. Their line was that I was secretly a Democrat—and a liberal Democrat at that.

"Let's be honest—he's a Democrat," John McCain told reporters during a trip to Overland Park. "He walks like a duck and he quacks like a duck and he is a duck."[10]

"Anybody with a liberal record like Greg's . . . that's not independence," chimed in McCain's 2008 running mate Sarah Palin. "That's someone who's trying to snooker you, Kansas."[11]

Politics ain't beanbag, to use the old expression, so I'm not complaining that this line of attack was unduly harsh in the context of our modern, and ritualistically negative, election campaigns. The larger problem is that the binary nature of our politics ignores the expressed aspirations of at least 43 percent of the American people. The two parties have a chokehold on the electorate's collective imagination. George Will illustrated this problem when he discussed my race six weeks before Election Day. "The Senate's intellectual voltage would be increased by Orman's election," he wrote. "But improving 1 percent of the Senate is less important than taking 100 percent of Senate control from Harry Reid, who has debased the institution to serve Barack Obama, whose job approval among Kansans is just 40 percent."[12]

I have watched George Will for over a decade on ABC's *This Week* and admire his intellect—and his love of baseball. He was pleasant when we talked in Shawnee, and he treated me respectfully in print, so I hesitate to single him out. But the approach to politics that he tacitly validated is hurting this country. Every close Senate race in 2014 was nationalized in this way. Discouraging voters from supporting candidates they believe would upgrade the caliber of Congress only ensures Washington's continued incompetence.

This moment in U.S. history demands more than that. Much more.

Voter dissatisfaction is not a new phenomenon. What is new is that the political center isn't holding. Faced with starkly ideological candidates and increasingly negative campaigns, moderate or Independent voters (which are not exactly the same thing, as I will discuss later) often opt out, particularly during mid-term election years when voter participation plummets. In addition, party identification is less frequently a source of pride in this country. As the year 2015 dawned, some 43 percent of Americans self-identified as "Independent"—the most in Gallup's polling history—despite the absence of a vibrant Independent movement in this country, and a dearth of high-profile, self-identified Independent candidates in American political life.[13]

Let's call these Independents what they are: a growing group of like-minded voters who are pushing past useless partisan divisions to define themselves as citizens seeking practical, workable solutions. They may not constitute a party, but they are a movement—and they deserve a definition as distinct as that of the two prevailing parties. So, if we can have Republicans and Democrats, then we can have Independents. Maybe you, the reader of this book, will come to define yourself as an Independent. I hope so.

To be sure, we Independents don't speak with one voice. A percentage of Independents find Congress too liberal, while another cohort thinks it's too conservative. We almost universally agree, however, that Congress has become a corrupt and self-serving institution that needs renewal. We are committed to seeking solutions, not succumbing to a dysfunctional political system. And we reject the notion that ideology is the only dimension that matters. True independence comes not through adherence to a rigid ideology but through putting our country ahead of a political party and the special interests that support it.

The duopoly's refusal to deal head-on with the effects of globalization and other sweeping social disruptions caused by technological advances has created not just uncertainty and frustration among the American electorate, but a deep anger borne out of the conviction that our elected leaders don't really care about us.

It is this perception that links the Tea Party to the Occupy Wall Street movement. More than eight in ten Americans believe that access to political power must be purchased with big donations to politicians. Guess what? They're right, as this book will show.

In their search for an alternative to the status quo, any alternative, American voters are looking at unorthodox choices. A Democratic Socialist who until recently refused to be called a Democrat won the New Hampshire primary in a historic landslide. That didn't happen by accident. And how about a New York real estate mogul-turned-reality TV star, with a sharp tongue and an instinct for bullying, who turned the Republican Party inside out. Don't blame the voters. Blame the two political parties. This is not a moment of time that appeared out of nowhere. It's a byproduct of decades of neglect, the logical result of a pampered political class that ignores festering national problems while putting its own interests ahead of the nation's.

Americans are desperate for something different.

A solid plurality of Americans know they've been underserved by our existing two-party system. These citizens believe we can do better. I agree with that. But *A Declaration of Independents* is more than a compilation of complaints about how our current politics has failed us. In addition to identifying the problems, this book will propose solutions. In these pages, I want to galvanize Independents and disaffected Republicans and Democrats into joining me in a cause—a mission no less encompassing than giving Americans an alternative to our corrupt, ineffectual, and polarized two major political parties. It's not as dramatic as Kennedy's summons to send us to the moon, but it's crucially important.

Part I of this book will chronicle my own personal path to political Independence. In charting the road I traveled in 2014 in the Kansas Senate race, I show the challenges of finding a new way amid hyper-partisanship, as well as the new opportunities that campaigns like mine offer for Independent candidates and voters beyond Kansas.

Part II will describe what's at stake if we don't fix the dysfunctional duopoly that controls Washington, D.C. It will detail how both parties have misled their voters and, in the process, created an environment of hyper-partisanship.

Part III will focus on the institutions and processes that both parties use to reinforce their hold on power—from crony capitalism to biased media outlets to rules that the partisans write to limit competition and accountability.

Finally, Part IV will propose an Independent path forward that will rejuvenate our country's politics and lift up every American.

Our American political system needs reinvention. We need problem solvers, not ideologues. We must have a sustained effort by high-caliber Independent candidates who can break through the Washington mindset that everything is a zero-sum game—that if it's good for Democrats, it can't be good for Republicans, and vice versa.

What we need is re-engagement by Americans who understandably view the current electoral process as little more than a choice between two bad options.

We need those voters, who realize intuitively that our country faces serious challenges and that our current leaders are ill-prepared to meet those challenges, to suit up and get involved.

We need our fellow Americans to take a stand against the corrupt, self-dealing practices of Washington, D.C., and send packing the politicians who are mainly interested in getting themselves reelected.

We need all well-intentioned Americans who want our country to be a better place to come together *en masse*, collectively declare their independence, and convert that 15 percent congressional approval rating into a 15 percent reelection rate. Doing this won't be easy. But as John F.

Kennedy suggested, Americans historically do not wilt in the face of difficulty. We rise to meet the challenge of the day.

We do things *because* they are hard. That's who we've been as a people, and who we need to be again.

If you're sick and tired of the brand of politics Washington is giving us, this book is for you. If you believe we deserve better than the leadership we're getting, this book is for you. If you're concerned about the future of our great country and its citizens, it's time to stand up and do something about it.

If you are ready to declare your independence, you have millions of other Independents ready to join you to remake America.

You're not alone.

PART I

The

MAKING

of an

INDEPENDENT

— ★★★ —

CHAPTER 1

A Natural-Born Independent

GROWING UP IN THE MIDDLE
IN MIDDLE AMERICA

———— ★ ★ ★ ————

ON A WARM JULY day in 1986, I waited, along with ninety-seven other rising high school seniors, in the Rose Garden of the White House for a glimpse of Ronald Reagan. For the fortieth president of the United States, this visit was an annual event. For us—teenagers from all over the country—it was the moment of a lifetime.

We were the delegates of Boys Nation, an American Legion sponsored forum designed to promote civic values and instill leadership in its young charges. Each state sent two delegates to a convention in the nation's capital. Housed for a week on a local college campus, we saw the sights of the city, enacted legislation, and elected our own president, who was tasked with handing that legislation to the real president of the United States. That was my job, although I didn't find out until minutes before the fact. I had just the day before been elected president of Boys Nation.

The Rose Garden event began with Ronald Reagan welcoming us to the White House by saying my name (among others). "Greetings," he said, "President Gregory Orman."

Five years before I was born, a Boys Nation delegate from Arkansas named Bill Clinton met John Kennedy in the Rose Garden and shook the president's hand. Clinton later said that this visit, coming only four months before Kennedy's assassination, "crystalized" his interest in public service. The year I was elected to head the Boys Nation delegation in Washington, D.C., Bill Clinton was chairman of the National Governors Association and already contemplating running for president.

I, too, found the nation's capital heady and inspiring. Looking back on the experience after three decades, I wish that the men and women who represent us in Washington exhibited the same level of idealism as the teenagers in that program. I've been told it's naïve to think that American politics can be reformed to the point that elected officials in Washington and the fifty state capitals put the interests of their constituents ahead of their own careers. I don't believe that. It's happened before; it can happen again.

THE HEART OF AMERICA

Boys Nation was a big deal in my hometown of Mankato, Minnesota. When I got home from Washington, D.C., in a ceremony covered by the local media, Mayor Herbert J. Mocol gave me the key to our city. The gift was decorative: It turned no latches or deadbolts. The event that precipitated the ceremonial honor, however, was quite real. It unlocked the possibilities in a vast world beyond the confines of Mankato and to the exciting potential of American government.

As President Reagan stepped out of the Oval Office for the short walk to the lectern in the Rose Garden, an audible hum of anticipation swept through the ranks of the boys waiting for him. The president was accompanied by a group of aides, along with the ever-present White

House press corps. The reporters weren't allowed to ask the president questions in that format, but we were.

The first question from our delegation came from "Senator" Scott Whitaker of Colorado. It was a good question, and it made news. Scott asked about the Strategic Defense Initiative. SDI was a controversial Reagan proposal for a defensive shield against nuclear attack. Partly because the highly speculative technology was still in the development phase (and partly because a Republican president was proposing it), Democrats in Congress considered SDI a waste of money. So did the media, which derisively referred to the program as "Star Wars." But SDI had freaked out the leaders of the Soviet Union, and now a Boys Nation representative wanted to know if the president was considering using it as "a bargaining chip" in arms talks with the Soviets.

Reagan's answer sent reporters present running to their phones to call their editors. He wouldn't bargain the program out of existence, as the Russians had asked, he said, but he would share the technology with them. The goal here, the president stressed, was "eliminating nuclear weapons once and for all."[1]

Minnesota had barely gone for home state hero Walter Mondale in the 1984 presidential election—the only state to do so—and Reagan was popular throughout America's heartland. Having a local kid get invited to the White House was considered news no matter who was in the Oval Office. So our civic leaders put together an event and invited the local press. Various elected officials and Mankato functionaries said glowing things about me, which I found curious, because none of them had laid eyes on me before. One state legislator even invited me to work on his upcoming campaign.

My favorite dignitary at the event was Mayor Mocol, a popular businessman of Lebanese ancestry who kept getting reelected by larger and larger margins. I have no recollection of my maternal grandfather, who was also Lebanese, but the way he was described to me I always imagined that the mayor was his clone. Suddenly, it was my turn to take questions from the press. As a novice, I had no idea how to finesse the Fourth Estate. I didn't know about reframing negatives, keeping "on message," or any other tricks of the trade. I just told the truth. One reporter asked if I intended to run for public office in the future.

"I might," I replied, "but I want to make some money first so I don't need the job and can do what's right."

The mayor was moved by that answer and gave me a big bear hug in front of everyone assembled. Actually, I'd spoken to my father about elective office at one point. His reflexive disdain for politicians and quick wit came through in his initial reaction. "Why don't you skip the internship," he quipped, "and go straight into crime?"

My dad had a natural aversion to people who advanced their own interests by spending other people's money, particularly if they had never learned the value of a dollar by earning it themselves. He suggested that if I wanted to pursue public service, I should accomplish something in another area of life, preferably becoming secure enough financially so that losing an election wouldn't upend my life. If I sought public office, he wanted me to be able to be my own man. So my answer during that press event was really his answer.

My dad, a registered Republican, taught me well. Tim Orman was the third-oldest boy in a Roman Catholic family of seven sons. His father, my Grandpa Ralph, grew up on a farm in Hastings, Minnesota. After graduating from high school, my Grandpa Ralph went straight to work in a Sears & Roebuck warehouse, where he labored for forty years. My father was raised to believe in self-reliance and exhibited a strong work ethic his entire life. In 1971, he opened a furniture store with one of his brothers in Stanley, Kansas. He commuted from Hopkins, Minnesota, every other week for almost twenty years before moving to Kansas full-time. To this day, he believes in low taxes and limited government, as do many small business owners who build their companies from the ground up. On the other hand, my father has never let any political party do his thinking for him. He believes handguns have no function other than to kill human beings and they should be banned. He considers access to medical care a basic right of all Americans.

My mother, Darlene Gates, was a Minnesota Democrat, and all that implies. She worked in a hospital and was an active member in the nurses' union. My mom also made sure her sons understood the way women were subtly and, in many cases, not so subtly diminished in our country. For as long as I can remember, my mom pointed out issues of gender inequality every time she encountered them. Like my father, she didn't march lock-step to anyone else's political agenda, either. He was a pro-gun-control Republican who favored universal health care; she was a pro-life Democrat. When I was growing up, it was not uncommon to find liberals who were vocally pro-life, especially those who were Catholics like my mother. My mother attended Minnesota Citizens Concerned for Life conventions with her Democratic friends. But her politics were always about more than just one issue.

My mom came by her Democratic Party affiliation honestly. Her father, Fred Gates, was Hubert H. Humphrey's chief of staff for twenty-five years. HHH, as he was called by headline writers, was a popular liberal Minnesota senator who was pulled into the vice presidency in Lyndon Johnson's administration. Humphrey was an optimistic, once-in-a-lifetime political figure who is still beloved by Minnesotans old enough to remember him. He will go down in history as the youthful mayor of Minneapolis who prompted the walkout of Southern "Dixiecrats" at the 1948 Democratic National Convention with his electrifying challenge on civil rights. The time had arrived, an impassioned Humphrey told the delegates, "for the Democratic Party to get out of the shadow of states' rights and walk forthrightly into the bright sunshine of human rights!"[2]

I have one clear recollection of meeting Humphrey as a boy. At the time, I had five brothers and sisters—and eleven uncles. Senator Humphrey immediately told me to call him "Uncle Hubert." He figured you needed two uncles per kid, and we were one short. We kids heard lots of stories about Hubert. Many of them revolved around his talent for negotiating with Republicans to get things done in Washington. Whether it was horse trading with Kansas senator Bob Dole on agricultural issues or working with Barry Goldwater on international affairs, this lifelong progressive knew the value of political compromise—and he had a talent for forging mutually satisfactory deals. (After the election in 2014, I had the chance to meet Senator Dole. When I mentioned my Humphrey connection to Dole, he recalled handing Hubert a quart of milk in the Senate Agriculture Committee many years ago to celebrate legislation they had fashioned together in support of dairy farmers.)

Given my start in life, perhaps it was inevitable I would end up as an Independent. But it would be a long journey, one that was also informed by my experiences in the business world, and by the changing landscape of American politics.

MY FIRST DECLARATION OF INDEPENDENCE

I declared my maverick political leanings publicly for the first time in the sixth grade when my elementary school held a mock presidential election. It was 1980, and John Anderson, an Illinois congressman first elected as a Republican, was running as an Independent against incumbent President Jimmy Carter and the Republican challenger I would meet in the Rose Garden six years later. I was responsible for managing Anderson's campaign at our school. Ultimately, Anderson tied Carter for first place in our school's election, which was no small feat given that Minnesota native Walter Mondale was Carter's vice president. Ronald

Reagan finished third, a result that shows the limitations of putting too much stock in the twelve-year-old vote. All I know is that I ran a positive campaign, mainly stressing the physical similarities between John Anderson and television personality Fred Rogers of *Mister Rogers' Neighborhood*.

A child psychologist would probably diagnose my independent streak as a way to bridge the gap between my parents. Perhaps there's something to that, but I think of it differently. My folks split up when I was five years old and my mom remarried when I was seven, so I don't really remember much of my parents being together. But I loved and respected them both—and still do—and couldn't ascribe to either of them any bad intent, which political partisans routinely do to each other. So I learned to consider my folks' respective points of view with an open mind and an empathetic heart.

I believe that's one of the real strengths of Independents–they're able to approach an issue with an open mind and see all sides of an argument. It's an attribute that has served me well in business, and, as I'll demonstrate later in the book, is something that's unique to political Independents.

What I do remember vividly about my childhood is being financially insecure. After remarrying, my mother had twins and then got divorced a second time. At thirty-three years old, she was a single parent raising six children.

The social science on the emotional impact of divorce on children is mixed. But the research into how raising children in a single-parent household closely correlates with poverty, lower academic achievement, and reduced future income is not much in dispute.

By age twelve, American children in non-married households are four times more likely to experience at least one year in poverty than children in married households. Adolescents in intact families are less likely to exhibit behavioral problems in school than children from single-parent families. They also get better grades. Boys and girls from such "Ozzie and Harriet" families, which mine was not, are also more likely to finish high school, which is the single biggest predictor of future income. They also are more likely to apply to college than kids from blended families or single-parent families.[3]

Social scientists rarely use terms like "broken family" anymore, and certainly some couples are better off—and their children happier—if they divorce. But as these statistics show, the net effects of our society's high divorce rate have profound public policy implications that only the most insensitive lawmaker would ignore. Single mothers, for instance, find that one of the biggest barriers to achieving financial security is the spiraling cost of child care, which is rising as fast as college tuition. What such data show is that conservatives' concerns about the erosion of the American family are genuine. But it also suggests that liberals' concerns about whether the U.S. has an adequate "safety net" for those living in poverty are not out of place.

I watched my mother struggle every month as she pulled a pile of bills out of her roll-top desk and tried to figure out which ones she absolutely had to pay and which ones could wait. My siblings and I benefited from the free and reduced-price lunch program at school, and we occasionally received cheese and other milk products from the Department of Agriculture. My mom wanted to do more for us, but she just didn't have the means. A skinny kid, I once asked her to help me buy a weight set so I could add muscle to my frame. She couldn't afford it. I can still recall the pain in her expression as she gently suggested that I try push-ups and isometrics.

The financial pressure she felt was rarely absent from our lives. It affected all of my brothers and sisters and continues to shape their decisions to this day. My older brother, Mike, didn't pay a dollar in rent for roughly fourteen years after graduating from college. He devised all sorts of ways to get free housing, including living in a house my dad owned in Minnesota, parlaying what was supposed to be a temporary housing allowance in California from the consulting firm Accenture into a years-long subsidy, crashing at friends' houses for months at a time, and even living for a while in his sports utility vehicle while showering at the gym.

Mike made partner at Accenture long before he ever paid for housing. Senator Roberts, my opponent in my 2014 Kansas campaign, thought it was cute to draw attention to the nice suit I wore during one of our debates, but growing up poor does leave an impression. I didn't take my thrift as far as my brother, but I did wait until I'd sold my first company before buying a home. Even after I was a successful entrepreneur I felt a gut-level aversion to borrowing money for a mortgage.

My older brother and I devised all sorts of ways to make money growing up. We mowed our neighbors' lawns in the summer and shoveled driveways in the winter. We scavenged through dumpsters for returnable glass bottles—a nickel for each one—and did other odd jobs. One of my schemes eventually entailed parental intervention.

This happened when I turned nine, and decided to go door-to-door offering to remove wasp's nests from the eaves of houses in our area. I wasn't exactly a licensed exterminator: My tools of the trade were an eight-foot pole and the client's water hose. My price was twenty-five cents per wasp's nest, which, as I look back on it, I earned in entertainment value alone. My method consisted of knocking the nest off the eaves with the stick, using the hose to frantically spray water over my own head at the wasps that went after me, and then running like hell. After one aggressive colony of wasps chased me down the street and stung me repeatedly, my mother took me to the doctor who solemnly informed me that I was allergic to bee and wasp venom and would have to quit the business or risk death. It took me decades before I realized my mother had put the doctor up to telling me that.

A safer and better-paying job was delivering the local newspaper. Mike and I both had paper routes, which provided spending money for clothes and extras. Once it gave me much more. After I knocked out my two front teeth swimming in an apartment swimming pool my friends and I had snuck into, the supplemental medical insurance plan I'd purchased through the Mankato Free Press paid the dental bill.

My father paid child support, but he didn't have much disposable income either. He was operating a small business in Kansas that survived month-to-month. He gave my older brother and me jobs working in the warehouse of his furniture store when we turned thirteen. He paid us $3.65 an hour, which was just over the prevailing minimum wage at the time. He meted that out over the summer, giving us $15 for each week and the rest in a lump sum in late August, so we'd have money to buy clothes and other necessities during the school year. One summer, my father told me that if the store had three or four slow months in a row, he'd have to close the doors. After that, I would sneak into the sales office to read the sheet where the daily sales were recorded. Eventually, my snooping became obvious, and my dad would simply ask, "What's the total?" He knew I was adding up the numbers in my head as I surreptitiously glanced at the sales sheet.

My dad expected a lot of us as store employees. He referred to my brother and me as "SOBs"—Sons of the Boss—and said we needed to work twice as hard for half the pay. We did our best. I worked an eighty-hour week during an offsite sale week, sleeping three of the nights in the warehouse as the "security" detail. I'm not sure what I would have done if someone had actually broken in. My father's advice was simple: "Call the police and then find somewhere to hide." I got an extra ten bucks for every night I slept in the warehouse.

Out of these experiences grew a desire to start and own my own business, and a determination to never be poor again. My parents instilled in me a work ethic that served me well in that pursuit, from public school in Mankato to Boys Nation to Princeton University, which I attended thanks to a combination of scholarships, student loans, work-study programs, and money saved from working summers for my father. In that sense, my success story is the type of up-from-the bootstraps success story cherished by conservatives. Yet my childhood also instilled in me a lifelong empathy for those caught in poverty's web, and it also gave me insights into what government should do—and should not do—for the poor.

In sum, my childhood deeply influenced my perspective on public policy. While I do not think Americans should be artificially propelled up the ladder of success, I also believe those of us who have climbed that ladder shouldn't pull it up from behind. I recognize that the programs that I benefited from growing up—from my time in Mankato to my four years in Princeton—gave me the opportunity to improve my life. Government has a role in helping to ensure equal access to opportunities for everyone. Yet, this is still a country where hard work has its rewards. Compassion and common sense aren't mutually exclusive.

This is where the Manichean nature of our modern politics fails us. If you listen to the Republicans at campaign time, the problem is that Democrats incessantly promote failed social programs that rob the poor of their incentive to work while impeding family formation. Meanwhile, in the Democrats' telling, Republicans are insensitive fat-cats who favor policies designed to reward "millionaires and billionaires."

If only things were that simple. The truth is much more nuanced—and, consequently, much more difficult to address in our current polarized environment. In my campaign I called the problem "the New American paradox." It's my contention, supported by vast amounts of data, that it's harder than ever for the average American to get ahead, but paradoxically, it's easier to do nothing with your life. Solving this paradox would require both sides to acknowledge that there is an element of truth in the other's thinking, something we shall later see is remarkably difficult for partisans to do.

MOTHER'S MILK

In the tenth grade, I was one of thirty kids who joined the YMCA's Youth in Government program, which was new that year to our community. It allowed high school students to participate in the political process by forming a mock state government, complete with lobbyists and journalists. The program was held over four days at the state capitol in St. Paul, Minnesota. I served in the mock Senate and was named clerk of the appropriations committee. Some 800 students took part in my first year: hundreds of kids writing and debating bills, participating on committees, engaging in horse trading to get their bills through committees and on to the floor calendar, and effectively participating in a legislative process.

It was like the real thing, only better. While there was media, the delegates weren't posturing for the cameras. Lobbyists were present, but participated in the process by providing information—not doling out campaign cash. No one was concerned about reelection, because as long as you stayed out of trouble, you were welcomed back. Kids passionately supported the bills that they had written because they felt like they were in the best interests of our state. There was disagreement, but it was civil. Bills that were poorly written or poorly thought through got voted down.

Professional, grown-up politicians might call me naïve, but I still feel today as I felt then: This is how the legislative process should work. Famed California politician Jesse Unruh, who ruled the legislature in

Sacramento when Reagan was governor there, was fond of saying that "Money is the mother's milk of politics." That's as true today, in state capitals and in Washington, D.C., as when Unruh said it. But in St. Paul's YMCA youth government, milk was just milk. Without political parties and reelection strategies, crony capitalism, or campaign cash we had our own little version of legislative utopia.

I participated in the YIG program and its companion program on National Affairs for three years. The National Affairs program was held in the Blue Ridge Mountains in North Carolina, where the YMCA had a camp. It was entirely a legislative program, structured in committees, where proposals were debated and then scored. If your proposal made it through three committees, it went to the general assembly floor. Anticipating what I'd be told three decades later by a Methodist minister in Manhattan, Kansas, my proposal the first year was to change the Aid to Families with Dependent Children program to eliminate the dollar-for-dollar reduction in benefits as participants earned money, replacing it with a more gradual reduction to give people an incentive to work. The second year, I proposed mandatory sex education to help address the issue of unwanted teen pregnancies.

As Governor of Minnesota's Youth in Government program, I attended the Youth Governor's Conference in Washington, D.C. One lecture was held at the Federal Reserve Bank. Wayne Angell, then a sitting Fed Governor (and a Kansan), addressed our group. When it came time for questions, I asked if the rising federal debt should be a concern to me as a seventeen-year-old who might have to pay that debt back some day. Angell responded that the national debt was statistically insignificant and not nearly as large as a percent of GDP as we experienced during World War II. That answer, which didn't fully make sense to me then, has proven wrong over time. It also reminds me that I was always fiscally conservative and conscious about the implications of debt, whether it was mine personally or the government's, which as a citizen I'd have a role in repaying.

As Boys Nation president in Washington, D.C., my most important job was to be an ambassador for the program. The next day, the staff was coy about where we were going. We lined up outside a venerable gray edifice, which turned out to be the Old Executive Office Building, and went through that to the White House press briefing room. We were heading in to meet President Reagan in the Rose Garden.

As we waited, someone handed me a yellow folder and said, "This is the legislation that the Boys Nation Senate passed this week. You have to present this to the president." I huddled with Boys Nation vice president Patrick Ungashick from Missouri. Pat told me he'd recently read a survey showing that a high percentage of young people admired Reagan. We were ushered out into the Rose Garden. Pat and I were situated on the stage behind the presidential podium, along with the Boys Nation program director.

Reagan came out and gave a few prepared remarks before taking a few questions from the boys. The time came for me to approach the podium. I presented him the legislation that we had passed and told him it represented the hopes and aspirations of our Boys Nation Senate. I told him, on a personal note, that the hearts and minds of the youth of today were with him. The president was exceedingly gracious. He accepted our legislation and made his exit. I breathed a huge sigh of relief, as I made it through the event without embarrassing the program.

As I look back on the Boys Nation program today, it's clear to me that the American Legion accomplished a lot more than simply giving a bunch of high school students a civics lesson. The program instilled an appreciation for real problem-solving—based on facts, intellectual conflict, and a genuine desire to find a solution. There were no artificial motives, no special interests or party bosses to please. There were no hidden agendas. Even though we knew the legislation we passed would have no real-world impact, we nonetheless approached the process with the dedication of idealistic teenagers trying to improve the lives of average Americans. Congress could learn a lot from that purposefulness and the no-nonsense approach to policy those ninety-eight boys demonstrated. I know I did.

CHAPTER 2

My Path to Political Independence

HOW THINKING LIKE AN ENTREPRENEUR
OPENED UP A NEW POLITICAL VISION

———— ★ ★ ★ ————

THE FIRST ELECTION I experienced as a voter was in 1988. Channeling my father in those years more than my mother, I had joined the College Republicans and volunteered to work as an advance man for George H. W. Bush at a New Jersey campaign event. When I went to the advance team meeting at a local hotel, the organizer asked if anyone had any experience driving a truck. Having driven my father's furniture store delivery truck, I raised my hand.

"Not a pick-up truck, a real truck," he shot back, giving me a glance that implied I was a spoiled college kid.

I explained that, in fact, I had driven a furniture delivery truck. He tossed me the keys. "It's out in the parking lot," he said. "Why don't you take it for a spin and tell me if you can handle it."

I drove the flatbed truck back that night to the student parking lot, where it was clearly out of place with all the students' cars. The next morning, I drove it to Trenton for Bush's event. Reporters were loaded onto it as Vice President Bush walked five blocks from a local bakery to a campaign event at Roman Hall, a neighborhood Italian restaurant that had a large event space. My job was to creep slowly in front of the vice president so that the national press corps could record him in action. Reporter Brit Hume wanted to sit in the cab of the truck with me, but the Secret Service waved him off. I can't blame Brit. The scene on the street was pretty bland, and the fumes from my barely idling diesel truck had to be unbearable.

Four years later, after Bush presided over what many conservative Republicans today call "Reagan's third term," the prevalent political mood in the United States was that America itself was stuck in idle. One prominent Texas businessman had a compelling diagnosis: We, the citizens, had handed the keys to power to two political parties whose main focus was staying in power. "We own this country," Ross Perot told an audience at the National Press Club. "Government should come from us."

It was March 18, 1992. I had been out of college for almost a year. The only presidential vote I'd cast in my young life had been for George H. W. Bush, and I was happy when he won. But here was a very different kind of person proclaiming something that hardly anyone in professional politics, from either party, had the gumption or political independence to say aloud. It was inexcusable, Perot asserted, for the United States Congress to run up a $4 trillion debt in peacetime. Both parties were to blame. Perot was tossing out ideas—line item veto, a ban on raising taxes, national referendums on new spending—about how to shake up the status quo. And he was doing so without using political jargon or weasel words.

"We've got to put the country back in control of the owners," Perot said. "In plain Texas talk, it's time to take out the trash and clean the barn or it's going to be too late."

It was obvious by then that if Ross Perot ran for president in 1992, he was going to do it as an Independent. Bill Clinton had essentially wrapped up the Democratic Party's presidential nomination the day before by winning the Illinois and Michigan primaries. On the Republican side, Bush's nomination was a foregone conclusion. Yet there was a restlessness in the air. It was also becoming clear that the American people weren't satisfied with their binary choice. Twenty-four years before Donald Trump roiled the 2016 presidential campaign, another businessman was tapping into a national dissatisfaction with government, offering words of basic common sense.

"I feel," he said, "that as owners of this country that if we're going anywhere you've got to send [elected officials] a message: 'You work for us; we don't work for you. Under the Constitution, you are our servants. Grow up! Work as a team. Serve the people. Solve the problem, move on to the next one. Build a better country and stop throwing away money we don't have!'"

Perot issued a challenge to his listeners. "Ordinary people," he declared, must demonstrate that they wanted the option of voting for an Independent presidential candidate by getting him on the ballot in all fifty states. Call and volunteer your support, he said. Make this happen from the ground up. Many Americans answered the call. At the Dallas-based Perot Petition Committee the phone calls flooded in: 2,000 an hour day after day. Hundreds of other volunteers swamped the building's lobby. People like Joe Odom, a local warehouseman for the Procter & Gamble Corp, who told a visiting reporter, "I just believe we're in a sad state of affairs in this country and the leadership is not getting the job done. It is like the latter days of Rome."[1]

What Americans also have in common with Rome, and others who have frittered away their good fortune, is that we've allowed ourselves to be led astray by political parties that value self-interest ahead of the common good. This is a recurring problem in our history. Theodore

Roosevelt spoke to it while announcing his break from the Republican Party in 1912. "Political parties exist to secure responsible government and to execute the will of the people," he said. "From these great tasks both of the old parties have turned aside. Instead of instruments to promote the general welfare they have become the tools of corrupt interests, which use them impartially to serve their selfish purposes."

Nearly a century after Roosevelt's words, Michael Bloomberg would sound a similar theme in announcing that he was leaving party politics. Originally a Democrat, Bloomberg had entered public life as a Republican. On June 19, 2007, however, he announced he was re-registering as an Independent. "We have achieved real progress by overcoming the partisanship that too often puts narrow interests above the common good," Bloomberg said in a written statement. "Working together, there's no limit to what we can do."

In 1992, I was drawn to Perot's message of debt reduction, tax code simplification, and political reform. I registered as an Independent and later joined Perot's United We Stand America party, which became the Reform Party. I was disappointed when Perot lost, but I managed to make a little money by betting that Perot would garner more than 15 percent of the vote in the general election. He actually attracted nearly 19 percent, even after quitting the race in July with no plausible explanation, and re-entering later. His showing under those circumstances proved to me even back then that Americans are receptive to the idea of a committed Independent presidential candidate.

A POLITICAL TOURIST

After Perot's 1992 campaign, I immersed myself in business. I had taken a job with the management consulting firm McKinsey & Company when

I graduated from college in 1991. I was grateful to have the position at McKinsey, in part because America was coming out of a recession when I graduated, and employment was hard to come by. I knew, however, that I wouldn't stay at McKinsey forever.

Having grown up with an entrepreneurial father and a penchant for making money any way I could as a kid, I always knew I would start my own business someday. One of my hobbies as a high school student was thinking up new businesses and then writing the associated business plan. I decided that when I graduated from college, I was going to start the first good business idea I had. In May of 1992, while still employed at McKinsey, I started my first company, Environmental Lighting Concepts, which designed and installed energy efficient lighting systems for commercial and industrial buildings.

While I had already decided that I would never enter politics unless I had the financial independence to be my own man while serving, I didn't realize how valuable a business background could be in the policy arena. Politicians often talk about the desire to bring business disciplines to Washington. This was one of the reasons I was attracted to Perot's candidacy. When they make these statements, they're generally referring to concepts like efficiency and accountability. By almost every measure, the private sector does a better job at exhibiting efficiency and accountability than the public sector. In certain federal agencies an employee is more likely to die while still employed than to be fired. It's hard to imagine any private company where that is the case. In the public sector, lifetime employment is alive and well. Accountability, not so much.

One overlooked area where the public sector can really learn from the private sector, however, is the private sector's approach to problem solving. Successful companies are nothing if not adept at addressing challenges. As my business career evolved, it became clear to me that there was a pattern to how successful companies fixed problems and thrived as a result. But in Washington, D.C., the intent isn't to actually solve problems. Often, it's to perpetuate them. (More on that later.)

By the spring of 1993, Environmental Lighting Concepts was profitable and growing rapidly. I found myself working at McKinsey during the workweek and at ELC at night and on the weekends. I didn't really have time for politics, or much else for that matter. As a result, I became something of a political tourist: I took in the sights and bought the branding that both parties were selling. I didn't really think for myself.

That tourism mentality began to dissipate during Bill Clinton's presidency. Under prodding from a Republican Congress, the executive branch fashioned fiscal policies that resulted in a balanced federal budget for the first time in forty years. The 2000 presidential election was the first time in many Americans' lifetimes in which fiscal debate centered on what to do with government surpluses. It felt to me as though our government was finally starting to act responsibly—and that the country would be positioned for another century of American leadership in the world. It was the first time in my adult life that I wasn't worried about the future of our country.

By this time, I was living in Kansas after having sold a majority interest in ELC to Kansas City Power & Light. I determined that the only way to participate meaningfully in the political process was to register as a Republican and vote in the primary. The real battle in most of Kansas was between conservative Republicans and moderate Republicans. With the exception of a good friend, who was a more conservative candidate, I supported the moderates.

But after watching George W. Bush and a Republican Congress run up $4 trillion in federal debt, expand unfunded entitlements, and ignore our growing health-care affordability crisis, I could no longer support the GOP. From January of 2001, when Bush took office, to Election Day 2008, our public debt had increased from $5.7 trillion to nearly $10.6

trillion.[2] If you add in our "entitlements deficit"—money owed to meet our obligations for government assistance programs, primarily Social Security and Medicare, and federal government pensions—the figure skyrocketed to nearly $53 trillion.[3]

It was, and still is, the most fiscally irresponsible era in our country's history. And it all happened on the Republicans' watch. If Republicans were no longer interested in living within our means, it was time for me to look elsewhere. Although I've felt stronger alignment with Democrats on social issues, I still thought they weren't fiscally prudent enough. But after the first eight years of this century, it was clear to me that Republicans weren't fiscally responsible either.

After eleven years as a registered Independent (or Reform Party member), which was bookended by my time as a registered Republican, I decided, with the encouragement of Democrats in Kansas, to explore running in the 2008 U.S. Senate race as a Democrat. Incumbent Pat Roberts was clearly part of the problem. While proclaiming to be fiscally conservative, he'd voted for 97 out of 101 Bush administration spending bills that passed and every tax cut bill, which helped explode the federal deficit. He sat on the Senate committee overseeing our Medicare program while it started to crumble financially. He also was Chairman of the Senate Select Committee on Intelligence in the run-up to the 2003 U.S. invasion of Iraq, which missed the boat on the intelligence agencies' and Bush Administration's erroneous assertions about Saddam Hussein's supposed arsenal of weapons of mass destruction. Someone had to run against him.

I did debate running as an Independent in 2008. Everywhere I turned for counsel, however, the advice came up the same: "You can't win as an Independent! So pick a party and run. If you win, you can work to change the party from the inside." I trusted the individuals dispensing this advice. I believe they genuinely believed the only way to accomplish the change that I wanted was to do it through a major party. I formed a campaign committee and began in earnest to explore the race as a Democrat.

I supported other Democratic candidates during that period of time, too, which was expected of me if I wanted to join their team, and I learned a great deal in the process. In the end I decided against running as a Democrat, partly because I realized how uncomfortable I felt wearing a party label. The idea that I was expected to agree to the party's perspective on every issue was unappealing. I wanted to be able to think for myself, to apply what I'd learned. I've never believed there were only two possible answers to any problem. I realized that neither party spoke for me anymore. And I didn't want to speak for either of them.

In hindsight, given my upbringing with a Democratic mom and a Republican dad—and my attraction to Ross Perot's campaign in 1992—I've always been an Independent. While I've tried both parties and supported candidates from both parties, I've generally been disappointed with the results of their leadership. In a sense, I view my experiment with both parties as being akin to an organ donor recipient who rejected both organs. It just wasn't natural for me.

I was also starting to form the belief that both parties were the problem. With extremists controlling the primary process and congressional districts growing increasingly partisan, our nation's elected officials were becoming more and more unyielding. They were also responsible for putting special interests in charge of our government. I knew we needed to do something different if we were to put America back on the right path. I knew we needed to empower Independents who weren't beholden to party bosses or special interests, but were rather citizen servants who put our country, not some political party, first. Most importantly, I knew I had to leave both parties behind and return to my Independent roots.

In November of 2010, I founded a nonprofit called the Common

Sense Coalition. I wanted to create an online community where the millions of Americans that the two parties were neglecting—people who were fiscally responsible and socially tolerant—had a voice. I wanted the Common Sense Coalition to be a place where rational voices dedicated to fact-based problem solving would be heard over the extremist voices that dominate the established duopoly. I've been committed to supporting independent causes ever since, as the best path to getting Washington working again.

When launching the Common Sense Coalition, I sent an email to some 5,000 people. If I had ever interacted with someone in my adult life and still had their email, they received my note. I told them that I believed we were on a path that, unless altered, would eventually lead to the elimination of the middle class in this country. I went on to relate the account of visiting Washington as a teenager and how a sitting Federal Reserve governor had blown off my question about rising federal debt. "As I observed our government at work over time, it became clear to me that good politics was bad policy," I wrote.

"We seem to have devolved to a point where we can't have an honest, fact-based discussion about issues and their solutions," the email continued. "If you want to talk about how we spend our health resources, you're referred to as an advocate of 'death panels.' Talk of modifying the corporate tax code to adopt a territorial system leads to references of 'extremism.' God forbid you should question the amount of money we spend on defense programs or how we spend it. That simply makes you 'unpatriotic.'

"Our political environment has become so charged and partisan that rational discourse is nearly impossible," I wrote.

I described how in an effort to elevate the level of political discourse and give voters a better resource for making decisions, I'd put together a group of dedicated people to form the Common Sense Coalition for

Change. I amplified on its sole goal: to leave a better America for future generations. An accompanying website highlighted issues we believed were important to creating that future and proposed common sense solutions to solving them. It also provided resources in the form of articles of interest, candidate information, and other tools to help voters make informed decisions. The site, I explained, was nonpartisan—and centrist leaning, "if that's possible."

We also allowed people to express their dissatisfaction with Washington and the lack of genuine leadership coming from both parties. The message clearly resonated with many people. More than 200,000 Americans "liked" our Facebook page. On October 1, 2013, as my wife Sybil and I honeymooned in Maine, the government shutdown occurred. We were shut out of Acadia National Park, which was closed down, along with nearly every other national park and monument in the country. Government workers were told to stay home. The Common Sense Coalition website posted a picture of Congress with the caption: "May I suggest the first 535 layoffs." That post received over 1.1 million "likes," the third-most liked Facebook post ever at the time.

While the Common Sense Coalition built a reasonable community and had lots of engagement, the impact we had on Washington, D.C., was non-existent. We eventually realized that the only way to change Washington was at the ballot box. To rely on the good will and judgment of elected officials and their willingness to embrace a sound, fact-based argument was naïve. They are in Washington to serve themselves, not the public. After spending seventeen years in the Senate, Olympia Snowe came to the same conclusion. A centrist Republican from Maine, Snowe determined that changing Washington from the inside was next to impossible. "The only way to change the dynamic, unless something miraculous happens, is from the outside," she said upon leaving the Senate in 2012. "It will happen when the public demands accountability."[4]

Over the years, a number of other organizations have committed themselves to goals similar to those of the Common Sense Coalition. In 1992, two former U.S. senators, Warren Rudman and Paul Tsongas, teamed up with former Secretary of Commerce Peter G. Peterson to form the Concord Coalition. While the Concord Coalition has focused on the issue of our budget deficits for almost twenty-five years, the problem has only grown. Despite the best efforts of a lot of very smart people, the group is no match for the forces at work in Washington, D.C. This isn't to say it hasn't had an impact. Who knows what our federal debt would look like without its efforts? But if you asked the founders what they hoped to accomplish when they established the organization, they'd say that where we are today is a long way from their aspirations.

Thomas Layton, who along with Charles Conn co-founded the Common Sense Coalition with me, is a San Francisco-based tech entrepreneur. With four daughters and a company to run, Thomas had better things to do with his time if the CSC wasn't going to produce results. I've always said the problem with Independents is they're independent. They don't work together. As a result, they work on multiple, independent initiatives when they should be working together. With this in mind, Thomas and I decided that our next move had to involve other like-minded organizations.

We found a shared sense of purpose with an organization called Americans Elect. Americans Elect was focused on changing the way we nominate and select a president. With the slogan, "Pick a President, not a Party," its approach was clearly consistent with ours. We worked with Peter Ackerman, the chairman of Americans Elect, to develop the Senate Fulcrum Strategy. Our strategy was simple: If we could prevent either party from having a majority in the United States Senate, we could use that leverage to get Washington back into the business of solving problems.

This "swing coalition," as we described it, would effectively be able to determine the party of the Senate majority leader, and, as a consequence, would influence which senators were able to chair committees. Most importantly, we'd also be able to hold the majority accountable. If it was unresponsive, we could switch our allegiances and support the other party's candidate for majority leader. We would be uniquely positioned to get government working again.

Finding suitable Independent candidates turned out to be a bigger problem than we anticipated. Many had been supportive of the Democrats or Republicans over the years and didn't want to leave their party. Others felt significant peer pressure. They didn't want to risk the social ostracism that they thought might come from running as an Independent. Many were simply skeptical. They realized the organizational and fundraising advantages that major party candidates had over Independents. After watching Independents and third-party candidates run for office over the years—and rarely get more than a few percentage points—they thought our plan was a strategy for public embarrassment.

My father always said to me that one concrete action was better than a thousand good ideas. It was time for me to look in the mirror. The question I had to ask myself was whether or not I believed enough in our strategy to take the step myself that we were asking others to take.

That was my thinking in early 2014, when I decided, as Theodore Roosevelt once urged his fellow U.S. citizens, to enter the arena myself. And although I thought I knew the extent of the problems the two major political parties had created for this country, running for office against that duopoly opened my eyes to the true extent of the crisis in American politics.

CHAPTER 3

An Independent Run

CAMPAIGNING FOR THE SENATE; FIGHT-
ING THE WASHINGTON ESTABLISHMENT

———— ★ ★ ★ ————

KANSAS MIGHT SEEM LIKE an unusual place for an Independent to launch a campaign for the United States Senate. Kansas hadn't elected a non-Republican to the U.S. Senate since 1932. Most pundits and political professionals agreed with the conventional wisdom that the state's Senate seats were the property of the GOP. Even though I ultimately lost my race, I don't accept that point of view. Kansas, the geographical center of the continental United States, has also long occupied a place at the center of America's cultural and historical evolution. As a consequence, Kansas has been considered one of our nation's emotional touchstones throughout our history.

Kansas, wrote famed *Emporia Gazette* newspaper editor William Allen White, is the "barometer" of the nation. "When anything is going to happen in this country, it happens first in Kansas," White wrote in 1922.[1] "Abolition, Prohibition, Populism, the Bull Moose, the exit of the roller towel, the appearance of the bank guarantee, the blue sky law, the adjudication of industrial disputes as distinguished from the arbitration of industrial differences—these things come popping out of Kansas like bats out of hell."

White's most famous essay about his state's politics, "What's the Matter with Kansas?" is still inspiring rebuttals and sequels. In 2004, liberal Kansas-born historian Thomas Frank penned a bestseller by the same name in which he examined, among other factors, the appeal of Republican politics to working-class voters.

Ever since its founding, Kansas has been the place where the nation's biggest issues have been addressed. It's not much of an exaggeration to say that the question that brought the nation to the point of Civil War was whether Kansas would be a free state or not. The first blood shed between abolitionists and the defenders of slavery was spilt in "Bleeding Kansas," a nickname the state earned four years before John Brown departed Kansas for Harper's Ferry—and four decades before locals began using the Sunflower as the state symbol.

In *The Wizard of Oz*, when Dorothy Gale tells her dog, Toto, "I've a feeling we're not in Kansas anymore," she's not just talking about the sepia-toned farm where she lives. She's talking about the American Heartland itself.

Kansans also pulled the lever disproportionately for Ross Perot. In 1992, as Perot was getting just under 19 percent nationally, 27 percent of Kansas voters chose Perot over Bill Clinton or George H. W. Bush. It was this independent spirit of Kansans and its historic place as a bellwether of U.S. political movements that I was relying on to propel our campaign and to change American politics.

The campaign was a learning experience for me every step of the way. It also reinforced every doubt I had about the current state of our two-party system—fortifying my conviction that nothing will improve until Independent candidates are a familiar staple of America's political life.

I announced my candidacy to represent this great state on June 4, 2014, in the warehouse of one of my businesses, a boxing equipment manufacturer called Combat Brands. We made the announcement there, in part, because I wanted to emphasize my business background and make it clear that I was different from the lifetime politicians that seem to dominate our politics today. More importantly, Combat Brands was a turnaround story. It was a testament to what can be overcome when a group of people come together around a common goal and work in good faith to solve problems. The business was formed when a business partner and good friend, Bruce Garner, and I acquired the assets and hired most of the employees of a company called Ringside, Inc. Ringside had experienced a slow but steady decline over the prior four years, having lost millions of dollars along the way. The first time I addressed the employees in a warehouse two years earlier, the faces that looked back at me were filled with worry. On that June day in 2014, however, they were in the audience not only to help me launch my campaign, but also to celebrate how far they had come as a business in two short years.

The rest of the audience was composed mostly of close friends and family—and the media. In those early days, the press tended to treat my Senate run as a novelty. I took pains in that announcement and over the next few days to explain why I was running as an Independent. "We've got problems we need to solve in this country that the politicians don't want to solve," I said. "I think everyone knows Washington is broken."[2]

"I didn't feel like either party fit me well as someone who is fiscally responsible and socially tolerant," I told a group in Wichita. "We're sending the worst of both parties to Washington—people who are bitter partisans who seem to care more about pleasing the extremists in their own party and the special interests than they do in solving problems."[3] I explained why I thought Senator Roberts was part of the problem, not the solution: "He's taken a sharp turn to the right recently, and ultimately I don't think he's representing the best interests of Kansas."

Nonetheless, the major party candidates responded predictably, like flip sides of the same broken record: The Democrat called me a closeted conservative; Roberts's campaign manager said I was a liberal masquerading as an Independent. Mostly, they ignored me, which was good. I was hiding in plain sight. Now my job was to get half a million dissatisfied but idealistic Kansans to see beyond the two-party paradigm.

BREAKING THE PARTISAN STOCKHOLM SYNDROME

I began my 2014 campaign in the usual way: talking to friends to gauge the support of those who knew me best and commissioning a poll. The first exercise was more heartening than the second. Most of my confidants were as frustrated as I was with the self-serving nature of Congress. Although none had any illusions that a campaign would be easy, especially running as an Independent, they were almost universally supportive.

The poll was less encouraging. It showed me running a distant third, which was to be expected. In detailed follow-up questions, the pollster recited the expected positive and negative messaging of all the candidates—and we remained in third place. Fully 35 percent of respondents said they wouldn't consider my candidacy because they viewed a vote for an Independent candidate as a wasted vote.

This didn't come as a surprise. For over a century, the two major political parties have repeatedly reinforced the wasted-vote notion, and it has taken root. Polling for the Common Sense Coalition showed similar results nationwide. Considering that the majority of Americans express disillusionment and even disgust with Republicans and Democrats, 35 percent struck me as too high a percentage of voters unwilling to buck the duopoly. It's as though they are programmed to ignore their own desires. What I think is happening is a version of the Stockholm Syndrome, the tendency of hostages to relate to the people holding them hostage. Although voters dislike what Republicans and Democrats are doing to our country—especially in Washington—they can't quite envision a world without them in charge. Americans are paralyzed, even when they are presented the opportunity to escape their captors.

What the poll didn't show, but what I am convinced is true, is that twenty-first-century American voters desperately want something different.

They want elected officials who tell the truth, even if that means relaying harsh facts. They want elected officials with the courage to stand up to the special interests that control the fundraising apparatuses in both parties. They want elected officials who don't go to Washington to enrich themselves personally or who view public office as a lifelong career. They want elected officials who care about this country's future—not in the lip-service way, but in the way that makes them willing to make hard choices and encourage their fellow Americans to do likewise. They want citizen politicians to serve as actual public servants. They want real leaders. I believed that more than I believed the poll numbers. I still do, notwithstanding the results of my 2014 Kansas campaign.

Nationally, the big political drama of the year was whether the Democrats could retain their Senate majority. The election returns that night provided a decisive answer to that question. Pat Roberts and his Republicans were put in control of the Senate—only four years after they wrested control of the House of Representatives from the Democrats. This outcome strongly suggested even greater gridlock in President Obama's last two years in office.

This development underscored a great anomaly of the Barack Obama era. Although Republicans never came close to beating him in his 2004 Senate race, his 2008 presidential race, or his 2012 reelection effort, other Democratic Party candidates fared less well while he was in the White House.

Kansans never caught Obama fever. As has happened in every presidential year after the Lyndon Johnson landslide of 1964, a majority of Kansans voted for the Republican presidential ticket in 2008, just as they would four years later. Pat Roberts ending up winning 60 percent of the vote in 2008, outperforming presidential candidate John McCain.

Thomas P. "Tip" O'Neill Jr., former Democratic House Speaker, is credited with coining the famous line "all politics is local." But as I was reminded in my 2014 campaign, the inverse is often true as well: All politics is national. This is not a new phenomenon. The last time a Republican lost a Senate race in Kansas was 1932. Even then, to make it happen took a third-party challenge that diluted the vote, along with Franklin Roosevelt's considerable coattails. It also took one more factor. The Democrats assigned Republican senator George S. McGill an unofficial running mate that year—a highly unpopular Republican president, Herbert Hoover.

Eighty-two years later, Republicans used the same strategy as a way of helping Pat Roberts. They tried to make Barack Obama my running mate. This was a more dubious tactic against me. I am not a Democrat and Obama was not president during anything nearly akin to the Great Depression as Hoover was—but it worked just the same. Joe Biden, of all people, helped the Republicans pull it off. This was frustrating for me for another reason. U.S. senators do not have running mates. Except that in my case, I really did have a running mate—literally. My running mate was my wife.

MY REAL RUNNING MATE

Sybil Niccum and I had our first meaningful conversation in July 2010 in a gym near my home. She was leaving for her daily run as I was just completing mine. We'd run into each other on occasion there, and in other social settings, but until then we hadn't exchanged a dozen words. We barely did that morning. I asked her if she was going running—a dumb question, as she was wearing running shoes and shorts and had earphones in her ears.

"Yes," she said without slowing down.

She had guessed what I planned to say next, which was "Maybe we could go running together," and apparently sought to avoid it. Undeterred, I asked her when she returned, "How far did you go?"

"Seven miles," she answered.

"That's great!" I enthused.

"Thanks," she replied noncommittally, as she walked away.

I figured I'd missed my chance, but another opportunity arose a little bit later when we found ourselves leaving the gym simultaneously. This time, I got straight to the point, suggesting that we go running together sometime.

"I'd love to," she said, "but I can't get here until 8:45 in the morning."

I found out later that she was politely giving me the brush-off—seeing my suit and tie, she pegged me for an eight-to-five businessman and thought that I wouldn't be able to run at 8:45—but I told her that would be fine. From that modest beginning I found a running partner and a friend. As we got to know each other on long morning runs, I learned two things. The first was that I felt completely at ease with her. The second was that my timing wasn't perfect. There was a reason she initially tried to brush me off—she had recently sworn off dating. As a guy with six sisters, I realized that this happens periodically and that I needed to move slowly. I decided to let the relationship develop, or not develop, on its own pace. It wasn't a seamless process. We went to a concert and then dancing, but she objected when I tried to kiss her goodnight. Summer ended and she returned to her job as a high school teacher. We'd been dating a month when Sybil wrote me a note saying she thought the timing was wrong for us. As a Spanish teacher and athletic coach, she found the first month of a new school year completely absorbing, she said. Also, her workday began at 6:30 a.m., too early for our morning runs.

I next saw her while running in the Kansas City Half Marathon. Although Sybil likes to start races in the middle of the pack, that's not where she finishes. She caught up to me at the four-mile mark, and we talked for a while before she pulled ahead nearly halfway through the race at milepost six. She finished five minutes before me and left before I crossed the finish line. But those fifteen minutes we ran together proved momentous: I asked her to watch a movie with me. She agreed, but upon one unusual condition: She was making cakes for all five of her high school classes and she was doing it in her pajamas. I needed to be similarly attired to be invited. I showed up in a pair of flannel pajamas my mother had given me for Christmas. Sybil let me in. When she realized she was out of cooking oil, we hopped in the car and walked the aisles at the nearby Walmart in our PJs to find it.

Who knows the exact minute we fell in love? Sybil later told me that, for her, it was seeing me play with my one-year-old niece Camilla. I think I loved Sybil from our first long distance runs together. But watching her interact with her students sealed the deal for me. Her life revolved around school from mid-August to mid-May. Spending time with "Miss Niccum" meant attending school plays and sporting events. I found myself often reflecting at these functions on how much I admired her. Sybil was special. She decorated her classroom with pictures of her various adventures. Having studied in Spain and Mexico and backpacked through Europe twice, she had lots of pictures to share. She had cut out letters on colored paper that spelled out "I want my life to be big," and posted them on her bulletin board. Her mission was to inspire her students to strive for more than they originally thought life held for them. Frankly, her mission inspired me.

As a teacher in a school in which over 70 percent of the students received free or reduced-price lunches, Sybil was on the front lines of educating at-risk kids. They would line up to talk to her before and after school—and often in between classes as well. Listening to her, I developed a keener appreciation for the problems of educating poor families, and an increasing admiration for the woman who was telling me about it. My part of the conversation often turned on my frustration with politics-as-usual in this country. I discussed running for office. She knew that I'd briefly considered running against Pat Roberts in 2008. Now I had a partner—and, as of September of 2013, a wife—who was as interested in public service as I was.

An American political campaign requires a candidate and a candidate's family who can greet relentless criticism with near-infinite patience. For Sybil that meant disregarding endlessly negative attacks on her husband, tuning out slurs on social media, and even ignoring attacks against her personally.

It wasn't always easy to show grace. In the last weeks of the race, our opponents started a whispering campaign: Sybil was headlining a late October rally for Planned Parenthood, according to a Kansans for Life posting on its Facebook page.[4] This was a lie. Sybil did indeed speak at campaign events that week. But the topic of discussion was not abortion and the sponsor was not Planned Parenthood; it was the importance of early voting. The events were hosted by such groups as Women for Kansas, which held an October 23 function in Wichita, and the Mainstream Coalition, which sponsored a similar one in Overland Park on October 25. Mainstream Coalition is a bipartisan group of political centrists. The same is true for Women for Kansas, which explicitly avoided abortion politics. Its mission statement is as follows: "To restore integrity, fiscal responsibility and balance to Kansas by electing moderate candidates to public office."

Although I expressed support during the campaign for a woman's right to make her own reproductive health decisions, I understood the difficulty of this issue for many Kansans. We tried to be sensitive to those feelings. We also believed in the goal of reducing unwanted pregnancies and felt that the pro-life community could be a helpful partner in the endeavor. We wouldn't have unnecessarily antagonized them.

From a tactical standpoint, we also understood that pro-lifers who are single-issue voters would support Pat Roberts, because of his rhetoric on the issue. We had hoped to attract voters from both parties who held divergent views on the abortion issue, however, and we would never have needlessly provoked one side by speaking at a Planned Parenthood rally. But polarization is the name of the game in modern politics. It's a strategy pursued relentlessly by partisan special interest groups, with the tacit concurrence of both major political parties.

When we tried to clarify what Sybil was actually doing, Kansans for Life added the logistical details of the Mainstream meeting, while repeating the misinformation about it being sponsored by Planned Parenthood. I've always suggested in my business dealings that "details sell the story." In this case, when we gave our opponents more details so as to tell the truth, they used those details to sell their lie.

CIVIL WAR IN THE HEARTLAND

One factor that convinced me that the political environment would be receptive to an Independent candidacy was the internal struggle consuming the Republican Party in Kansas. Attempts to purge GOP moderates, led by the state's Republican governor, Sam Brownback, had split the party, leaving a vacuum in the political center.[5] Brownback had been elected governor in 2010 after serving in Washington, first in the House and then in the Senate. Once in office, he decided that the state capital's Republicans weren't conservative enough for him. Specifically, they weren't conservative enough to rubber-stamp the plans he had for the state budget, which included large tax cuts accompanied by deep spending decreases in education and social services.

"Brownback and his whole group there, it's an amazing thing they're doing," supply-side economics evangelist Arthur Laffer gushed to *The Washington Post*. "It's a revolution in a cornfield."[6] But fourteen of the state senate's thirty-two Republicans, led by senate president Steve Morris, hadn't signed up for a "revolution." Although fiscally conservative by any traditional definition, they found some of Brownback's cuts, particularly in education, economically and socially counterproductive—and joined with Democrats in the state senate to block them. The governor responded by tacitly encouraging arch-conservative challengers to take these moderates out in the 2012 Republican primaries. "There's a war," Steve Morris told the Associated Press.[7] He was right about that, and wars have casualties. Morris was one of them. Backed by local and national Tea Party groups, and campaign money provided by Americans for Prosperity (the right-wing political action group founded by the billionaire Koch brothers), the Kansas Chamber of Commerce, and Kansans for Life, eight such insurgents defeated the moderates in 2012.

The day after the 2012 primary, Democratic leaders in Topeka held a press conference inviting moderate Republican and Independent voters to join them. "The welcome mat is front and center at the Kansas Democratic Party," said Paul Davis, the leader of the House Democrats.[8] Two years later, with Davis running for governor—and the state's budget a mess—one hundred prominent Kansas Republicans, including Steve Morris, signed a letter endorsing Davis over Brownback.[9]

My own reaction was a little different: Why not use the shambles Brownback had made of things to show voters that there ought to be more than two choices in American politics? I wasn't the only one with that thought. Infighting between moderates and conservatives is a perennial feature of Republicanism in Kansas and elsewhere. Usually, after the primary season is over the party unites to take on the Democrats. The Brownback machine's attack on the moderates was so vicious it made reconciliation impossible. Organizations with names like Traditional Republicans for Common Sense, Reroute the Roadmap, and Republicans for Kansas Values were springing up around the state. Pat Roberts and the rest of the Kansas congressional delegation in Washington, D.C., were complicit in the Brownback purge. They never spoke out against it, inched rightward on various policy issues themselves, linked themselves to Brownback on social media, and served as honorary co-chairs of his reelection campaign. They pandered in this way because they didn't want the Brownback cabal to gin up primary opposition against them. It's an understandable impulse, but it demonstrated precisely why the current political duopoly is such a dead end.

In Senator Roberts's case, his rightward lurch didn't spare him from a primary challenge. Milton Wolf, a forty-two-year-old radiologist who practiced in the Kansas City area, announced his candidacy on October 8, 2013. Although unknown to rank-and-file Kansas Republicans, Wolf had strong conservative credentials, as well as an interesting historical footnote to his personal pedigree. The biographical oddity is that he's a blood relative of Barack Obama.[10] The president's grandmother was his mother's cousin, making him Obama's second cousin once-removed. His mother and Obama's mother were childhood friends in Wichita. But there was no love lost between Wolf and his cousin Barack. "Most of you know that President Barack Obama and I are cousins," he told an audience early in the campaign. "Like I've said before, you cannot choose your family but you can choose to rise up and stop your family from destroying America."[11]

Such comments, along with Milton's involvement with Tea Party organizations, his regular column in the conservative *Washington Times*, and frequent appearances on Fox News made him a potentially formidable challenger to Roberts. In his announcement, he criticized Roberts for voting to raise the federal debt limit and for voting to confirm fellow Kansan Kathleen Sebelius as the Obama administration's Secretary of Health and Human Services, the agency tasked with implementing the Affordable Care Act. Wolf, of course, was outspokenly opposed to the law. But his underlying pitch to his supporters was more basic. "I'm sorry," he said, "no one should be in Congress for four decades."[12]

I didn't disagree. More to the point, I welcomed a challenge that would preoccupy Roberts through the early August primary and necessitate his spending some of his $1.5 million campaign war chest. I was beginning to see a path to winning. My first order of business was hiring a campaign manager. Anticipating that the Roberts camp would try to paint me as a liberal Democrat, I decided I wanted a Republican heading the campaign. But finding a credible Republican to take the job was difficult. Notwithstanding the civil war within the state party, any respected political professional knew that their days serving GOP candidates would be over the moment they joined a general election campaign against an incumbent Republican senator.

This is one of the big challenges of an Independent campaign. The duopoly's dominance of America's political life extends to campaign advisors. In Washington, where congressional aides are discouraged from socializing with those from the opposite party, imagine the reaction if a campaign operative decided to work for the enemy. As a result, campaign staffers have suited up in Republican red and Democrat blue.

Sometimes, however, the needle is shiny enough to be found in the proverbial haystack, and so it was I discovered Jim Jonas. Jim had worked in the presidential campaign of George H. W. Bush and the 1996 campaign of Tennessee senator Lamar Alexander—two Republicans I respect. More recently, he had been one of the founders of Unity '08, the predecessor to Americans Elect, a bipartisan organization that sought to field a presidential ticket pairing a prominent Democrat with a prominent Republican. Although committed to other clients, Jim was so excited about the campaign he agreed to spend three days a week on mine. This wasn't an ideal arrangement, but Jim showed his dedication by working many more days than his contract called for. By mid-September, he had effectively relocated to Kansas.

After our launch event, and press conferences in Topeka and Wichita, I headed to western Kansas, Pat Roberts's stronghold. Those first trips around the state were eye-opening. Although the Republican primary was only months away, there was little evident enthusiasm for the incumbent. In Dodge City, Roberts's adopted hometown, we didn't see a single Pat Roberts yard sign. Steve Morris joined us on this trip. Steve was still smarting over his defeat at the hands of the Brownback cabal; not because of the fact that he'd lost a Republican primary, but how. During his 2012 primary, Americans for Prosperity blanketed his district with postcards that read, "Unhappy that Obama and five Supreme Court justices are forcing you to accept ObamaCare? Thank Steve Morris. He voted to restrict Kansans' right to opt-out of ObamaCare if the law was upheld. Steve Morris' vote prevented you from having the option to say NO to Obama's radical agenda."[13]

This was a flat out lie. Actually, during his last legislative session as state senate president, Morris voted for a constitutional amendment stating that Kansans could not be forced to buy insurance. The measure was not only a direct rebuke of ObamaCare, but it took aim at the provision most loathed by Kansans: the individual mandate. A former Air Force major and Vietnam War veteran, Steve may be the most honorable man I've ever met. He deserved better from his fellow Republicans. But in a low-turnout primary, these smear tactics worked well enough to unseat one of our state's most dedicated public servants. Now he was escorting me throughout the western Kansas towns he knew so well.

THE NEW AMERICAN PARADOX

In Dodge City, we met with a group of local leaders that included retired schoolteacher Ethel Peterson, a Democrat who had served in the Kansas House for four decades. At first Ethel was skeptical why any Democrat should consider supporting an Independent. When the conversation turned to education policy, I talked to her about "the New American Paradox." It's my belief that it's harder than ever for the average American to get ahead and, yet, paradoxically easier to do nothing with your life. As a lifelong educator, Ethel was intimately familiar with the correlation between educational attainment and economic opportunity.

Altering the New American Paradox will require addressing the summer learning deficit for lower income kids, among other measures. High income kids simply have access to more enriching opportunities during the summer. They read more, and have more parental involvement. They continue learning during the summer, while lower income kids tend to regress, leading educators to conduct remedial lessons during the first weeks of each new school year. As I discussed this issue in Dodge City, I suggested that these programs didn't necessarily need to be staffed by licensed teachers. This last point brought a spirited rejoinder from Ethel.

"Why wouldn't we take advantage of the availability of licensed educators if we could?" she asked.

A local community college official then interjected by recalling his own experience in a summer program. He said the biggest impact on his life came from a college student who was working in the program. I wrapped up the debate by saying, "If this is what we're arguing about, we've won." If we were contending over who the teachers would be, then clearly we agreed that the program was necessary and worth government support.

I don't know whether I won Ethel over that first day, or whether it took more conversations. I do know that she became a strong supporter and a friendly face at future Dodge City events. That evening ended at Youthville, a local center for at-risk kids. Dodge City native Aaron Estabrook, a veteran of the war in Afghanistan, accompanied me. We arrived after 7 p.m. to a staff that graciously showed us around the campus, explained what they were doing, and told of the challenges of a constrained funding environment. As the summer sun set around 10 p.m., I thanked the executive director for staying so late. He had a telling response.

"In thirty years, Pat Roberts, our hometown senator, hasn't visited us once," he said. "I would have stayed until midnight to share with you what we're doing."

I myself went to catch the midnight train back to Kansas City. It was two hours late, but as I finally settled in my seat for the seven-hour ride I kept replaying in my mind what I'd seen and heard that day. Even though we were only at 7 percent in the polls, I had taken heart. It would be morning before I was home, but by then I realized that the opportunity for an Independent candidate to unseat Roberts was real.

ROCKETING THROUGH THE GRAVITATIONAL PULL

One of the first strategic decisions we made was to start advertising early in July, five weeks before the Republican primary was over. It turned out that Roberts had his hands full with Milton Wolf, meaning he wasn't paying attention to some pesky Independent. While we ran the risk of depleting our financial resources too early, we wanted to increase my name identification with the voters—on our own terms. It's a rule in politics that it's better to "define" yourself than to let your opponent do it for you. I had the rare opportunity to pitch myself as a candidate before either major party candidate really started paying attention. The goal was to reach the high teens in the polls before the Republican primary was decided. That wouldn't put us in first place, but it would be respectable in a three-way race and we figured the press and the voters would take our candidacy seriously.

As in a track meet, there's a danger for a runner making a move too soon. The risk was that we would deplete our resources by advertising before voters were really paying attention. Having sworn off any money from special interests or lobbyists, we knew how difficult future fundraising would be after my friends, colleagues, and family had contributed. We also knew the Roberts campaign, with their longstanding ties to K Street lobbyists, would be able to replenish their funds quickly if they were able to beat Milton Wolf. It was important that we didn't waste a single dollar.

There's also peril in waiting too long, especially for third-party candidates. Unless you surprise the pundits and the public with a strong early showing, there's a gravitational pull that is exerted on Independents. The two parties erode away their support by characterizing them as spoilers with no chance of victory. Voters want their ballot to matter. Advertising early also helped us with our signature gathering. As a statewide Independent candidate, I needed 5,000 signatures from registered Kansas voters. We didn't want to barely reach that number either, because Kansas's secretary of state is notoriously partisan and could find plenty of reasons to disqualify signatures. Three years earlier he'd initially rejected the Americans Elect presidential petition drive on the grounds that fewer than 100 of the 32,000 signees had dated the form improperly.

We decided to take a chance that Kansans were ready to hear from me. We had raised just over $600,000 from donors in our first month. Most of the contributions came from friends, family members, and people who had worked with me in the private sector. I also had a number of close friends who put themselves on the line with their networks to get contributions for me, a candidate who had barely registered in the polls. We were about to commit to spend all that money on one ad.

Our first political ad was a thirty-second spot depicting two teams, one in red and one in blue, engaged in an unwinnable contest of tug of war. When it was shown to me, I thought a viewer might misconstrue the message and believe that the moral of the story was that one side could actually pull the rope across the finish line and win the contest. This is how Republicans and Democrats think. I suggested ending it instead with a wide screen shot that showed the rope actually anchored behind each of the teams, showing that no one could ever prevail.

My idea was greeted with polite criticism, so I deferred to my team's judgment. Good thing, because the ad was incredibly well received. It seemed to resonate with everyone who saw it. While campaigning in parades or other public events people would spot me and talk spontaneously about the tug of war spot. It gave us an immediate bump in the polls. The first public survey that came out after the primaries put me at 23 percent, just two points behind Democratic nominee Chad Taylor and only nine percentage points behind Senator Roberts, who'd bested Milton Wolf in a much closer race than anyone anticipated.

PROBLEM SOLVING, NOT PARTISANSHIP

In mid-August, we embarked on a nine-day bus trip through Kansas. We called it our Problem Solving Bus Tour and put the mantra "Problem Solving, not Partisanship" on the side of our coach. This is one clear advantage of being a political Independent. There's no requirement for an Independent to engage in empty games to support a particular political party. Independents can focus exclusively on solving problems. This point was reinforced for me when Angus King, the Independent senator from Maine, called me to get acquainted. He said that being an Independent was wonderful because he could work with either side of the aisle on problems that he thought were critical.

The bus tour was a great opportunity to meet with the Kansans who were on the front lines of solving problems every day. At Sybil's suggestion, we set a goal to engage in a community service project in every city we visited. We did so to highlight our belief that the job I was seeking was about serving the people of Kansas, not the other way around. It was a learning experience every step of the way. I've lived in Kansas for almost two decades, spent summers here as a boy since the 1980s, and started businesses in the state; Sybil is Kansas-born, Kansas-raised, and Kansas-educated. Yet both of us were constantly acquiring new information about the people I wanted to represent in Washington and gaining new and deeper understandings of their needs.

As we peeled tomatoes in a Lawrence food pantry, we were told that close to 30 percent of Douglas County residents were food-insecure. More than 10,000 individuals had accessed the food bank at one point or another during the past year. A Methodist minister in Manhattan, Kansas, described to us in great detail the problem of the "benefits cliff." His church was focused on helping those in need, and he was keenly aware that there was a point at which for every dollar a person receiving public assistance earned, a dollar in benefits was taken away from them.

This problem was not new to me, or to U.S. policy makers. Bill Clinton had made it a big part of his first presidential campaign. In "Putting People First," the Democrat's 1992 campaign manifesto, the Clinton campaign called for tweaking the tax code, strengthening the safety net, and imposing conditions on receiving assistance—all in ways that would alter the equation to aid the working poor. Instead of being penalized economically for transitioning from welfare to work, they would be rewarded. Clinton's proposals were enacted into law; so were Republican ideas about making work a requirement of welfare. The upshot was a marked decline in the poverty rate. But it didn't last forever and two decades later, this Christian pastor made a persuasive case that it was time for another round of fixes in addressing poverty.

The campaign had its light moments. In the town of McPherson, our public schedule included having Sybil compete in a triathlon that benefited a local charity. I teased Sybil that this was one race she might not want to win. Let one of McPherson's citizens get the medal, I suggested, only half in jest. When the race was over, it appeared that she had gotten second place among all the female contestants. We decided she should stay behind for the awards ceremony, while the campaign bus tour went ahead to the next town. When it came time to announce the female winner, they called Sybil's name. She protested that she'd really finished second. Apparently not: The person we thought had won was a man wearing his girlfriend's number.

As we traveled the state, we found that our campaign was drawing Kansans from across the political spectrum, with a shared conviction that they were fed up with Washington. Sometimes that belief was all they had in common. But they could talk to each other anyway, we found. Everyday Americans don't show up, even at overtly political events, with talking points written for them by partisan political professionals in some windowless Washington office for the sole purpose of scoring points at the other party's expense. They come with actual questions, albeit sometimes misguided ones.

"What are you going to do about all the gays in the White House?" one woman asked me at a meet-and-greet in a Great Bend, Kansas, bar and grill.

That was a new one to me, and my first thought in answering was concern for the feelings of a gay campaign aide present at the event. I replied that I knew of no problems along those lines and that, in any event, my own views toward sexual orientation were guided by a spirit of inclusiveness. She seemed to accept this answer, but a younger woman didn't let the conversation end there. She told the first woman about her own friends and family members who were gay, the implication being that she found the older woman intolerant. Instead of being defensive or combative—remember, these were citizens from the American Heartland, not cable TV combatants—the first woman thanked her for sharing those experiences. We moved on to other discussion topics. I was struck at how two individuals with opposite perspectives could talk about their differences without rancor or insult. It reminded me of the old adage, "It's hard to hate up close."

The experience also demonstrated for me how powerful an Independent candidacy can be for bringing people together. At rallies for partisan candidates, the audience is generally handpicked to create as supportive an environment as possible for the candidate. Hecklers occasionally sneak in, but they're often ushered out of the rally as soon as they make themselves known—often with other rally-goers screaming at them and, in some cases, engaging in physical intimidation or even violence. As an Independent, I had Kansans from across the ideological spectrum attend campaign events, because the events themselves weren't tainted with a partisan tinge. Everyone was welcome, as were divergent points of view. What we learned, which I'll describe in greater detail in

Chapter 11, is how much common ground exists among voters from across the political spectrum. It's our politicians and parties who divide us as an electoral strategy.

Most of all, I was impressed by how far people would travel to see us. Kansas is a big place, and people often drive long distances to see loved ones. But traveling seventy-five miles to share a few minutes with a first-time Senate candidate running third in the polls showed me how badly Kansas voters wanted something different in their politics. We had a couple of videographers who traveled with us during the bus trip. What they captured always amazed me. Kansans were getting it.

For me, some of the most fun was marching in parades. Folks are happy at parades, and it was enjoyable to interact with smiling people. Sybil's mother, Seana, had her Ford F-150 pickup truck decaled with "Orman for Senate" paraphernalia. She'd drive in parades with her similarly adorned vintage horse trailer in tow. Riding up front in the cab were our dogs, Lucy and Mala, usually clad in patriotic apparel. My father, a natural-born salesman, attended almost every parade. He worked the crowds enthusiastically, as did a rotating group of volunteers, Sybil's friends, and other members of the large Orman clan. We had one of our staffers wear a horse costume and entertain the crowd with his antics. He usually stole the show.

The parades became less fun once Pat Roberts started considering me a threat. It seemed best for me to walk the parade route, instead of riding in a car, to be more accessible to voters. Invariably, walking and greeting voters left us lagging behind the float in front of us; when the distance became too great and we risked slowing down the parade, our team of volunteers and I would start running to catch up. It's hard to imagine a more innocent activity and one less likely to be misconstrued. But in today's hyper-partisan political arena, nothing is innocent. By September, the GOP attack machine was sending camera-toting "trackers" to our events and seeding the crowd with political operators who would ask planted questions as I walked along the parade route. These weren't really questions: They were shouted accusations, such as "Will you vote to repeal ObamaCare?"

My opponents would splice such queries together in a video that would show me running to catch up with the parade—never mind that I'd answered the question dozens of times that day—to create a visual effect that I was literally running away from tough questions. This sophomoric stunt supposedly bolstered one of Pat Roberts's more dubious anti-Orman narratives: namely, that I was ducking the issues. Knowing that voters didn't have the same shorthand understanding of what an Independent stood for, I had committed to answering any question that a voter asked me.

Eventually I learned how to defang the trackers. I would simply answer every question they lobbed at me by saying, "It's really disappointing that Senator Roberts skipped the hearing on the Ebola virus." I knew they wouldn't run with that answer regardless of the question they asked.

But the nastiness soon became more pointed. Telephoned threats from anonymous phone callers were a regular occurrence at my campaign headquarters. This particularly put Sybil on edge, as she was now pregnant with our first child. Knowing how vulnerable we were on a parade route, she worried that we might be targets of deranged individuals who were lapping up the venom being spewed by the other side.

For me, the most galling moment came at a parade in the college town of Manhattan, Kansas, while walking alongside a volunteer named Jade Lane. One coward shouted from the crowd that Jade wasn't a real American because he was campaigning for me.

This would be an ugly thing to say to any citizen of this country. It was a particularly disgraceful remark to make to Jade, a former Army Ranger who served in Iraq and Afghanistan and was awarded the Purple Heart after being shot through his shoulder and knee in combat. This was the flip side to the two women in the diner who had aired their differences with civility. It showed me how ordinary people can be stirred to hate by skilled political professionals. We noticed a rather abrupt change in tone the first week of September. Only later did we really find out why.

NATIONALIZING THE RACE

On Wednesday, September 3, Democratic nominee Chad Taylor informed the Kansas secretary of state's office that he was withdrawing from the race. After winning the nomination in a low-turnout Democratic primary, Taylor had been stagnant in the polls and was raising little money. Speculation that he might bow out had bubbled up earlier, but the Shawnee County district attorney mostly kept his own counsel. It was reported in the press Taylor had spoken privately with Senator Claire McCaskill, a Missouri Democrat, and that other Democrats hoped Taylor would quit, in the hope that a two-way race would be tougher for Roberts to win.[14]

This perception was undoubtedly true, but the Roberts campaign immediately made it into something else.

"Chad Taylor's withdrawal from the U.S. Senate race reveals a corrupt bargain between Greg Orman and national Democrats including Senator Harry Reid that disenfranchises Kansas Democrats," said Roberts campaign manager Leroy Towns in a written statement. "It makes clear what has been obvious from the start: Orman is the choice of liberal Democrats and he can no longer hide behind an independent smokescreen."[15]

The curious phrase about "disenfranchising" Kansas Democrats was more than a throwaway line: It was a new Republican tactic. Under

Kansas election law, September 3 was the last day Taylor could remove his name from the ballot. But Kansas secretary of state Kris Kobach attempted to nullify the law, telling Democrats that if they didn't choose another nominee Taylor's name would remain on the ballot. The state Supreme Court swatted down this cynical gambit, ruling that Kobach had no authority to do anything of the kind. In response, the Roberts campaign attacked the Kansas Supreme Court on the grounds that it had "disenfranchised"—that word again—the 65,000 Democrats who'd voted for Taylor in the primary.

In Chapter 10, we'll discuss how both Republicans and Democrats rig the election rules to give their respective parties an advantage. Needless to say, the actual disenfranchisement of voters has become a staple of the duopoly, as both parties seek to maintain their control over our politics and avoid accountability at the ballot box. It was almost laughable that the Roberts campaign would use such a word in response to a challenge from an Independent.

This episode did more that suggest collusion between Roberts and Kobach. It also revealed the Roberts campaign's negative line of attack against me for the next two months. The man implementing that strategy, however, would not be Roberts's veteran campaign manager Leroy Towns, the man Pat Roberts described as his "alter ego." The week Chad Taylor withdrew, Towns was unceremoniously fired, essentially on the orders of Senate Republican Leader Mitch McConnell. The Roberts campaign had raised a meager $62,000 in August, wasn't filming or airing ads, and was still reeling from reports that that senator didn't live in Kansas anymore—and rarely visited the state. A briefing paper given to McConnell about the competitive Senate races in the country showed that GOP plans to take the Senate were threatened by Roberts's listless campaign.

Roberts wasn't going to lose to any Kansas Democrat, the private polling numbers showed, but he was in danger of losing to me. The exact impact of my victory on control of the Senate wasn't clear—more on that later—but McConnell didn't want to find out. He called Pat Roberts to angrily tell him his campaign needed to be retooled, immediately. McConnell didn't issue threats exactly, but he made it clear that the national Republican Party would be sending resources and manpower to help Roberts and that he ought to accept them. Roberts cursed at McConnell in frustration, but before their conversation had ended he'd agreed to go along. Towns was gone the next day.

In his place, the Republican Party dispatched three veteran Republican hired guns, none of whom had Kansas roots or any particular connection to Pat Roberts.[16] They made no secret of their plans to go negative.

"We are going to be very aggressive now that it has become a national campaign," Roberts said at a political forum sponsored by the Kansas Chamber of Commerce in Wichita. This statement managed to be simultaneously candid and disingenuous: It was Roberts and his new team of hired guns who were intent on making the race "a national campaign." Their methods would prove both crude and effective.[17]

I had hoped that legendary Kansas senator Bob Dole, whom I deeply respect, could somehow remain neutral. Roberts and the junior senator from Kansas, Jerry Moran, had disappointed Dole on the United Nations Convention on the Rights of Persons with Disabilities—a treaty that Dole, who still suffered from the severe battle injuries he received in World War II, strongly supported. In May of 2012, Moran had gone so far as to endorse the treaty, saying that it advanced "fundamental values by standing up for the rights of those with disabilities." In December of 2012, however, both Kansas senators voted against the treaty—leaving the United States in the company of Congo and Guyana as the only countries that failed to ratify the pact.

Yet Dole, who turned ninety-one years old that summer, had known

Pat Roberts for decades. Dole was also too much a devout Republican to sit out an election. He had noticed even before I got in the race how difficult the environment was for Senator Roberts, and after a trip to western Kansas had conveyed this concern to Scott Reed, a former Dole aide who was plugged into the GOP establishment in Washington, D.C., where he worked for the U.S. Chamber of Commerce. "There wasn't the enthusiasm I expected for Pat," Dole told his former aide.[18]

In June, two young RNC aides had told Roberts that their polling showed that his residence in Alexandria, Virginia—he hadn't lived in Kansas in years—was bothersome to voters back home. Until Mitch McConnell called him in early September, according to post-mortem reporting I read later, Pat tended to dismiss worried intra-party critics as upstarts who knew vastly less about the Sunflower State than he did. That was surely true, but it didn't matter. The party professionals may not have known a sunflower from an oil well, but they knew how to win midterm elections in heavily Republican states.

Their playbook was neither extensive nor uplifting. As *The Washington Post* put it, Republicans had a simple blueprint for taking the Senate: "Don't make mistakes, and make it all about Obama, Obama, Obama. Every new White House crisis would bring a new Republican ad. And every Democratic incumbent would be attacked relentlessly for voting with the president 97 or 98 or 99 percent of the time."[19]

This would have been a difficult case to make against Chad Taylor, a local prosecutor with no real connection to Washington or the president. It should have been impossible against me; I wasn't a Democrat at all. But the well-oiled Republican juggernaut didn't let facts get in the way of a good narrative. And the GOP machine found a willing collaborator in Pat Roberts.

This period of our campaign demonstrates another challenge for Independents in breaking through the red/blue paradigm in the minds of voters. In Part II, we'll describe in detail what both Democrats and

Republicans have done to condition voters to believe there are only two choices and to reinforce the environment of hyper-partisanship that has put our country on an unsustainable path. The practical effect of all that conditioning was that when I introduced myself as an Independent, many Democrats heard "Republican"—and vice-versa. In effect, what many partisan voters were hearing was that I wasn't one of them, and, therefore, by the process of elimination, I must be from the "other" party.

A FACT-FREE ZONE

The incumbent senator didn't meet his new campaign manager until September 5, the day before our first debate at the state fair in Hutchinson. Roberts prepared a thick briefing book on the many statewide issues he expected to be the focus of the debate. The thirty-three-year-old political operator, who was born a year after Pat Roberts was first elected to Congress, told Pat that the binder was unnecessary. He handed the seventy-eight-year-old incumbent a single sheet of paper with a simple new campaign strategy: morph Greg Orman into a puppet of Barack Obama and Harry Reid.[20]

Although I was looking forward to being able to discuss issues that mattered to people, I was still nervous. There was a rumor floating around before the debate that Roberts wouldn't show up, which created an odd vibe. It was my first debate, and I had never previously witnessed one at a Kansas State Fair. While I'd always tried to be respectful of Senator Roberts, my team wanted me to be particularly respectful during the debate.

As Sybil and I arrived on the fairgrounds, we were met by a member of my team, Valerie Martin, who had watched the earlier debate between

Governor Brownback and Paul Davis. It was a bare-knuckles affair, and Valerie had an inkling ours might be, too.

"All bets are off," she told us. "This is a free for all."

Roughly half the audience supported each candidate. Pat may have only had the RNC's one-page blueprint for twenty-four hours, but it wasn't complicated and he had absorbed it quickly. It was clear from the opening bell that his strategy was to position the contest as being between himself and the duo of Harry Reid and Barack Obama. Having supported candidates from both political parties in the past, I had come to expect this line of attack. If anything, Pat overdid it. He invoked the Senate majority leader's name so many times that by the third question the audience was booing every time he invoked Reid. At one point, Pat looked to me for help. The audience was shouting so loudly that he couldn't get a word in as he was trying to answer a question and he said, "Greg, could you give me a hand?" Eventually, the audience didn't wait for Roberts to answer. They simply preempted him and shouted "Harry Reid" before he could answer a question.

To a debate participant, the reaction of the crowd can be misleading. It's natural to believe that if you've won the live audience, you've won the debate. This is not always the case. Typically, many more voters see the debate on television—and many more than that see only a clip or two from it, sometimes courtesy of a paid, and opportunistically edited, attack ad. Among those watching the debate via live stream were political reporters who didn't pick up the audience interaction. It might have shaped the coverage of the race if they had, but all they heard was the comments of the debate moderator and the candidates themselves. As a result, it looked to some as though I was letting Roberts pin a label on me.

A couple of times during the state fair debate, Roberts claimed paternity for some highly popular Kansas program. He said, for instance, that he was "the father of the crop insurance program."[21] When I shook his hand at the end of the debate, I quipped privately that I had been afraid he was going to say he was my father, too. Pat, known for his sense of humor, was able to laugh.

Three times during that debate I agreed with something Roberts said. This shouldn't have surprised anyone. As an Independent, it was perfectly reasonable that I'd share some common ground with a Republican. As a businessman who finds the Democratic Party often fiscally irresponsible, Republican positions resonate with me on certain issues. But the media are so conditioned to the blue/red partisan dynamic that they didn't know what to make of my answers. The idea that a candidate in a debate might seek to find some common ground with his opponent as a basis for solving problems was almost heretical to some in the media. Their belief seemed to be that if Pat had said, "The sky is blue," it was my job to say, "He's wrong. It's red"—or some variation on that theme.

The Roberts campaign didn't waste any time taking advantage of my candor. Not content that I had agreed with Pat three times, they cut-and-pasted a clip together to make it look like I had agreed with him four times, and then they pushed the video out on YouTube. The press called them out on this subterfuge, but a tone had been set. At the second debate, which was tailored to allow candidates to give more detailed answers, Roberts preemptively attacked. "Trying to get Greg Orman's position on an issue, any issue, is like trying to nail Jell-O to the wall," he said early in the session. "Kansas needs someone in the Senate with conviction and backbone. My opponent has neither."[22]

By way of response, I offered detailed policy proposals, some of which were closer to the standard Republican view, such as amending Dodd-Frank restrictions on community banks, and some of which were closer to the Democratic Party stance, such as fixing the nation's immigration problems with comprehensive legislation. The closest I came to personal criticism was to assert that Roberts and his fellow Republicans in Washington, along with Senate Democrats, have created gridlock in the nation's capital. "Both parties are failing Kansas," I said. "I'm running as an Independent to reject the false choices that the two-party system has presented us with."

Before the third and final debate, I would learn later that Roberts's wife and daughter expressed their displeasure to the campaign's new general consultant about the senator's relentlessly negative campaign. "It's all about Obama," they were told. "That's the way we win."[23]

Despite this attempted intervention, Roberts was all-in by that time, determined to win through hyper-partisanship, irrespective of what any family members thought. When the moderator brought the last debate to a close by asking each of us to say something nice about our opponent, I tried to be gracious and sincere. "I will have to say that every time I've had an opportunity to talk privately with the senator, he's been a gentleman with a great sense of humor," I said. I also praised his service to our country as a U.S. Marine.

Then it was Roberts's turn—and he couldn't resist two last digs. "I would say that you are a very well-dressed opponent," he said, looking over my dark suit, light-blue shirt, and a blue tie with white and red stripes. "I admire your accumulation of wealth," he added. "I have a little question of how you got there from here, but I think that's the American dream and I would hope that we could make that possible for everybody up and down every small Kansas community."[24]

His passive-aggressive comments struck some of the press as tacky. (" . . . the defining moment may have been the final question," noted *The Wichita Eagle*, "when they were asked to say something nice about each other—and Roberts didn't".)[25] To me, his jabs were mostly ironic. Roberts and the Republican machine had spent millions of dollars portraying me as Harry Reid's most loyal soldier (and Barack Obama's personal rubber stamp). I met Senator Reid in 2007, but don't really know him. I have read, however, that his reputation as a young boxer in Nevada was that he would punch his opponent after the bell. That's essentially what Pat Roberts did—an apt reminder that the two major political parties campaign—and govern—exactly the same way.

CLOWN CAR POLITICS

The last week of our campaign was filled with tactical trivia. First the Republicans misled Kansas State football coach Bill Snyder into endorsing Roberts on camera, an endorsement they promptly aired as a TV ad. According to Coach Snyder, he thought the endorsement was being filmed for a private fundraising event, not for broadcast on the state's airwaves. Dodging fallout from that sleight-of-hand, the Roberts campaign responded with mock anger to a crack I'd made in response to the steady stream of conservative surrogates who trekked to Kansas to call me a liberal Democrat. This roster included Ted Cruz, Sarah Palin, Mike Huckabee, Rick Santorum, and two dozen other national Republicans. On October 31, the GOP's "Clean Sweep Bus Tour" came to Kansas featuring four former or current Republican governors: Chris Christie of New Jersey, Mike Pence of Indiana, Bill Haslam of Tennessee, and Haley Barbour, who'd served as governor of Mississippi and was a well-known Washington lobbyist and fixture.

"Greg," a reporter asked me, "how can you compete with the turnout machine that the Republicans have on display today with the big bus tour, with everybody endorsing Senator Roberts and Governor Brownback?"

"It sort of seems like a Washington establishment clown car to me," I replied. "You know, every day a new person comes out of the car."[26]

No one would have minded my wisecrack except that Bob Dole was also one of the Republicans who'd come to Kansas to endorse Pat. So the Roberts campaign quickly asserted that I'd called Bob Dole—a wounded World War II combat veteran, Republican icon, and Kansas's favorite son—a clown. I hadn't, but this is what passes for a "gotcha" moment in politics these days. Feigning outrage, Roberts called on me to apologize.

Instead, I sent Dole a private email explaining what I meant, expressing my respect for him, and saying I'd never think of calling him a clown or any other name. The former senator publically characterized it as an apology, while I felt it was more of a clarification of what I'd said. Whatever it was, Fox News and various right-leaning websites couldn't get enough of this little non-story in the last days of the campaign.

My team wanted me to run a negative ad blasting Pat for living in Northern Virginia, not Kansas, but that's not how I wanted to end the campaign. I'd decided early on to avoid personal attacks in favor of a strategy that dovetailed with my reason for running. I wanted to project an image that was positive and focused on solving problems. Most people say that in modern politics, winning is everything. But my view is that how you win is important, too. If you get elected by talking about issues and opportunities, you have a mandate to get something done. If you get elected by tearing down your opponent, you have a mandate for further hatefulness and partisanship.

It was always clear what the 2014 campaign was about for the two parties. For Democrats, this election was about stopping the Republicans. For Republicans, it was about stopping Democrats. During the campaign, I told voters we didn't need an election that accomplished nothing. With a solidly Republican House of Representatives and a Democratic incumbent in the White House, the ingredients for gridlock were already firmly in place. What we needed was to send both parties a message that it was time to stop the bickering and start solving problems. If the basis of my campaign was personal attacks on Senator Roberts, that message wouldn't be received.

By November, the lead I'd had in the polls had dwindled to virtually nothing, as Roberts's relentless portrayal of me as a liberal Democrat in an Independent's clothing had taken its toll. The Republican machine's organized get-out-the-vote efforts would finish the job. This organizational advantage is something that Independents are going to have to tackle if we want to be successful in changing the environment in Washington. As I describe in Part IV of the book, I think the tools available today make it eminently possible to replicate the ground game of the major parties.

One last kick in the shins would come our way on Election Day when Vice President Joe Biden was in theory trying to help Democrats with their own get-out-the vote drive in a Connecticut campaign.

Throughout the campaign, I had been asked by political reporters which party I would caucus with in Washington. This was not an academic question. In each house of Congress, control of the gavel, the legislative calendar, and the chairmanship of every committee is dependent on one factor: which party holds the most seats. It's winner-take-all every two years. In 2014, thirty-three states held their regularly scheduled Senate elections, plus three others because of death or retirements. Going into the election, Democrats held fifty-three seats and the Republicans held forty-five. Two officially Independent senators, Angus King and Vermont's self-described "democratic Socialist" Bernie Sanders,[27] caucused with the Democrats; the vice president could break all ties if the Senate was divided fifty-fifty. The upshot was that Republicans needed a net pickup of six seats.

The wrinkle was that no one knew which political party I would caucus with, because I hadn't committed one way or the other. I hadn't refused to address the question; it was just that my answer mystified a political press and political establishment that could only process a binary response—Republican or Democrat.

In late August, while Chad Taylor was still in the race, I was asked by MSNBC host Steve Kornacki which party I'd caucus with. My answer was that my plan was to caucus "with whichever party is willing to actually . . . start trying to solve problems as opposed to just pleasing the extremists in their own base."

For the next two months I made the same point in many interviews. "I'm going to caucus with whichever party really wants to solve problems in the country," I said the morning of the election. "Either party, if they're willing to solve our problems, I'm willing to work with them. In some cases, I agree more with the Republican position on issues, and in other cases I agree more with the Democratic position on issues."[28]

Yet the country's political establishment, including political reporters, couldn't seem to get their minds around it. "What Will Greg Orman Do?" *The New York Times* wondered in a headline. NBC News called me "the most interesting man in politics this November." *The Huffington Post* wrote about "The Orman Factor."[29] The press was so obsessed with this issue that they began to call people who had donated to my campaign to determine if they had an insight into my thinking. In a couple of cases, they wanted to know if the donors would be angry if I chose one side or the other. To my knowledge, every donor who was asked that question indicated that they trusted me to make the right decision.

My goal was to use my vote to organize the Senate as leverage to get both parties to start genuinely focusing on solving problems. I made it clear that regardless of the initial decision that I made, I wouldn't hesitate to use my vote to hold the majority accountable—particularly if I was the swing vote that decided who would be in the majority. I believed (and still believe) that my approach was the best way to get Washington working again for Kansas and for America.

Among those who thought this was some kind of code was the vice president of the United States. In an Election Day interview on a Connecticut radio station Biden gave the Republicans the words they needed to sell their storyline. "We have a chance of picking up an Independent who will be with us in the state of Kansas," he declared.

Republicans quickly seized on the line, sending out an abbreviated clip in a blitz of last-minute automated calls to voters throughout Kansas. "Joe Biden admitted that Greg Orman will become a Democrat in the U.S. Senate even though Orman is denying it to Kansas voters," the automated calls stated.

"Greg's never spoken to the vice president in his life," Jim Jonas countered to the media. "Greg is an Independent, and he's not going to Washington to represent the Democrats or the Republicans."[30]

Most of the Kansans on the receiving end of those robocalls never heard that. Some wouldn't have believed it anyway. The damage was done. Biden's blunder was the last straw. Some people in my campaign just wrote it off as the gaffe-prone Biden being Biden. Others viewed the Republicans' twisting of his words as Roberts's last little dirty trick of a spitefully run campaign. It's not clear to me that it was an innocent gaffe.

One of the first rules of dealing with the media is: "You get to choose the words; they get to choose the punctuation." As an example: "I know some people think Larry's a crook, but he's the most honest man I know," would become in the hands of an unscrupulous reporter or political hack, "Some people think Larry's a crook." Or even worse, "Larry's a crook."

I found myself thinking that Biden must have known my opponents would punctuate his words. I'm not saying the Democratic vice president deliberately colluded with a Republican senator to defeat me. I am suggesting that the two parties are so rigidly entrenched that their leaders literally cannot process the idea of a truly Independent member of Congress anymore, notwithstanding that independent-minded voters are a solid plurality in this country.

On election night, Sybil and I were ensconced in a Drury Inn suite separate from the rest of the top campaign staff. A "watch party" for supporters was underway at the Overland Park Convention Center less than a mile away. In a few minutes those of us in all three of those rooms would learn if my next job would be serving in the Senate—or whether we'd all be remembered as participants in the supposed fool's errand of challenging the existing duopoly in U.S. politics.

Sybil and I were alone when the knock came on the door. Jim Jonas, my campaign manager, and Dave Beattie, my pollster, were standing in the hall, looking resigned to bad news. Dave spoke first, but the looks on their faces had already told me what I needed to know.

"You're not going to win," he said simply.

This bluntness masked Dave's emotions. For nearly a decade he and I had worked together on a variety of political causes. This wasn't just a job for him. He shared my yearning to give power to Americans the two parties had left behind. I asked Jim to get Senator Roberts on the telephone. While Pat had been prickly with me in public—and at times mean-spirited—he was gracious that night. He said he appreciated some of the ideas I'd advanced in the campaign and wanted to work with me to make some of them a reality. I congratulated him and wished him luck in his continued service in government.

My attention quickly turned to what I was going tell the Kansans who'd thought enough of our cause to flock to the convention center. They'd arrived that night hoping for a victory party. They would hear a concession speech instead. I viewed this address as more important than the one I'd have delivered if the election had gone my way. In that case, the people of Kansas would have been the ones sending the message.

As Sybil and I drove to the convention center, the whole campaign poured through my mind. In 2012, Mitt Romney was faulted for writing a victory speech in advance but not preparing a concession speech. All candidates who have ever put themselves forward for elective office can understand Romney's mindset. Thoughts about losing don't help a candidate. Even when defeat comes, it is hard to accept. To buoy my spirits as we drove in silence to the last event of the 2014 campaign, I thought about how far we'd come. I decided that my job that evening was to assure those who had invested so much of themselves in the campaign—and people outside the state who had supported us from afar—that this was a beginning, not an end. Although I lost a Senate race in Kansas, the idea that Independents could win seats in government, and that we must start doing so, was the idea I wanted to convey.

We had taken on the entire Republican establishment, along with a handful of Democrats, and right up until Election Day the contest was still in doubt. We had come a long way. Still, I could barely hold it together as Sybil and I climbed the steps to the podium.

Looking out on the sea of faces attending my concession speech—Republicans who thought their party had veered too far right, Democrats who found the national party too liberal, other Democrats who'd caught our nonpartisan bug, Independents frustrated with both parties, Kansans who just wanted government to work again—I felt strongly that they'd deserved a better result.

"While Senator Roberts won tonight," I said in my concession speech, "we did not lose. We not only ran against Senator Roberts, we ran against the whole Washington establishment."

Whether or not I ever again ask Kansans to elect me to office, I'm going to keep challenging the political duopoly—fighting to ensure that Americans have a government that puts the interests of Americans ahead of the interests of either political party.

PART II

A

DYSFUNCTIONAL

DUOPOLY

★★★

CHAPTER 4

The New American Crisis

THE CONSEQUENCES OF THE FAILURE OF THE TWO-PARTY SYSTEM

——— ★ ★ ★ ———

LIKE NEARLY EVERY ICONIC national symbol these days, the phrase "American Exceptionalism" has become a political pawn in the endless and distracting bickering between Democrats and Republicans. For much of Barack Obama's tenure in office, conservatives have groused that the forty-fourth U.S. president didn't understand the famous phrase, and was insufficiently proud of the United States. In foreign countries, this critique tended to leave people scratching their heads. *Of course* America is exceptional, they said, and the ascension to the presidency of a child born to a white mother from Kansas and a black exchange student from Kenya is itself evidence of that truism.

Is there any validity to the conservatives' broader complaint that modern American progressives are too quick to blame the United States for the world's problems and too focused on what is wrong with the country? Perhaps, but pointing out America's shortcomings is not unpatriotic—in fact, it's quite the opposite, if it leads to improving our country.

Yes, America is exceptional. Since our founding in 1776, we have built our country on the unique principles of equality, self-government, and social mobility. While those principles might not strike a twenty-first-century American as noteworthy, they certainly were 250 years ago. They are the basis for the American Idea—that unique set of principles that drove our founding as a nation. Until this country came along, the idea that you could change your station in life was barely a consideration. If you were born the son of a farmer, you became a farmer. If you were lucky enough to be born into a family with wealth and power, you inherited that wealth and power. In general, we have strived as a nation to build on these ideals. While it hasn't always been a straight line, over the last two-and-half centuries, we've made progress in improving the lives of Americans by staying true to our principles. Like the unfinished pyramid on our dollar bill, America, as a nation, is constantly striving to improve herself, evolving to meet each new challenge as it arises. And America has been a force for good in the world.

"No American will think it wrong of me if I proclaim that to have the United States at our side was to me the greatest joy," Winston Churchill wrote after World War II ended.[1] U.S. history is filled with examples of our nation and its people rising to meet great challenges. Whether facing off against global fascism and mass genocide during World War II, rebuilding Europe with the Marshall Plan, standing up to the expansion of Communism and the suppression of almost two billion people during the Cold War, or brokering the peace accord between Egypt and Israel, when the alarm bells rang, Americans answered the call. We were revered in the world. Americans could go almost anywhere and be welcomed—a tacit admission of the status our country held around the globe.

Today, however, we stand at an inflection point in our history. The course we choose will determine whether the twenty-first century is another era of American leadership or if our preeminence comes to an end, as it has for other dominant world powers throughout history, leaving our descendants the depressing task of writing the epitaph of a once-great nation.

Our political dysfunction is not only affecting our status in the world, but it is also hindering our ability to live up to our national ideals. One hundred and eighty-five years after Alexis de Tocqueville wrote about America's "great experiment" in democracy, our system of self-government is being compromised by a campaign finance system that allows special interests to buy politicians and elections. The parties have become a duopoly and are behaving like one—dramatically limiting competition and, by extension, limiting accountability. Social mobility, once a source of national pride, is in jeopardy as a result of these troubling changes.

My stump speech on the 2014 campaign trail echoed this theme. It started with a simple message:

> We all know our system of government is broken. We are sending the worst of both parties to Washington—bitter partisans who care more about pleasing the extremists and special interests in their own party than they do moving our country forward.
>
> As our elected leaders draw childish lines in the sand and refuse to cooperate, inaction has replaced leadership in solving our most pressing issues. Neglect is the result.
>
> Without political courage and meaningful action, our problems have grown to almost unmanageable proportions. . . . The sum of our public debt and entitlement deficit is now almost half a million dollars for every American family. And while we're spending more and more money as a country, it's harder than ever for the average American to get ahead.
>
> I'm concerned if we don't start addressing these issues, our

standard of living, our status in the world, and the very existence
of the middle class in America is at risk.

The cynicism surrounding politics makes it easy to dismiss any candidate's stump speech. But the facts supporting those assertions are brac-
ing. Most voters are aware that our public debt is a huge problem. As a
percentage of our nation's gross national product it's approaching the
levels we faced during the height of World War II.

Think about that: During World War II, the United States mobi-
lized over sixteen million soldiers, sailors, airmen, and Marines. We were
fighting in Europe, North Africa, and the Pacific. Twenty-four million
more Americans marched into defense plants to power the war effort.
Three million cars were manufactured in this country in 1941. For the
entire duration of the war only 139 private automobiles were made.
Instead, Americans built hundreds of thousands of the tanks, planes,
ships, rifles, and artillery pieces that won the war. By the time of Japan's
1945 surrender, half the world's industrial production was taking place
in the United States.

The result of that massive investment in victory was a national debt
exceeding annual gross domestic product. Nonetheless, over the next
twenty-five years we dramatically reduced that ratio while simultaneously providing medical care to 600,000 wounded soldiers, sailors, airmen, and Marines, and enacting a GI Bill that sent millions of veterans
to college and vocational schools or put them in their own homes. We
did all this while rebuilding Europe, constructing an interstate highway
system, and sending a manned spacecraft to the moon.

In contrast, since the turn of century we've engaged in a war of choice
in Iraq—a war that neither established stability for Iraqis nor has yet been
paid for by Americans. Our wars in Iraq and Afghanistan, which have
now lasted longer than the Vietnam War or the American Revolution,

have overwhelmed the Veterans Administration's healthcare system and led to the rise of ISIS. We have ignored our impending retirement and health-care crises while social mobility in America has come to a grinding halt. In America today, if you're born in the bottom 20 percent of the economy, the overwhelming likelihood is that you'll die there, too.

Here are two charts that illustrate the slow death of the American Dream. The first, produced by the Pew Charitable Trusts Mobility Project, shows that, contrary to the up-by-the-bootstraps Horatio Alger tales that Americans take pride in, upward mobility is a rarity today. It shows that 43 percent of Americans are stuck on the bottom rung of our economic ladder.

Americas Raised at the Top and Bottom Are Likely to Stay There as Adults

Chances of moving up or down the family income ladder, by parents' quintile

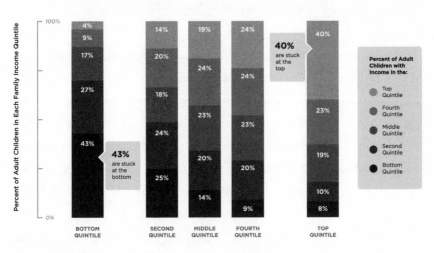

The second chart shows that kids of high income parents earn significantly more as adults than kids of low income parents.

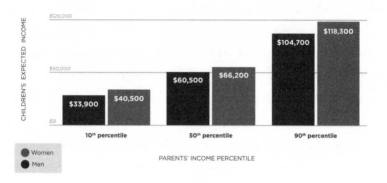

These charts represent a threat to our nation's well-being as well as its vision of itself. Economic mobility has always been a defining American characteristic. Its ethos is literally carved in stone on the base of the Statue of Liberty, the implied promise being that the USA is the place on earth where human beings—whether born here or naturalized as American citizens—can reach their potential.

Americans intuitively know that this is important. Although very few of us have memorized all the facts and charts, we understand what's going on—and comprehend the implications. In past years, survey after survey has shown that a large majority believe this country's future is in jeopardy. Sixty percent of American voters believe the nation is in decline.[2] Three-fourths believe our children and grandchildren will not be as prosperous or happy as the current generation.[3] That sad belief constitutes the undoing of the sacred social contract that is at the very foundation of the American Idea. A solid majority of voters now believe that working hard and playing by the rules may not be enough to succeed in our country today.[4] That fear is the death rattle of the American Dream.

Our fellow citizens are angry, justifiably, about our broken politics and self-absorbed leaders. In 1776, as our founders signed the Declaration of Independence, they did so knowing they were risking their fortunes and their lives. Today, many of our elected leaders won't even vote on legislation that confronts the hard issues because their votes might affect the outcome of their next election. Their notion of sacrificing for their country is to fly coach class. The common interests of our nation have given way to the self-interest of our elected leaders.

RIPE FOR DEMAGOGUERY

Donald Trump's bombastic and bigoted rhetoric is not the answer, but the two governing parties have failed us so miserably that millions of Americans have been drawn to him as the opposite of today's officeholders. Even some people who would never vote for him applaud him for raising one of the right questions: how politicians are bought by campaign donations. When he gives politicians money, The Donald told *The Wall Street Journal* in a July 29, 2015, interview, "They do whatever the hell you want them to do."[5]

Asked about this comment a week later by Fox News' Bret Baier during the first Republican debate of the 2015–2016 election cycle, the New York City real estate tycoon was only too happy to explain. "When they call, I give," he said. "And you know what, when I need something from them two years later, three years later, I call them. They are there for me. That's a broken system."

Although many Americans, including the nation's political establishment, disapproved of Trump for his many dubious policy pronouncements and hurtful, inflammatory statements—millions of voters applauded the man for his candid and succinct description of the endemic corruption that is strangling government in this country and impeding our ability to meet the many crises that threaten our well-being.

Because our government's finances are so large and complex, we have no clue about how many pigs are at the trough gathering their special-interest perks and payments. There are thousands of Donald Trumps—albeit without his flair or his hair or his forthright acknowledgment of what political donations do—who are gaming the system and getting rich off the taxpayers. They manipulate tax policy and bankruptcy laws, profiteer off the Pentagon, and benefit from a thousand little loopholes, subsidies, and special pleadings that are quietly inserted into federal and state law by pliant politicians doing lobbyists' bidding. To perpetuate this gravy train, these lobbyists, bundlers, billionaires, and special interests donate hundreds of millions of dollars to political campaigns, essentially rigging U.S. elections.

Armed with a friendly Supreme Court decision and abetted by Congress and both political parties, political slush funds known as super PACs have turned presidential politics into an arms race among rival billionaires and wealthy multinational corporations. In 2015, super PACs and other outside groups that can raise unlimited sums from businesses, individuals, and unions, in some cases without even disclosing their identity, amassed a $360 million war chest for the 2016 presidential campaign. This amount dwarfed the money collected by candidates themselves. Donations of $1 million or more accounted for half of the money.[6] If Americans were getting better government for all these donations, it might be worth it—a self-imposed tax on the wealthy for the good of the country.

Unfortunately, the power of money will likely only grow more pervasive as time goes on. With a $4 trillion annual U.S. budget to fight over, what we spend today on campaigns only represents a small fraction of what's at stake financially. Without meaningful reforms to our system of campaign finance or a dramatic change in the intentions, attitudes, and allegiances of the people we elect to represent us in Washington, D.C., the interests of average Americans will likely continue to take a back seat to the interests of the donor community.

In 1968, Americans tired of war wanted a new direction in Vietnam, but neither party would give it to them until a Minnesota Democrat with no moneyed interests behind him challenged the president of his own party. This public servant's name was Eugene McCarthy. Senator McCarthy didn't start campaigning until six weeks before the New Hampshire primary—not two years before, the way it is done today—and he never really started fundraising at all. He had no campaign infrastructure, no media consultants, no advertising budget, not even enough money to stay in hotel rooms. The total amount he'd raised when he entered the campaign was $400. Asked by skeptical reporters how he intended to challenge an incumbent president of the United States on that kind of budget, Gene McCarthy quipped, "We'll live off the land."[7]

He did, too, staying in supporters' homes and relying on unpaid college volunteers who cut their hair and shaved their beards and put away their tie-dyed shirts to go door-to-door for their candidate. "Get clean for Gene" was their slogan. When McCarthy came close to upsetting President Lyndon Baines Johnson in the New Hampshire primary, LBJ withdrew from the race. Think about that: $400, one determined senator, and a group of committed young people forced one of our most powerful presidents in history from running for reelection.

Today, even a protest candidate running on the issue of eliminating special interest money believed he had to raise $1 million to run in the Democratic primaries. This would-be reformer was Harvard professor Lawrence Lessig. His sole platform consisted of a sweeping proposed election reform law he calls the Citizens Equality Act. It would require campaigns to be financed by a combination of small private donations and public funds. It would also end the practice of members of Congress choosing their voters—instead of the other way around—by doing away with gerrymandered districts. The Citizens Equality Act also called for making Election Day a national holiday. His plan would "give Congress a chance to lead," in Lessig's words.

"Congress doesn't have that chance right now since they are so dependent on getting reelected," he said. "If we reformed elections you could have more Congress members thinking about what makes sense, not whether my lobbyist is happy."[8]

Apparently, a million dollars doesn't go nearly as far as $400 in McCarthy's day. In November 2015, Lessig dropped out of the race after sixty days.[9]

The situation wasn't always as dire as it is now. Despite fits and starts self-government has risen to the occasion time and time again throughout this nation's history to serve the greater national good. For most of our nation's history, independent-minded Americans took on the most complex and difficult problems, sometimes at great cost to themselves. In the 1830s, Massachusetts lawyer and legislator Horace Mann convinced authorities in his state that American-style democracy depended on an educated populace. So was born the "Common School"—the notion of universal education. In the process, whether you were rich or poor, you had the opportunity to improve your life through public education.

As rapid business consolidations threatened to impede competition in the marketplace to the detriment of consumers in the late 1800s, Congress stepped in. The efforts were spearheaded by Senator John Sherman of Ohio, an abolitionist Republican and younger brother of the famed Civil War general William Tecumseh Sherman. John Sherman led passage of a federal antitrust act that still bears his name. After the turn of the century, when John D. Rockefeller's Standard Oil dramatically raised the price of kerosene, the primary home heating source—and a market in which it had a near monopoly—President Theodore Roosevelt lowered the boom on Rockefeller and broke up Standard Oil. Shortly afterward, in 1910, California reformer Hiram

Johnson challenged the power of the western railroads, as detailed in Upton Sinclair's best-selling exposé *The Octopus*. Johnson was elected to the U.S. Senate on the Progressive Party ticket using the slogan, "Kick the Southern Pacific railroad out of politics."

By necessity, political reform of this kind means challenging the entrenched status quo—challenging the duopoly. Independent-minded Americans, even if they are operating within the two entrenched parties, have historically been at the forefront of political progress.

America has faced crises before; actually our country has confronted multiple crises at the same time, just as we do now. Often they were worse. In the Dustbowl days of the 1930s, we had more disruptive weather than today. In the Great Depression of the 1930s and early 1940s we had a far worse economy than anything seen in recent times. Nazi Germany and the Imperial Japanese Navy were deadlier to the United States than al-Qaeda and ISIS. Crime rates were worse in the 1960s than they are now.

The difference is that in the twenty-first century we seem unable or unwilling to tackle our problems. Here are two easy examples:

Everyone in Washington knows that the Social Security disability program is rife with fraud and waste, and is in need of overhaul. Crafted during the Eisenhower administration, this program originally limited payments to workers who were fifty or older, or to disabled children. It was envisioned as a supplemental payment to Americans who had literally worked themselves to the bone—and couldn't continue. Annual payments rose steadily, but were still below $20 billion annually when Ronald Reagan became president two-and-a-half decades after the program began. It's now costing $143 billion annually, which even after adjusting for inflation is a three-fold increase.[10] It's clearly being abused, as government auditors have revealed.[11] Claims related to soft tissue and other hard to verify musculoskeletal injuries have skyrocketed. These claims have increased dramatically during a period of time when far fewer Americans are engaged in manual labor. But try getting Democrats in Washington to even discuss fixing it.

Meanwhile, Medicare Part D, the drug benefit passed by a Republican Congress at the behest of George W. Bush, is the very definition of an unfunded mandate. Underwritten by general revenues, it is projected to cost taxpayers between $850 billion and $900 billion over the next ten years, a price tag roughly equivalent to the cost of ObamaCare over the same period. And since these are times of perpetual deficit financing, the net result is that Bush and a compliant Congress added more than $1 trillion to the national debt between 2003 and 2023—*in one facet of a single government program.* As for reining in costs by negotiating prescription drug prices, well, Republicans won't hear of it.[12]

These two examples show why we need a renewal, a new "Declaration of Independents." The two parties are effectively at an impasse. As long as they keep getting reelected they have no incentive to change.

SUMMER SOLDIERS AND SUNSHINE PATRIOTS

The only way for our country to address the political stalemate gripping our nation is for a real movement of Independents to take hold. Abundant evidence exists that Americans are ready for this. It's present in the Americans who have gravitated to unconventional choices in the 2016 presidential contest—looking for anyone who demonstrates the kind of independence from special interests and the Washington elite that they are craving.

As this movement takes hold, however, there are other citizens who have chosen to opt out of political engagement or running for office. Faced with the bitter partisanship and negative campaigning in elections that increasingly pit very liberal Democrats against very conservative Republicans, independent-minded candidates have walked away from politics—along with millions of nonaligned voters who would support them. Although opting out of the political process is understandable, it is unfortunate because it has allowed political intractability to take root, at precisely the time when we could change Washington.

This is the reaction that entrenched political incumbents hope for. By opting out of the process, Independent voters are tacitly supporting the status quo without realizing it. With approval ratings for Congress at historic lows and most incumbent officeholders registering below 50 percent in approval ratings, these politicians recognize that they can't win reelection selling a positive vision of themselves. They want to make you hold your nose and vote.

If you are dissatisfied with business as usual, the political pros are banking on one of two responses from you: (1) They want you to vote against the challenger because you have been led to think he's reprehensible and at least you know what we get with the incumbent; or (2) they want you not to vote at all because you feel like you're choosing between shingles and the flu. Social science and practical experience reveal that you'll remember negative ads better than positive ads and feel more motivated by them. This induces challengers to also run negative campaigns, further reinforcing your aversion.

In this war of negative ads, the incumbent generally has an advantage, because the current officeholders typically have more money with which to spread negative messages. Incumbents have this edge because political fundraising is always transactional in nature. And incumbents have something tangible to sell to donors: access to their office and their vote. This truism came into stark relief for me during my campaign against Senator Roberts. As *The Hill* newspaper reported in an article entitled "Lobbyists Try to Save Roberts," Kansas's longtime incumbent senator was raising $1.5 million every two weeks from lobbyists representing various special interests.

"Sen. Pat Roberts is leaning heavily on K Street as he tries to save the

Senate seat he's held for 18 years," it began. It quoted an unnamed prominent Republican as saying approvingly, "[Senator Roberts] is raising 100 grand a day. I'm serious. Ask any lobbyist of anyone in Washington if they've gotten a call from Pat Roberts. It's amazing what a little fear will do to somebody."[13]

Another source for *The Hill* didn't mind being quoted on the record. He was former Republican senator Tim Hutchinson from Arkansas, who walked through the Washington revolving door after leaving Congress and now makes a hefty salary lobbying his former colleagues—and slipping them huge checks. "I got a call from Pat," Hutchinson told the newspaper, "I was glad to get it."[14] Hutchinson works for a huge law firm and lobbying outfit named Greenberg Traurig. That it views democratic self-government as one big business opportunity is revealed in the opening pitch on its website.

> In 1791 Washington, D.C. became the seat of the U.S. government and headquarters for most federal agencies. With so much of the federal government concentrated within 70 square miles, a unique business community has developed in and around Washington. As each new administration and the ever-shifting political winds usher in new legislation and regulation, companies worldwide are profoundly impacted.

It's safe to say that the man whom the capital city is named after would shake his head sadly at reading those words. George Washington personified the very opposite of the "sunshine patriot" described by Thomas Paine in his fiery essay *The American Crisis*. General Washington instructed his officers to read that pamphlet to the Continental Army before their bold Delaware River crossing in the harsh winter of 1776. Its first lines are its most famous. "These are the times that try men's souls," Paine wrote. "The summer soldier and the sunshine patriot will, in this crisis, shrink from the service of their country; but he that stands it now, deserves the love and thanks of man and woman."

While I understand why voters would opt out of American politics as currently practiced, Paine's plea reaches across the centuries to remind us that we can't afford to shirk our obligations as citizens.

A FAILURE OF LEADERSHIP

Much of our discontent is driven not by the nature of the problems themselves—we have indeed faced even greater challenges—but by the fear that our political system can no longer handle difficult issues.

Democrats and Republicans have demonstrated repeatedly that they have no interest in addressing hard issues. Historically when we've had difficult problems as a nation, both parties would come together, develop a solution, and move that solution through Congress together. That doesn't mean there weren't debates or even heated arguments—there were. In the end, though, both parties put the interests of our country ahead of self-interest and partisanship.

But today, to disagree with the other party's position also involves challenging its fundamental loyalty to America itself. It's depressing how quickly partisan politicians question the other side's patriotism. It's not uncommon for prominent conservatives—and the occasional Republican politician—to express doubt that President Obama "loves America." For his part, the president routinely disparages and questions Republicans' motivations on everything from the Iran nuclear deal to the budget process. Each side should look in the mirror.

In today's over-caffeinated conservatism, for instance, compromise is literally a dirty word. Senator Ted Cruz, a freshman Republican from

Texas, for one, rose to national prominence among movement conservatives by advancing the proposition that negotiating with the White House on the federal budget is a betrayal of principle. The Tea Party activists who egged on Cruz and his allies are fond of invoking their supposed loyalty to the U.S. Constitution. They are historically illiterate. The Constitution itself is a quilt of political compromises—and over much more momentous issues than whether the top income tax rate in this country should be 36 percent or 39.6 percent. Today's conservatives also express deep admiration for Ronald Reagan. But it was Reagan, negotiating with Democratic House Speaker Thomas P. "Tip" O'Neill Jr., who forged the compromise in the winter of 1982–1983 that preserved the solvency of Social Security for a generation by accepting the recommendations of the Greenspan Commission—recommendations that included (Republican) curbs on future spending growth and (Democratic) proposals on how to raise more revenue.

That kind of statesmanship doesn't happen today. Here's a case study: In 2011, when the Obama administration sent a pro forma request to Capitol Hill to raise the debt ceiling, Republicans demanded budget cuts over the next ten years in the same amount that the ceiling would be raised. Obama's budgeters, desperate for political cover and scrambling to manage the highest annual budget deficits in history, responded by proposing a crude cudgel, a device to control spending known as "sequester"—across-the-board cuts for every government department and agency, no matter whether such cuts were arguably warranted or profoundly debilitating. It's an idiotic way to balance the books, and Obama officials later conceded they didn't think Congress would go for something so dumb.[15] They shouldn't have been surprised. The House and Senate tentatively accepted the proposal with the caveat that a so-called "Super Committee" would first see if it could find bipartisan spending cuts to stave off the automatic reductions.

Composed, in theory, of the brightest legislators and negotiators from both sides of the aisle—but still beholden to their respective party leaders—the Super Committee was no more able to come to agreement than the full Congress had been. Under the terms of the sequester, if the recommended cuts weren't enacted, automatic cuts to both the Defense Department and discretionary non-defense spending kicked in. Entitlements, the real driver of the deficit, were untouched. The theory had been that Democrats would recoil at the notion of cuts to domestic programs, while Republicans could never stomach a reduction in defense spending. This would force these "super" legislators to critically examine entitlement programs and finally make the tough, courageous decision to reform them.

Despite having a year to come up with recommendations, the Super Committee couldn't agree on a single cut to send to Congress for its consideration. As a result of the sequester, the U.S. Army is now below its critical readiness level, and programs supporting returning and homeless veterans have been slashed, along with mental health services for those with head injuries and post-traumatic stress. Promising studies at the nation's research universities were curtailed, necessary infrastructure projects delayed, and the gross national product slowed down. It took the surprise resignation announcement of House Speaker John Boehner to help get it done, but in October 2015, Congress added $80 billion to the budget above sequestration levels for the next two years, divided between military and non-military. The intent of this two-year measure was to push the issue past the 2016 elections, thereby allowing politicians to avoid the hard decisions that might threaten their political futures.

The episode is a perfect example of Washington dysfunction. It demonstrated how elected leaders from both parties place the interests of their own futures over the future of our country. They lack the courage to make the hard decisions to put our country on a more sustainable path. I believe that public service without courage inevitably becomes self-service. As I said on the campaign trail, that's exactly what we have today in Washington—a bunch of "self-servants."

It's going to take a new generation of real public servants to break the gridlock in Washington.

It's going to take leaders who put the interests of America ahead of the interests of their parties or the special interests that support them.

It's going to take real citizen servants who are willing to go to Washington, D.C., as problem solvers, not partisans, who understand that protecting the future generations of Americans is far more important than protecting their own political futures.

It's going to take replacing current members of Congress with independent-minded men and women who will restore our nation's can-do spirit and our commitment to our nation's founding ideals—and ending once and for all any debate about whether America is still exceptional.

CHAPTER 5

Why Washington Doesn't Work

THE STRUCTURAL CHANGES THAT HAVE
LED TO GRIDLOCK

—— ★ ★ ★ ——

ON OCTOBER 2, 2013, Bob Butler, a ninety-two-year-old U.S. Navy veteran from my town of Olathe, Kansas, arrived in Washington, D.C., to tour the World War II Memorial. Bob had served in the Pacific aboard the *USS Dayton*, a light cruiser launched in 1944 and named after the Ohio city that helped raise the money to build her through a civic bond drive. On this day, he was part of a Kansas City contingent of World War II veterans invited to the nation's capital under the auspices of a group called Heartland Honor Flight, which brings aging servicemen from the Greatest Generation to see the capital city's memorials.

Often these veterans are greeted by one of their own, former senator Bob Dole. Without fanfare or an entourage, Dole welcomes them personally to the soaring monument that pays homage to their sacrifice. On October 2, 2013, however, the veterans were met with barricades, not welcoming handshakes.[1] Even though the World War II Memorial is never closed to the public, on this occasion it was blocked off by the National Park Service, on orders emanating from the Oval Office. The old warriors were pawns in a chess game waged between the Democrats who controlled the White House and the Republicans who controlled the U.S. House of Representatives.

It was the perfect symbol of what Washington has become: a sandbox for spoiled and selfish career politicians from both parties who ignore the desires, rights, and wishes of the American taxpayers who pay their salaries.

While I've studied the trend toward hyper-partisanship and think I have a good knowledge of its roots, it took a meeting with Bob Dole after my 2014 race before I realized that what I think of as "common" knowledge actually isn't well understood at all. After the election, I heard from a handful of people that the former senator and 1996 Republican presidential nominee appreciated the issues I'd raised during my campaign and wanted to meet me. As a longtime admirer of Dole's, I jumped at the chance. His office was more than happy to accommodate me on my next trip to Washington, D.C., which happened to be on St. Patrick's Day. I arrived at his law firm office, Alston & Bird, just before 11 a.m. and we spoke for about an hour.

After exchanging pleasantries, Senator Dole commented, "If you were a Republican you'd be in the Senate right now." While Dole wasn't expressing that he preferred me to Roberts (obviously he didn't) he just knew the weight of the Republican brand in Kansas. I knew he was right. In the last poll our campaign completed prior to Election Day, more than two-thirds of voters who said they were voting for Roberts indicated they were doing so not because they liked him, but because they wanted a Republican-controlled Senate. During the campaign, I had been counseled that the best way to get elected was to signal publicly that I'd caucus with the Republicans if I were elected.

While I figured that strategy might be the surest way to win, I also realized that I'd then owe my election to the Republican Party. Kansans would expect me to tow the Republican line. I wouldn't be in a position to execute the Senate Fulcrum Strategy or hold anyone accountable or otherwise bring the kind of change that Washington so desperately needed. I'd just be another red state Republican in Congress. I'd rather play golf.

This doesn't mean that I had precluded the idea of ever caucusing with Senate Republicans or working with them on certain issues. But running as an Independent wasn't a gimmick, and if I won I had no intention of leaving the voters of Kansas feeling as though they had been misled. I didn't want to be another politician who would say or do anything to get elected, and I was unwilling to go to Washington as a party drone. Saying that I would effectively "become" a Republican wasn't in the cards for me.

I put it to Bob Dole this way: "I know that, but would I be accomplishing anything." He thought for a bit and finally conceded, "Probably not."

He went on to say that he didn't understand the dysfunction in Washington today. "In my time, I considered the Democrats to be my friends. In fact," he added, referring to the former Democratic Senate leader, "George Mitchell and I still talk almost every week." With sadness in his voice, he then made an observation that struck me. "I don't know why it's gotten this bad," he said.

POLITICAL SEGREGATION

Washington's gridlock can be traced back to the demise of two all but extinct groups: the New England Republican and the Southern Democrat. As I mentioned to Dole: "When you ran the Senate, there was ideological overlap. Many Southern Democrats were more conservative on a lot of issues than the New England Republicans. You could count on Democrats to be partners in getting things done because you agreed on many issues."

Today there is no such ideological overlap in Washington, D.C. The most conservative Democrat is more liberal on almost every measure of ideology than the most liberal Republican.

The process that led to this state of affairs took a long time to develop—and we'll explore it more in Chapter 7—but it's a peril that our founders identified and cautioned us about. In his farewell address as president, George Washington warned of the "baneful effects" of partisanship. John Adams, Washington's successor in office, wrote, "There is nothing which I dread so much as the division of the Republic into two great parties, each arranged under its leader, concerting measures in opposition to each other."[2] James Madison, writing in the Federalist Papers, lamented "the propensity of mankind" to form mutually antagonist political groups that encourage the most trivial partisan differences to "kindle their unfriendly passions and excite their most violent conflicts."[3]

Pumping the brakes on such passions have traditionally been political moderates. What I didn't say to Bob Dole, but believe to be true, is that in our current crisis moderates are partly the authors of their own misfortune. I've long held the view that moderates in both parties are the victims of the rule rigging and negative campaigning that they themselves have historically supported. They made the assumption that if it was good for the party, it was good for them as incumbent officeholders. Unfortunately, they didn't think through the ultimate consequences of their support until it was too late. With heavily partisan districts and an electorate conditioned by negative campaigning to reflexively dislike the other side—as well as the "traitors" within their own party who compromise—moderate politicians helped to create an environment that was ironically hostile to them.

Why we no longer have ideological overlap in Washington, D.C., can be traced to a few root causes. First, since the middle part of the twentieth century, Americans have been effectively sorting themselves in ways that align geography with demography with ideology and cultural preferences. This process of self-segregation has been studied by various political scientists and demographers, including Austin-based political author Bill Bishop, who dubbed it "The Big Sort" in a book of that name. His subtitle tells it all: "Why the Clustering of Like-Minded America is Tearing Us Apart." We don't just have Republican and Democratic precincts anymore. We have Republican and Democratic churches, Republican and Democratic television shows, Republican and Democratic supermarkets, Republican and Democratic book clubs, fast-food restaurants, and neighborhoods.

This phenomenon began with the development of the automobile culture and the interstate highway system, which made it much easier for people to live and work in different places. As a result, the suburbanization of America took place, with significant "white flight" out of the inner cities that created a gulf between American communities of different races. We also experienced significant migration from rural areas into suburban America as mechanization made it easier to farm with fewer hands and jobs moved from the country to areas surrounding cities.

Over time, our communities became more homogenous, which meant that we grew less likely to encounter people with ideologies and opinions different from our own. "In 1976, less than a quarter of Americans lived in places where the presidential election was a landslide," noted Bill Bishop. "By 2004, nearly half of all voters lived in landslide counties."[4] He quotes playwright Arthur Miller, who, in 2004, asked apparently without irony, "How can the polls be neck and neck when I don't know one Bush supporter?"[5] The answer to that question is clustering. I encountered this phenomenon myself during the 2012 Presidential election. In 2012, as the presidential campaign was in its final weeks, a good friend, Wynne Jennings, and I were discussing the election. Wynne was convinced Romney was not only going to win the election, but would do so comfortably. I thought a Romney victory possible but unlikely. This difference in perception led to Wynne proposing he bet me that Romney would win the popular vote by seven percentage points. "I'm happy to take that bet," I told him, "but tell me why you think that way."

Wynne's response was telling. He said, "Everyone I talk to, everyone I know, is voting for Romney."

Wynne isn't a naïve person. He served in senior executive positions at large and small companies for decades. The fact that he thought Romney was going to win by such a large margin is simply emblematic of the echo chamber—of the right or the left—that many Americans live in. As Bill Bishop notes: "America may be more diverse than ever coast to coast, but the places where we live are becoming increasingly crowded with people who live, think, and vote like we do."[6]

And not only are we isolated from other opinions by where we live, but by how we associate socially with others and from whom we garner news and information. "This social transformation didn't happen by accident," Bishop added. "We've built a country where we can all choose the neighborhood and church and news show most compatible with our lifestyle and beliefs. And we are living with the consequences of this way-of-life segregation." The results of organizing ourselves in this way are more lasting than the result of an election we don't like. "The Big Sort has not been simply a difference of political opinion," Bishop writes. "The communities of interest—and the growing economic disparities among regions—won't disappear with a change in Congress or a new president."[7]

These maps illustrate how that process led to a greater concentration of Democrats and Republicans in America from 1960 to 2012. As a result, Presidential elections have become more lopsided in the majority of American counties.

1960 Presidential Elections
RELATIVE VOTESHARE

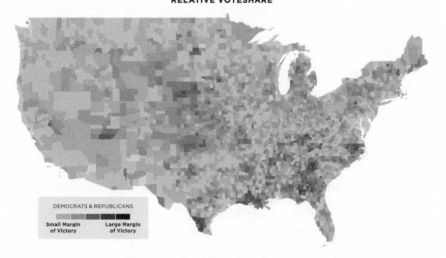

2012 Presidential Elections
RELATIVE VOTESHARE

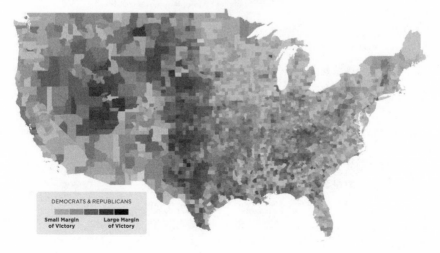

ELIMINATING COMPETITION/EMPOWERING EXTREMISTS

Congressional districts became more homogenous as well, thanks to migration, self-segregation, and modern Americans' remarkable mobility. This phenomenon was made worse by gerrymandering, the age-old practice by which the duopoly creates voting districts to ensure that the odds are stacked in their favor. In an effort to create a safe path to reelection for themselves, incumbent politicians from both parties produce redistricting schemes that create as many "safe" Republican and Democratic districts as possible. The intent of these redistricting efforts is not, contrary to popular belief, to pack as many voters from one party into a district as possible. The intent is to give one party an advantage (invariably, the party that controls the politics at the state level) in as many districts as possible

The illustration that follows was produced by a gentleman named Stephen Nass, who posted it on Facebook. It was subsequently reproduced widely on the Internet and on various news sites, including *The Washington Post*. In this hypothetical example, a state with five congressional districts is made up of 60 percent Democrat and 40 percent Republican voters.

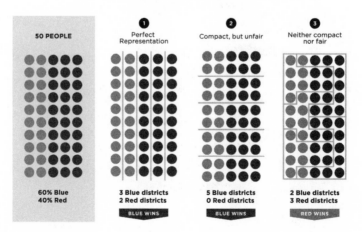

Gerrymandering, Explained
Three different ways to divide 50 people into five districts

50 PEOPLE	**1** Perfect Representation	**2** Compact, but unfair	**3** Neither compact nor fair
60% Blue 40% Red	3 Blue districts 2 Red districts	5 Blue districts 0 Red districts	2 Blue districts 3 Red districts
	BLUE WINS	BLUE WINS	RED WINS

Adapted from Stephen Nass

Depending on how the lines are drawn the Democrats will get a minimum of two and a maximum of five seats. Gerrymandering generally
gives one party or the other more seats than they would be entitled to—
based solely on the composition of voters. This allows one party to effectively decide the outcome of elections without a ballot ever being cast!

Gerrymandering goes back over two hundred years, when a Massachusetts governor, Elbridge Gerry, redrew the state senate districts to benefit
what was then the Democratic-Republican Party. One of the districts was
so distorted it resembled a salamander—thus the Gerry-Mander, as the
press of the day called it. The shaded area on this map of Massachusetts
shows Gerry's contorted district from 1812.

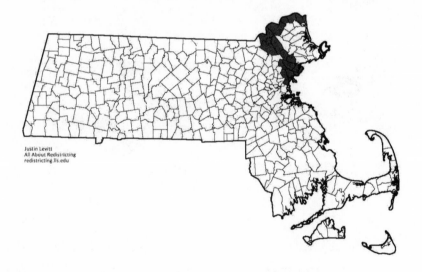

For the last two centuries, it has turned out that cynically drawing
legislative and congressional districts was much easier to lampoon than
to kill. Over the past few decades, with the advent of data-driven politics, it's been perfected. Every ten years, when the U.S. completes the
census, state legislatures throughout the country go through the process
of redrawing voting districts. While a small handful of states, such as

California, have recently adopted nonpartisan redistricting commissions, it remains a very partisan process in most states.

Pennsylvania's seventh congressional district is an illustration of gerrymandering at work over the last 80 years. Over time, this district has gone from being reasonably compact and appropriate to being an unrecognizable mess.

Evolution of Pennsylvania's 7th District

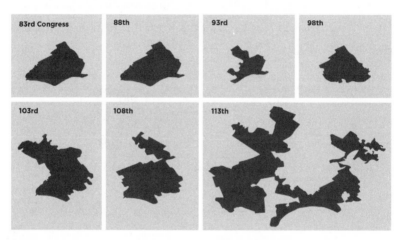

Shapefiles maintained by Jeffrey B. Lewis, Brandon DeVine, Lincoln Pritcher, and Kenneth C. Martis, UCLA. Drawn to scale.

Rigged redistricting subverts the principles of democracy. The essence of our democracy demands that voters pick their leaders. In reality, politicians are picking their voters. Democrats and Republicans alike are sorting the electorate in ways that curtail competition and limit their accountability. Should we really expect anything different from either Democrats or Republicans? This behavior is common for duopolies in business, so why would the two parties behave any differently?

The result of rigging the system in this manner has been the elimination of competitive House races. Over the past four decades, as gerrymandering has magnified the effects of migration and clustering, the number of competitive House seats has fallen dramatically, which the following chart illustrates.

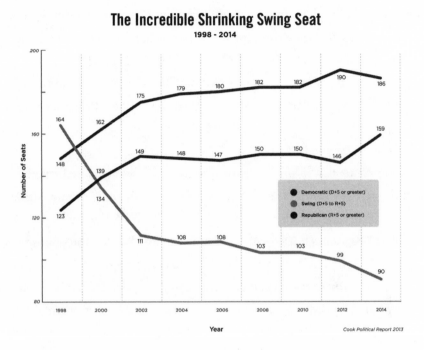

The Incredible Shrinking Swing Seat
1998 - 2014

Cook Political Report 2013

As a result, the general election result is a foregone conclusion in the vast majority of elections for the House of Representatives. Since 1980, there has only been one election cycle (1994, when Republicans took back the House of Representatives) when over 10 percent of the congressional races had a margin of victory less than five percentage points. The vast majority of general election races are blowouts.

Most of us civilly engaged Americans think of it as our patriotic duty to vote in November. Every proposal to make Election Day a national holiday reinforces this notion. However, the races that really matter in most of America today are the partisan primaries, which the vast majority of us skip. Fewer than 10 percent of Americans vote in primaries, meaning that our truly decisive elections are dominated by political activists and voters who harbor the most rigid ideological views—on both the left and right wings—on the American political spectrum.

Just as congressional districts are red or blue, so too do we consider most states the domain of one party or the other. As a result, party-dominated primaries determine the outcome in most Senate and guber-natorial races. That's why Pat Roberts only raised $62,000 in August for his general election campaign. After winning the primary, he thought the race was over. Pat planned to go back to his home in Virginia until Election Day, when he would return to Kansas for a victory party.

The most vivid example in 2014 of a primary being the race that counts came in Virginia's seventh congressional district. The incumbent in this heavily Republican district was Eric Cantor, a handsome, articu-late, mainstream conservative from Richmond who'd risen through GOP ranks to become House majority leader. Cantor had led the opposition to the Democrats' huge stimulus bill, spoken out against ObamaCare, opposed administration tax increases, and publicly defined the Keynesian economics favored by Democrats as "the idea that the government can be counted on to spend money more wisely than the people." Cantor was such a staunch defender of Republican principles that President Obama went to Cantor's district a couple of times to bad-mouth him.

You'd think all that would be enough, even in a very conservative district. Democrats certainly did. They nominated a little-known pro-fessor from a little-known college, Jack Trammell, to run against him. Trammell figured on being on the losing end of a general election GOP shellacking, but Eric Cantor wasn't the Republican who ran up the score. Trammell lost to another obscure professor named Dave Brat, a man almost no one in this country had heard of until he upset Cantor in a low-turnout primary. One factor in Cantor's primary defeat was that the same gerrymandered lines that made this district hospitable for Republicans in November left it susceptible to being controlled by arch-conservative voters in the summer primary. And the election that took out Eric Cantor hinged mainly on the white conservative grass-roots' strong opposition to illegal immigration.

When Cantor signaled that he was receptive to discussing how immigrants brought to the U.S. without papers could be put on the path to U.S. citizenship, the self-appointed culture warriors of the far right went on the warpath. Laura Ingraham held a rally for Brat; Mark Levin promoted Brat on the radio; Ann Coulter trashed Cantor on his behalf.

So a critical mass of our elected leaders are now the people who appeal to the most radicalized members of the voting population. In this brand of extremism, compromise with the other side is viewed as appeasement. It's a sin almost akin to treason. What this leaves us with is a never-ending game of political chicken—with each side waiting for the other to blink. It's the reason Bob Dole's Senate career was marked by accomplishments, while the last decade of federal legislative life has largely been characterized by stagnation. In the first six months of 2013, a non-election year, Congress enacted a total of fifteen significant bills, which is to say they weren't ceremonial "joint resolutions" praising Mother's Day. This was the lowest number since legislative tracking began in 1948. Even that 2013 number is inflated: One of those fifteen legislative actions that year was a law keeping the nation's air traffic control system functioning because Congress forgot to exempt FAA operations from the sequester. Another legislative achievement, if we can call it that, was a bill specifying the size of the precious metal mold used for commemorative coins at the National Baseball Hall of Fame in Cooperstown.

These numbers only get worse when we add together congressional action of all types. When President Truman ran for reelection in 1948, he gained traction by running against the 80th Congress—the "do nothing Congress," he called it. But the 80th Congress passed 1,739 bills. The 113th Congress passed 223 bills. The "do nothing" was eight times as busy as the last completed Congress occupying Capitol Hill.

THE PRICE OF PARALYSIS

Gridlock leads to bigger government. So many of the programs our government has put in place, Social Security, Medicare, and now elements of the Affordable Care Act, are not subject to the annual appropriations process. Absent legislative action, which requires cooperation between Democrats and Republicans, these programs will only grow unrestrained. Fully 70 percent of the 2015 budget is either interest on the national debt, which we have to pay to avoid a global financial meltdown, or entitlements that are on autopilot.

Congressional gridlock means that eleven million people are living in the United States without benefit of citizenship. Congress can't find the collective will to do anything about it: not to deport them; not to authorize them to remain here legally (if temporarily); not to devise a path for citizenship for them. It also can't agree on steps to safeguard U.S. borders, implement the e-Verify system to hold employers accountable, tighten our leaky immigration system, or modernize our system of legal immigration.

A gridlocked Congress has ignored the fact that the cost of college education is spiraling out of control, due in part to government programs that are, ironically, intended to make college more affordable. As tech companies are asking for more H1-B visas to meet their hiring needs, our legislators allow the potential of our country to deliver those workers from within to be suffocated by a system of higher education that only the children of privilege can afford.

Congress continues to allow our social safety net to be structured in such a way as to discourage people from improving their lives, as they are cut off from benefits if they earn too much. Single mothers, especially, must disregard these disincentives if they want to work to make a better life for their families. All working-class families are forced to make gut-wrenching decisions about how to provide day care for their children.

The deadlock in Congress means we cannot deal with basic issues of economic fairness. The federal minimum wage has not kept pace, either. It was raised once during Bill Clinton's presidency, but then was stuck at $5.15 an hour for ten years until a three-step increase was enacted by Congress in 2007 and signed into law by President George W. Bush. The last part of that increase took place in 2009—to $7.25 per hour— and hasn't been increased since. According to the Bureau of Labor Statistics, the cost of child care has risen twice as fast as inflation in the last twenty-five years. "We basically had to remake our entire budget around daycare," a thirty-seven-year-old new mother named Amber Sparks told *Bloomberg News*. Sparks returned to her job for a Washington labor union when her baby turned three months old. "We'll eat out a lot less, and have a lot less discretionary spending," she said. "We live in an apartment building and I don't think there's any way we'd be able to afford a home and pay for daycare and pay for student loans."[8]

Amber Sparks speaks for millions of Americans. The chart below shows how much her fears are rooted in economic reality. As it demonstrates, child-care costs have risen at twice the rate of inflation over the past 25 years:

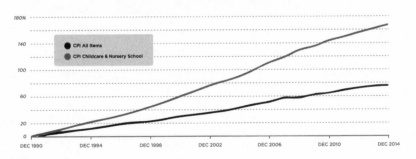

Little People, Big Bills

Childcare costs have surged at more than twice the pace of overall inflation since 1990

Note: Charts December year-over-year percent change in each seasonally adjusted index, normalized to December 1990 levels.
Source: *Bloomberg News*

As Congress has debated the pros and cons of the Affordable Care Act for the past six years, it has allowed health-care costs to continue to consume an ever-increasing portion of our paychecks. Private sector health-care costs have been rising for decades, with health care for a family of four on a PPO now costing an average of $24,671 per year.[9]

Congress passively allows our tax system to confer advantages on that same group of people by taxing earnings from working at a higher rate than earnings from capital, even as globalization has led to stagnated wages, with the vast majority of income gains going to the top 1 percent. And what about our tax system? It's become a 70,000-page monstrosity so riddled with loopholes and bedeviled by complexity that most middle-income Americans have to hire a third party to prepare their taxes, and even then they have no certainty that they've complied with the law and the maze of IRS regulations. Does Congress care about that fact? It sure doesn't show it.

Congress cannot act even when both sides of the aisle agree on an issue. Meaningful reforms are needed in a criminal justice system that imprisons a higher percentage of our people than any other country in the world and leaves them devoid of meaningful options when they are released. For the past two congresses, Republican Rand Paul, supported by Democrat Cory Booker, introduced the REDEEM Act to the Senate, which expunges the records of most non-violent and juvenile offenders. Not surprisingly, it hasn't even made it out of committee. This inaction is so egregious that it has offended both right-wing Republican mega-donor Charles Koch and left-wing Democratic mega-donor George Soros. The two billionaires joined forces to accomplish justice reform with a goal of reducing the prison population in America by 50 percent.[10] Meanwhile, Congress can't even muster the will to address the most obvious reforms. Could it be that the millions of dollars spent on lobbying and campaign contributions by the for-profit prison industry (and unionized prison guards) is what is paralyzing Capitol Hill?

Congress also won't hold up-or-down votes on presidential appointees in a timely manner, including much-needed federal judges. It can't decide which military installations should be kept open or closed. It won't approve an annual budget, as required by the Constitution. It can't even schedule a debate on whether to authorize military action against the Islamic State. This roster of challenges is a direct result of the inability of Democrats and Republicans to work together to solve problems. In the Senate, threatened filibusters are so common that it takes sixty votes to do almost anything, which is a formula for structured gridlock.

Congress has let symbolic votes replace governing. Fifty times over the past few years the House, on straight party-line votes, called the roll on legislation that would repeal ObamaCare or key elements of it. The Republican leadership scheduled those votes knowing, beyond any doubt, that their measures would not become law. The bills couldn't pass the Senate, for starters, and if by some miracle they did, the president made it clear he would veto them. The apparent intent was to influence elections—to try to dupe the voting public into thinking that Republican control of Congress meant the repeal of the Affordable Care Act.

EMPTY PROMISES

During my 2014 campaign, the rhetoric that Republicans employed against me—and against most other of their election opponents around the country—denied the reality of Congressional gridlock and offered instead an empty promise: "Elect us and we'll repeal ObamaCare," Republicans promised.

I was clear in that election about my perspective on the Affordable Care Act. I pointed out that this country had a health-care affordability issue before the ACA, and we have a health-care affordability issue after it was passed. While I believed some of the insurance reforms in the ACA were necessary—such as allowing kids to stay on their parents' insurance until age twenty-six and eliminating the ability of insurance companies to dump customers or raise their rates to unreachable levels after they became ill—I also believed we should have done more to drive down the cost of care before expanding a broken system. In 2010, I went so far as to make a campaign contribution to Republican Scott Brown's Massachusetts Senate campaign, supporting his effort to prevent the ACA from becoming law. But in my 2014 race I labeled the promise of a Senate repeal vote for what it was, political theater, pointing out that people who said they were going to rescind ObamaCare in the next Congress were making promises they couldn't keep. A plainer way to say it is that they were lying. I said I had no intention of going to Washington to engage in such empty gamesmanship.

Yet turning politics into a game is exactly what both parties have done—a game of chicken. In the winter of 2013–2014, both parties conspired in a partial government shutdown. Ostensibly, the subject of contention was raising the nation's debt limit. The real issue was partisan politics, especially the year before a presidential election, and the insincere grandstanding that goes with it.

The first time Congress balked at raising the debt limit was in 1953—while Dwight Eisenhower, a popular Republican president, was in the White House. Eisenhower, a fiscally restrained chief executive, proposed a modest raise in the debt ceiling from $275 billion to $290 billion (currently, it's $18.7 trillion). Ike was anticipating a rise in the country's debt because of programs ranging from aiding the nation's returning veterans to new road building, which in time became the interstate highway system. Opposition was led by Senator Harry Byrd, a Virginia Democrat, who argued that the Eisenhower administration should look to make cuts before asking Congress to raise the debt limit. This argument struck some as backwards.[11] "No one likes to contemplate a larger debt

burden," said *The Washington Post* in a 1953 editorial. "But the debt figure is the consequence rather than the cause of government spending."

Similar assertions are still made today, but the upshot in 1953–1954
was that Congress used its leverage wisely. The Eisenhower administration did find ways to curb spending. It also identified new sources of
revenue, chiefly in the sale of excess gold, and the debt ceiling was raised
the following year.

In 2013, nothing that sensible took place. Led by Ted Cruz, the freshman Texas senator already exhibiting presidential ambitions, congressional Republicans balked at raising the debt ceiling. Unlike their fiscally
conservative predecessors from the 1950s, they didn't nudge the president for cuts in federal spending: They said they wouldn't authorize the
federal government to pay its bills unless the administration agreed to
quit spending money to implement ObamaCare. Since Cruz and fellow
mutineers knew that Obama wouldn't comply with that demand, this
wasn't a negotiation. It was grandstanding.

Except for a small band of Tea Party-fueled true believers over on the
House side of the Capitol, Cruz's colleagues hated him for forcing this
issue—even though they didn't dare buck the conservative radio hosts
egging him on. There is no endgame to this, responsible Republicans
told themselves. This cannot end well, they said. But they accepted the
government shutdown anyway.

For their part, President Obama and the Democrats performed with
no more integrity. For one thing, they tried to pull a similar stunt on
George W. Bush a few years earlier. In 2006, every single Senate Democrat voted against the Bush administration's request to raise the debt
ceiling. Some Senate Democrats held their noses and followed the herd.
Others senators seemed to relish sticking it to Bush. Among the latter
category was a certain freshman from Illinois. "The fact that we are
here today to debate raising America's debt limit is a sign of leadership

failure," Barack Obama said on the Senate floor on March 16, 2006. "It is a sign that the U.S. government can't pay its own bills."[12]

After he became president, Obama cringed visibly when questioned about his previous posturing. "I think that it's important to understand the vantage point of a senator versus the vantage point of a president," Obama told ABC's George Stephanopoulos in 2011. "When you're a senator, traditionally what's happened is, this is always a lousy vote. Nobody likes to be tagged as having increased the debt limit for the United States by a trillion dollars. As president, you start realizing, you know what, we, we can't play around with this stuff. This is the full faith and credit of the United States. And so that was just an example of a new senator making what is a political vote as opposed to doing what was important for the country."[13]

If that was really the only problem—a zealous freshman senator getting ahead of himself—our country wouldn't be in such a mess. But that's hardly the extent of the problem. Democrats voted that way in 2006 because they were told to do so by their Senate leader, Harry Reid. Among other of Reid's colleagues who were voting to have the government stop paying its bills in order to score political points against George W. were Joe Biden and Hillary Clinton, both of whom harbored presidential ambitions of their own. How did they imagine they'd explain such a vote later?

No matter. In the years 2011 through 2013 when it was Republicans who were voting to shut the government, these Democrats were quick to label them irresponsible or extremists. And what about those Republicans: how was it that Ronald Reagan requested, and was granted, eighteen separate increases in the debt limit while he was president, without Republican saying a word against it? It happened another seven times under George W. Bush—again, with no GOP opposition. Among those who routinely supported raising it for a Republican administration were many of the fiscal conservatives who can't stomach it when Obama does the same thing. Included in that number are Pat Roberts, and Sam

Brownback when he was in the U.S. Senate, along with Jim DeMint, the South Carolina firebrand who even after he left the Senate pulled strings from his perch at the conservative Heritage Foundation. DeMint openly encouraged Ted Cruz to take a step that DeMint himself refused to take with a fellow Republican in the White House.

In theology, the term for elastic principles of this kind is called "situational ethics." In politics, it's derided as "flip-flopping." Most people know what it really is: hypocrisy. Whatever it's called, it's become standard operating procedure in our nation's capital.

The current environment in Washington reminds me of the story of the two Russian farmers who were each farming their small one-acre plots of potatoes. Over time they'd grown to hate each other. They hated each other for so long they no longer even remembered why. One year, one of the farmers saved up enough money to buy a cow to provide milk for his family. The other farmer was envious and angry. He was walking on his land, kicking everything in sight out of anger—a rock, the dirt—eventually he kicked an old lamp and out came a genie.

"I'll grant you one wish—anything you want, riches for you and your family, an end to poverty, world peace," the genie told the fortunate farmer. "What do you want most in the world?"

The farmer, without thinking, blurted out, "I want my neighbor's cow to die."

Democrats and Republicans are more interested in seeing the other party fail than they are in seeing our country succeed. They'll do anything to accomplish that goal, including putting our country at risk.

FALSE PROPHETS OF CIVILITY

Like the Wizard of Oz, who madly pulled the levers of power that manipulated the affections and fears of the residents of Emerald City, many members of the ruling duopoly claim to no longer remember what originally motivated them to behave so callously—or even derive much enjoyment from their machinations. This sad state of affairs was proven by sequestration, which we discussed in Chapter 4. It became law on March 13, 2013, because of partisan gridlock and not because it represented the will of the Congress. Quite the opposite: "One hundred percent of Congress opposed it, and we're doing it," explained Representative Peter Welch, a Vermont Democrat. "That's a sign of a dysfunctional institution."[14]

Given a chance to change the tone in Washington, D.C., however, these same politicians, even those who profess to want a better environment, refuse to take even the smallest of steps.

During Obama's first term, former White House aide Lanny Davis, a Jewish Democrat, teamed up with Mark DeMoss, a conservative Christian active in Republican politics. Davis contrasted the schoolyard trash talk he heard from both sides with the pride most Americans felt, regardless of political party, when George W. Bush stood on the rubble at Ground Zero with a retired firefighter. Davis also recalled the bipartisan joy after Osama bin Laden was killed that led to Americans spontaneously gathering at the White House.

"Both the left and the right—and the leadership of both political parties—are responsible for this politics of demonizing political opponents," Davis explained. "It's shameful."[15] Davis and DeMoss drafted a "civility pledge" and sent it in May of 2010 to every member of the House and Senate, as well as every governor, along with some facts and polling numbers they thought would get the elected officials' attention.

Two out of three Americans consider a lack of civility a major problem, while almost three-fourths believe the problem is worsening. More than two-thirds of those who responded to a survey about health-care legislation answered affirmatively when asked if Americans "should be ashamed of the way elected officials acted" during the congressional debate. Fully 83 percent agreed with the statement that "People should not vote for candidates and politicians who are uncivil." Almost half said they were "tuning out" of government and politics as a result.[16]

The accompanying "civility pledge" Davis and DeMoss included with this information consisted of only 32 words: (1) I will be civil in my public discourse and behavior; (2) I will be respectful of others whether or not I agree with them; (3) I will stand against incivility when I see it.

In May of 2010 they sent it to every member of the House and Senate, as well as every governor. Exactly three people out of the 585 who received the letter were willing to sign the pledge. (They were Republican House members Frank Wolfe and Sue Myrick and Independent senator Joe Lieberman, a personal friend of Davis.) Less than a year later, Davis and DeMoss shut down the Civility Project "for lack of interest."

Obviously, Democrats and Republicans alike came to the same conclusion—that the current environment in Washington works well for incumbents. They realized that having the obligation to behave civilly would deprive them of a potent weapon in their quest for reelection, the ability to demean and denigrate the other side. In short, civility is a hard virtue to cling to when you need incivility to win.

While that may be a formula for electoral success, it's also a formula for legislative failure. During my campaign, Independent senator Angus King offered me encouragement, but said that he couldn't campaign against a colleague as it would prevent him from working with Senator Roberts in Washington. That's a position only an Independent would take today, as evidenced by the failure of the Civility Project. As for most other people in official Washington, they just really want the other farmers' cows to die.

If we genuinely want to change Washington, we must make fundamental reforms. But those reforms will come not from party partisans gridlocked in government. They happen only if we crack open the gridlock through Independent action.

CHAPTER 6

Selling the Party Line (and Dividing America)

HOW REPUBLICANS AND DEMOCRATS BRAINWASHED THEIR BASES

———— ★ ★ ★ ————

IN MY CAMPAIGN, MANY of the Kansans I met seemed energized by the possibility of breaking out of their traditional voting habits. They liked the idea that Kansas was a part of the national dialogue again, instead of simply being a reliable red state where the election would be called the moment the polls closed. They liked that Kansas mattered again.

Many of the Republicans I spoke with, however, seemed to be torn between relating to our message and what our campaign was bringing to the state and feeling a reflexive obligation to support my opponent, particularly in light of impending battle for control of the U.S. Senate. Those conversations followed a typical pattern. The prospective voter would say, "Greg, I really like what I'm hearing from you, but we need the Republicans to take control of the Senate."

"I understand your goal," I'd reply. "But can I ask you a simple question: Why?"

Almost invariably, the answer was variation on the same theme. "Because," they'd say, "we're going to repeal ObamaCare."

"How?" I'd answer. "How are you going to do that when the guy whose name is on the law owns a veto pen?"

At that point, many of these voters would go on to say that a Republican Congress would bring the nation's runaway entitlement programs under control. "George W. Bush tried that in 2005," I'd tell them, "when he had a Republican House and Senate to work with—and he didn't get to first base. How are you going to do that with divided government and no real mandate?"

As a last line of defense, some voters would say. "Well, we're going to prevent Obama from appointing liberal judges."

"You're right," I'd say. "A Republican-controlled Senate could theoretically bottle up the appointment process." But I would also tell them that when Democratic Senate Leader Harry Reid changed the filibuster rules for judicial appointments, Republican Leader Mitch McConnell went to the floor of the Senate and pointed out that Republicans had confirmed 215 Obama judicial nominees, rejecting only two. "That's a confirmation rate of 99 percent," McConnell said.[1]

Ultimately, then, the turn-the-Senate-Republican rationale boiled down to wanting to block 1 percent of Barack Obama's judicial appointees from holding gavels on the federal bench. (No one, at the time, assumed Justice Scalia would pass away.) Astute voters tended to realize at that point that their desire for a Republican Senate wasn't grounded in substance, but was rather driven by a desire to see their "team" win.

This tribal mentality isn't a good enough reason for choosing our nation's leaders. But it's one that Republicans and Democrats have spent billions of dollars and the better part of two centuries marketing. So if we Independents want to offer an alternative narrative, we need to hone our arguments—and be attuned to what the American people really desire.

Deep down most of the Republicans I spoke with revealed to me that, mainly, they just want government to spend the money we entrust it with wisely. They want to slow the rate of growth of government and its tendency to creep into more and more parts of our daily lives. They don't think government is inherently bad, or that its role in their lives is unimportant, just that it never seems to stop growing. Some of them want a smaller federal government; all of them want a smarter and more efficient one.

After acknowledging that they hadn't fully thought through *why* they wanted a Republican Senate, I'd touch on things they really cared about. I'd point out that roughly 70 percent of the federal budget is no longer subject to the appropriation process but instead goes for "entitlement" programs (and interest on the debt) that partisan politicians have no incentive to examine for effectiveness or fairness.[2] What all Americans are truly entitled to, including the beneficiaries of these programs, is a political system that manages them prudently and funds them adequately. That takes compromise, intellectual honesty, and a willingness to negotiate in good faith with officeholders who may not necessarily agree with your own priorities. In other words, it takes good governance—the kind we are sorely missing these days.

In those conversations with Republican-leaning Kansans, I'd continue: "The only way to actually get government spending under control is for Democrats and Republicans to work together. And the only way to do that is to send them a message that they can't go to Washington and hide behind their party label—they actually have to get something done. The only way to send that message is to elect me."

That pitch may sound self-serving (obviously, I wanted Republicans in Kansas to vote for me), but the statement was grounded in reality. It also has a much broader application beyond my candidacy. Until independent-minded, disaffected, and moderate voters from both parties re-engage in the electoral process in a meaningful way to challenge the status quo, a 94 percent reelection rate guarantees business-as-usual in Washington, D.C., and in the state capitals also controlled by the duopoly.

SHOW VOTES AND FAILURE THEATER

As we saw in the previous chapter, one now-familiar feature of that status quo is the scheduling of roll call votes in Congress with no real-world consequence. Congressional leaders allow their members to go on record supporting legislation popular in their districts or with the respective conservative and liberal wings in each party—knowing it will never be enacted. These votes are an electioneering tool, but one with a "Groundhog Day" feel to it. Taking aim at the Republican leadership in the House and the Senate, the conservative blogger known as Ace of Spades described the posturing and pandering as "Failure Theater."[3] Even Ted Cruz, that congressional show horse, decries them as "show votes on legislation that has no chance of becoming law."[4]

"The leadership loves 'show votes,'" Cruz added, pointing out that the true goal is to appease the grassroots without altering the basic equation on the federal budget or any other issue. "In 2010, we were told that Republicans would stand and fight if only we had a Republican House. In 2014, we were told that Republicans would stand and fight just as soon as we won a majority in the Senate and retired Harry Reid. In both instances, the American people obliged. Now we're told that we must wait until 2017 when we have a Republican president."[5]

While I'd argue that Senator Cruz is guilty of the same behavior in forcing the government to shut down in 2013 without any real hope of accomplishing legislative change—the ultimate "show vote"—it's hard to argue with his critique of his own leaders and the misleading campaigns that they've engaged in to stay in power. Invariably, this sort of misleading campaign won't end in November 2016. No doubt in the midterm elections of 2018, the Republicans will be explaining away their lack of accomplishment by blaming the Democrats in the Senate. If they maintain their majority in 2016, their 2018 campaign messaging will be oriented around needing sixty votes in the Senate to bypass the filibuster. If they lose the majority in 2016, they'll once again blame the failures of Washington on a Democratic Senate. The Democrats, who have little hope of regaining their majority in the House of Representatives until after the 2020 census, will continue to possess a political foil regardless of the outcome of the race for the White House in 2016 or the control of the Senate in 2016 or beyond.

Meanwhile, there's no reason to believe that without a vibrant Independent movement—one that includes officeholders elected as Independents—to force their hands, that Republicans and Democrats will find ways to work together effectively. The dynamics of their reelection campaigns all but guarantee it.

Both sides realize the only way to truly avoid risking electoral defeat is to take as extreme a position as possible in an effort to prevent a primary challenge. These positions won't overlap in any meaningful way, which guarantees inaction on Capitol Hill—unless one believes that "show votes" and never-ending partisan skirmishes constitute action. This incessant bickering will, however, lead to a constant stream of fundraising emails, Twitter and Facebook posts, and direct mail appeals to voters about how the earnest representative or senator is working tirelessly to advance the partisan agenda. Much of that mail will even be sent at taxpayer expense. All the while, our elected officials will be spending their time raising money and dining with lobbyists. The only way to get them to actually focus on problem-solving is to make continued inaction a liability at election time.

The time to starting doing this is soon. I thought of this while talking to Bob Dole. Just as the members of the "Greatest Generation" are passing from the scene, so are politicians who remember when Washington was a city that worked. Olympia Snowe is one of those disappearing public servants. A longtime moderate Republican from Maine, Snowe pointedly discussed the price of political neglect in her farewell address to the Senate in December of 2012. "I fear we are losing the art of legislating," she told her colleagues. "It is regrettable that excessive political polarization in Washington today is preventing us from tackling our problems in this period of monumental consequences for our nation."

She went on to say, "Our problems are not insurmountable if we refuse to be intractable. It is not about what's in the best interests of a single political party, but what's in the best interests of our country."[6]

LIES, DAMN LIES, AND CAMPAIGN RHETORIC

Two-and-a-half decades ago, as Bill Clinton and Ross Perot prepared to challenge an incumbent Republican president, political writer E. J. Dionne penned an unlikely best seller, *Why Americans Hate Politics*. Although the book was written from Dionne's liberal perspective, its prescription for addressing Americans' disturbing lack of faith in their government did not advocate for the triumph of liberalism at the expense of conservatism. Rather, Dionne postulated that the problem was increasing polarization, fueled by a two-party system that imposed on Americans a series of "false choices" to pressing issues of national concern that prevented us from expressing our true preference.

Many voters, he pointed out, prefer an "intelligent 'both/and' politics to an artificially constrained 'either/or' approach." Democrats and

Republicans speak of "issues," he added, but only in ways calculated to start arguments instead of produce solutions. Instead, Dionne suggested speaking of "problems"—a formulation more suggestive of challenges to be solved by reasoning together.

I believe that in framing possible policy solutions as "either/or" choices, both parties lead us to believe that there are only two answers to any problem. Generally, these answers have been hyper-distilled to such an extent that they're troublingly simplistic. At that point, they become litmus tests. Even worse, they are made into labels that harden a false choice into a single word: "pro-choice" or "pro-life," for example. Even on that ideologically and morally charged subject, the great majority of Americans have nuanced views that wouldn't pass muster with party gate-keepers. Over time, Americans have internalized the false choice paradigm promoted by the two parties. So much of what we believe about the two parties and their positions on issues is not grounded in reality, but rather has become a part of our conscious understanding of the parties—thanks to decades of messaging, false advertising, and phony framing of the issues.

Let's look at an example. If I asked you which party, on average, spends more, your reflexive response would likely be, "the Democrats." The reality is more complex.

Go back with me in time to 1963, the year the federal government started running persistent annual budget deficits. It turns out that since then, on average, we spend more and have higher deficits as a percent of GDP when we have a Republican administration. If you're a Republican, I know you will recoil at that statement and question its accuracy. But facts are stubborn things as John Adams told us. Don't take my word for it—look it up.

Others of you will insist that who controls Congress matters as well when it comes to creating budget deficits. I'm not arguing that point; I agree. I am just saying that it's just not as simple as campaign messaging would have you believe. I'm also not suggesting that Democratic fiscal policy, by contrast, is the answer. I think both parties suffer from the same condition—a desire to spend our money to advance the interests of the people who keep them in power. My point is that we are being duped by the campaign messaging and branding strategies of *both* parties. In their zeal to get one over on the other side rather than solve problems, the two parties even work against their own stated interests—provided that such double-dealing will help them raise money or win elections.

A classic example is how Democrats manipulated immigration reform legislation. During the Obama presidency, this subject has become a line of separation between the two parties. Obama won office in 2008 and again in 2012, in part by presenting himself to Latinos and Asians as immigrant-friendly and portraying Republicans as the opposite. But it was Obama himself who helped deliberately sabotage a delicate compromise forged by Senator Edward M. Kennedy, John McCain, House Democrats, and the Bush administration. The window for this historic deal opened in late spring of 2007. It closed a month later.

Support was strong in the House of Representatives, but in the Senate the chamber's most conservative Republicans found the proposed legislation too lenient to illegal immigrants. Meanwhile, the Senate's most left-leaning Democrats heeded organized labor's behind-the-scenes lobbying against it on the grounds that it would let too many temporary workers in the country.

A bloc of Senate moderates in both parties, headed by John McCain, along with principled liberals, led by Kennedy, forged a tenuous working majority and in June of 2007 their bill seemed headed for passage. Both top Senate leaders, Republican Mitch McConnell and Democrat Harry Reid, publicly expressed support. So did President Bush. Those on the fringes kept working against it, however. Right-wing Republicans Jim

DeMint and Jeff Sessions attempted to essentially filibuster the measure with a flurry of amendments. Pro-labor Democrat Byron Dorgan of North Dakota offered a sly amendment, one that would sunset the guest worker provision after five years. This eroded just enough Republican support for the bill to upend the compromise—as its sponsors knew it would. That was their intention. This is what is called a "poison pill" amendment: Their true aim is to undermine the carefully crafted compromise and, in the process, kill the legislation.

Dorgan's measure failed the first time, but on June 6, 2007, he offered it again. This time it passed by one vote, with Barack Obama and Harry Reid—along with four conservative Republicans—switching their votes to support the amendment.

"Who is the senator from North Dakota trying to fool?" an angry Ted Kennedy demanded of Dorgan. McCain would ask the same thing about Obama, but the damage was done. The fragile coalition supporting the legislation fell apart by summertime, meaning that 12 million newcomers to America would remain in the shadows. Reid apparently didn't want to see George W. Bush in the Rose Garden signing the bill; likewise, Obama didn't want McCain, the Republicans' likely presidential nominee in 2008, claiming credit. They'd calculated that they could undermine Hispanic aspirations while simultaneously campaigning for Hispanic votes by blaming Republicans for the stalled legislation. Their cynical strategy paid off.[7]

For Democrats who don't want to believe that Senator Obama helped torpedo immigration reform in 2007, just examine the record of the Democrats in 2009 and 2010. During the 111th Congress, Democrats enjoyed overwhelming majorities in both the Senate and especially the House of Representatives, where they had a huge seventy-six-seat advantage over the Republicans. With President Obama in the White House, it was a period of busy legislative activity. Democrats passed laws attempting to address pay inequity, children's health care, mortgage relief, Pentagon reform, Iran sanctions, children's nutrition, food safety, and dozens of other issues. They passed stimulus legislation of unprecedented size and provided incentives for first-time homebuyers and alternate energy. Democrats marshaled through the Wall Street Reform and Consumer Protection Act, informally known as Dodd-Frank, the names of its co-sponsors. They also passed the Patient Protection and Affordable Care Act. Given all these passed bills, it's clear that had Democrats been so inclined, they could have passed a sweeping immigration reform package in 2009—or at least enacted an incremental approach such as the DREAM Act, which conferred permanent resident status on young people who had been in America for years and were serving in the U.S. military or attending an American college. But they did not do it.

In subsequent years, the Democrats' alibi would be that they had no significant Republican support for immigration reform. This excuse doesn't wash. For starters, Dodd-Frank passed with no GOP votes in the House and only four in the Senate. ObamaCare was enacted without a single Republican vote. Secondly, Democrats *would* have gotten some Republican support for immigration reform, which is less toxic to Republicans than ObamaCare. In fact, in 2013, the Senate did pass comprehensive immigration reform with the support of fourteen Republican senators. The House, which at that time was deeply red after the 2012 election, refused to take up the matter. When the Democrats controlled all the levers of power in Washington, they never tried to make immigration reform happen.

In a classic example of partisan gamesmanship on both sides, the Republican Party position on immigration is just as disingenuous as the Democrats'. Most Republicans assert that because undocumented workers have broken the law they can never qualify for full citizenship. While hardly any of them follow Donald Trump's example and call Mexican immigrants "rapists" and drug mules, it was Republican presidential nominee Mitt Romney himself who in 2012 advocated the antidote of "self-deportation." It was Senator Pat Roberts of Kansas who called for "humanitarian deportation." Regardless of the words they use to describe their respective positions, the altered rhetoric is a distinction without a difference in policy.

That raises the question of why the Chamber of Commerce would support so many of these anti-immigrant candidates. The Chamber's stated policy position on the issue of undocumented workers favors giving them legal status. Yet it backs candidates that pander to the most nativist elements of the GOP base by openly advocating mass deportation, which would hurt the Chamber's member companies—and the economy. These candidates clearly are quietly telling the Chamber that their stated position on immigration is merely campaign rhetoric intended to secure votes back home, and that they have no intention of following through once they're safely ensconced in office.

This is the kind of corrupt bargain Ted Cruz accused the GOP congressional leadership of striking regarding the issue of whether or not to fund Planned Parenthood. "If leadership is correct that we can never win against the president, why did it matter to win a Republican House?" he asked in an op-ed for *Politico*. "A Republican Senate? If Republican majorities in Congress will acquiesce to and affirmatively fund the identical Big Government priorities that Obama supports, then what difference does it make who is in charge of Congress?"[8]

Not to be shown up, House Speaker John Boehner went on *Face the Nation* the weekend after announcing his retirement to lambast Cruz, if not by name, then by deed. Asked by host John Dickerson in a live interview whether GOP hardliners are "unrealistic about what can be done in government," Boehner's voice rose passionately in response.

"Absolutely, they're unrealistic!" he replied. "But, you know, the

Bible says beware of false prophets, and there are people out there spreading noise about how much can get done."[9]

"I mean this whole idea that we're gonna shut down the government to get rid of ObamaCare in 2013, this plan never had a chance," Boehner added. "You know a lot of my Republican colleagues who knew it was a fool's errand, really they were getting all this pressure from home to do this. So we got groups here in town, members of the House and Senate here in town, who whip people into a frenzy believing they can accomplish things that they know, *they know*, are never gonna happen."[10]

It's ironic that the leader of a House of Representatives that voted fifty times to repeal ObamaCare, voted to approve the Keystone XL Pipeline in spite of dubious chances of its passage, and held dozens of other votes that would never become law would level such a charge. Cruz was trying to galvanize movement conservatives. But his point applies to liberals, too: The real constituency for members on both sides of the aisle is the status quo.

Even as the predicable propaganda was being spread in the bowels of Republican and Democratic Party message factories—with the stated goal of helping their side win the next election—neither political establishment was positioning itself for meaningful change. Regardless of which party controls the Senate or the Oval Office, immigrants won't be deported or, alternatively, given a path to citizenship. Social Security Disability won't be reformed. We'll still be paying more than the rest of the industrialized world for pharmaceuticals and routine health care.

ANTI-ESTABLISHMENT BACKLASH

Millions of Americans know that their party's leaders are paying lip service to their real concerns. It's why so many voters are embracing Donald

Trump, a candidate who—rhetorically, at least—wants to blow up the whole system. Others were drawn to Bernie Sanders in the Democratic primaries because of his longstanding opposition to "establishment" forces and his everyman political style. There's an obvious paradox here. When firebrands such as Ted Cruz and the House Republicans who undermined John Boehner's Speakership disparage "show votes" and maintain that compromise is a dirty word, they have the right diagnosis, but the wrong prescription. We need more compromise, not less, but it must be real compromise, which means, by definition that each side gets at least some of what it wants.

As I worked to make clear in my Senate race, I want members of Congress to stop wasting time, quit pandering to their base, and refrain from misleading the public. I want them to roll up their sleeves and do the hard work of solving our problems—even if that means sharing the credit with their adversaries—and explaining to Americans that fixing some solutions will be painful. I want them to show some courage. That's what being an Independent citizen servant is all about.

If the problem were solely the result of two ideologically polarized parties moving away from each other on the ideological spectrum, it would be bad enough. But the root cause of the respective political parties' stubbornness can often be traced to their campaign sponsors. They are not into compromise. They are industry- or ideology-motivated organizations whose entire lobbying presence in Washington or the state capitals revolves around a single issue or narrow cluster of issues. Oftentimes, they have a vested financial interest in maintaining the status quo.

How else do you explain the Republican reluctance to allow Medicare Part D to negotiate prescription drug prices? As the champions of free market enterprises who profess to believe the private sector is more efficient than the government, why would Republicans want to prevent government from using a tactic that any self-respecting capitalist would use to lower costs? By the same token, many Democrats voted for the recent changes in the 2014 budget bill that allowed big banks to make risky derivative bets inside their government insured subsidiaries. When the campaign coffers of Democrats who voted for those changes were examined, we interested investigators learned that, on average, they had received twice as much money from financial services industry donors than Democrats who voted against the bill.[11]

As we heard in Chapter 1, California Assembly Speaker Jesse "Big Daddy" Unruh said "money is the mother's milk of politics"[12]—but today, a better analogy might be heroin. Our elected officials are addicted to campaign cash, and like any addict they want more and more. They're also willing to do just about anything to get it, including protecting the status quo for the benefit of their campaign sponsors—even if it means breaking every promise they made to voters to get elected. Their addiction is killing our politics. Governance has devolved into eighteen months of political theater meant to establish the issues upon which the next election will be run, followed by six months of campaigning. The goal of all of this activity is simple—to get reelected without upsetting establishment forces by challenging the status quo. Even the supposedly anti-establishment Ted Cruz routinely campaigns for the establishment guys on his side, just as he did against me in Kansas.

Americans are starting to understand this hypocrisy more clearly. They're no longer being led astray by divisive politics that's intended to distract attention from Washington's failure to address the underlying economic insecurity that most Americans are feeling. As a result, many are leaving the two major parties in droves. Millennials are increasingly disinclined to even join either one of the entities in the duopoly. Others, who have remained in the Republican and Democratic parties, are supporting candidates who might not share their values on historic "hot button" issues, but who give them hope that Washington will start addressing their real needs. Millions of Americans are more willing to forgive imperfections that would have historically rendered a candidate "unelectable" in exchange for a leader they believe will be in their corner —fighting for them and not the economic and political elites.

Many of these disaffected voters through their behavior are also asking an obvious question of establishment politicians: "Why do you want to be in Washington in the first place if you're not going to get anything done?"

One of the answers to that question is outsized personal ambition and greed. Those are human traits that will always be with us. Voters, however, should also be asking a question of themselves: "Why do I continue to support politicians of either party, when they only exist to protect the status quo and the interests of the donor class?" For disaffected voters from either party who are willing to ask themselves that question, I'd ask you to join the ranks of political Independents. We can then collectively chart a new course for all Americans and show how our politics—and our lives—will be transformed when we give up partisanship and think for ourselves.

CHAPTER 7

The Rise of Weaponized Partisanship

HOW D.C. DYSFUNCTION HAS POLARIZED
AND PARALYZED HALF OF AMERICA

———— ★ ★ ★ ————

AFTER PAT ROBERTS WON his 2014 Senate primary against Milton Wolf, a high school classmate of Sybil's began attacking me on her personal Facebook account. Sybil was Facebook friends with this person, who had been supporting Wolf. With the Republican nomination settled, she threw herself behind Pat as her candidate. Actually what she did was threw herself *against* me, repeating and passing along every scandalous criticism she dug up on the Internet or that was fed to her by like-minded partisans.

Since Sybil and this woman shared well over 100 mutual Facebook friends, my wife read these attacks with dismay. The information this person was sharing online ranged from simply name-calling to recounting rumors of political donations I'd never received and stances on issues such as gun control that I'd never taken.

After one particularly nasty post, Sybil appealed directly to the woman. "I'm not sure where you are getting your information, but you have been misinformed," Sybil wrote. "I'd love to have you and your family over for dinner and you could ask him any questions you may have."

In reply to this overture, the woman asserted that she had no desire to visit the home of "someone who is clearly a liberal." Sybil did not respond in kind, saying only that if she changed her mind, the offer remained. Although she never heard from the woman again, the unfounded attacks apparently continued on Facebook.

This little story illustrates how successful partisan conservatives (in this case) and partisan liberals have been at introducing toxic additives into our nation's political discourse. Republicans aim these poison darts at Democrats. Democrats shoot them at Republicans. Independents get caught in the crossfire. In so doing, the two political parties are exploiting an innate human reflex to demonize the other side.

In 2013, the Bipartisan Policy Center retained two respected pollsters, Democrat Mark Mellman and Republican Whit Ayres, to research this phenomenon. For an experiment, they devised two education reform proposals that described options on reducing class size, increasing teacher pay, and the like. The first they called Plan A; the second was Plan B. But when they asked voters about them, Plan A was described as the Democratic Party plan, and Plan B as the Republican plan to half the survey sample. Thus primed, Democrats preferred "their party's" plan 75 percent to 17 percent. Yet when the exact same details were called the "Republican Plan," only 12 percent of Democrats liked it. The same dichotomy was present among Republicans. Only Independents answered the question irrespective of which party label was put on it.

"Thus, policy positions were not driving partisanship, but rather partisanship was driving policy positions," Mellman observed. "Voters took whichever position was ascribed to their party, irrespective of the specific policies that position entailed."[1]

In all fairness, what their research also showed was that some self-identified Republicans and Democrats were willing to think beyond the partisan labels and judge each proposal on its merits. Unfortunately, it was a small percentage of voters.

The implications of this finding are huge. It suggests that Republicans and Democrats have been maddeningly successful in their relentless habit of demonizing each other. As a result, political tribalism has infected millions of American voters, making them literally incapable of considering any position espoused by the "other" party. This threatens the possibility of intellectually honest governance for the rest of us, the plurality of Americans—43 percent by the summer of 2015—who want solutions to problems instead of political parties waging "permanent campaigns" designed to keep problems festering so they can raise money and stir up their respective activist bases.

"Politics is the art of the possible," nineteenth-century German statesman Otto Von Bismarck famously observed. The Mellman-Ayres poll suggests that twenty-first-century politics in the United States has deliberately been made the art of the impossible.

Partisanship is not a new phenomenon, but the situation has obviously gotten seriously aggravated in this country when neighbors refuse to even discuss their political differences with each other. Concerns over the corrosive effects of partisanship predate the founding of the United States, and have long been a source of concern to those who value good governance. As I mentioned earlier, George Washington cautioned his countrymen—and future generations of Americans—about this problem. "Since the bond of Union is now complete and we once more consider ourselves as one family," he wrote in 1790, "we must drive far away the demon of party spirit and local reproach."[2]

John Adams didn't merely "dread" the effects of partisanship, as we noted earlier; he saw it as the most significant threat faced by the new national government. "This, in my humble apprehension, is to be dreaded as the greatest political evil under our Constitution," he wrote.[3]

Madison's warning seven years later about mankind's "propensity"[4] to form mutually antagonistic political associations implies that partisanship is more than a hazard of elective politics—it's human nature.

Modern social scientists tend to agree. New York University professor Jonathan Haidt has concluded that human beings are hard-wired not to synthesize data empirically and arrive at objective conclusions, but rather to sift through available information—a politician's voting record, a columnist's contentions, Internet rumors—looking for facts and anecdotes that back up their existing world view.

We saw this in full display during our election, as partisans from both parties would take the thinnest shreds of "evidence" and turn them into full-blown narratives that "uncovered" who they thought I really was. In one instance, at a town hall meeting in Lawrence, Kansas, I was asked about the affordability of higher education. I recounted a discussion I'd had with a university president who callously suggested that easy access to college loans undermined concerns about affordability. My response was that just because a student can go deeply in debt to pay the freight doesn't really make college affordable. I told the audience that his statement reminded me of Mitt Romney's comment about how everyone had a rich uncle who would lend her money.

Then, for the next three minutes everybody in the town hall endured a lecture from a partisan Democrat in the crowd who decried my unmitigated gall for assuming everyone had a rich uncle. The fact that I was mocking Romney's famously clueless declaration to young people that they should "take a shot, go for it, take a risk, get the education, borrow money if you have to from your parents, start a business"[5] was lost on her. She took each of my statements out of context and constructed a story about how I thought students should have to go deeply in debt to afford college. She clearly had already made up her mind about me and had a partisan filter that was so thick that it prevented her from actually hearing what I said.

The two political parties count on that kind of reaction from their part of their faithful—and go out of their way to instill it. While my liberal critic was constructing her own narrative about me right through her ideological prism, Kansas conservatives made it a practice of building stories around every little detail and spreading them around the state. One instance involved a fundraiser I held. The event did indeed occur in New York City—that part was true. It was also true our fundraising team was soliciting donations in advance of the event, which is customary. Donors who gave $2,000 or more were listed as "hosts." One such individual was Jonathan Soros, the son of the famed hedge fund titan and prolific Democratic political donor, George Soros. I had never spoken to Jonathan (or George for that matter), and I'm told the contribution that he made was inspired by the campaign finance reforms that I was proposing. Jonathan's donation represented less than one-tenth of 1 percent of the money our campaign spent. We had dozens of longtime GOP donors who gave us significantly more money. No matter. The Republicans used the Soros donation as "evidence" that I was a liberal. What's worse, other Republicans believed them, because their partisan filters had them looking for evidence that I was really a Democrat.

Jonathan Haidt, author of *The Righteous Mind: Why Good People Are Divided by Politics*, marshals evidence that we are born to be advocates, not impartial judges. The ability to reason, he suggests, has not evolved to help us learn, but to help us spin.

"When it comes to moral judgments," he asserts, "we think we are scientists discovering the truth, but actually we are lawyers arguing for positions we arrived at by other means."[6]

Other researchers concur. Studies by Dan Kahan, a professor of law and psychology at Yale University, have shown that when members of the public were asked whether a PhD scientist who is a member of the National Academy of Sciences should be considered an "expert" on climate issues, they'd only agree to that proposition if the mythical expert's view matched their own.[7] Meanwhile, a team of clinicians led by Valparaiso University professor Kevin Goebbert showed that both sides in the climate change debate use recent weather events to bolster their position—but that neither side was even able to accurately recall the weather they'd just experienced.[8]

Even our elected leaders, who have access to the best available data, tend to grab on to whatever information they can to reinforce their beliefs. As an example, on February 26, 2015, Senator Jim Inhofe, a Republican from Oklahoma, strode onto the Senate floor with evidence that he believed revealed global warming to be a hoax. This smoking gun he carried with him? A snowball. The way Senator Inhofe reasoned, if global warming were really happening it wouldn't be so cold in the nation's capital. In February.

If Jim Inhofe were merely the author of *The Greatest Hoax: How the Global Warming Conspiracy Threatens Your Future*, his publicly mocking the "hysteria on global warming" wouldn't be so out-of-place. But Inhofe was also the chairman of the Senate Environment and Public Works Committee, a key cog in the federal government's machinery for fighting climate change.

"In case we have forgotten, because we keep hearing that 2014 has been the warmest year on record, I ask the chair, 'You know what this is?'" he said. "It's a snowball, from outside here. So it's very, very cold out. Very unseasonable."

"Catch this," he then told the presiding officer, before tossing the blob of snow.

Actually, it wasn't "very" unseasonable. Snow wasn't unseasonable at all—it was the middle of winter. But Inhofe went ahead to list recent cold temperatures across the United States, some of which were quite chilly.

As the chairman of the Senate Environment and Public Works Committee, this perspective mortified many Americans and much of the rest of the world. How could a sitting U.S. senator in a position of responsibility regarding the official U.S. response to climate change cite such flimsy evidence to support his perspective?

What is going on here? Aren't human beings rational enough to evaluate information that doesn't fit our preconceived notions? Are we really that tribal? It turns out that those are two different questions. The answer to the second is that yes, we are that clannish. We like to stick to our cultural group. But we do so for reasons of self-preservation—and that's the answer to the first question. We are rational, but we are rewarded with social benefits for conforming to the majority view within our own group. Peer pressure is huge, particularly in politics.

"If anything, social science suggests that citizens are culturally polarized because they are, in fact, *too* rational—at filtering out information that would drive a wedge between themselves and their peers," writes Kahan. "For members of the public, being right or wrong about climate-change science will have no impact. Nothing they do as individual consumers or as individual voters will meaningfully affect the risks posed by climate change. Yet the impact of taking a position that conflicts with their cultural group could be disastrous." He cites as an example a hypothetical barber in a rural South Carolina town. "Is it a good idea for him to implore his customers to sign a petition urging Congress to take action on climate change? No. If he does, he will find himself out of a job . . . "[9]

John Adams and James Madison decried party passions, yet each emerged as a leader of his own political party: Adams as a Federalist, and Madison of the forerunner of the Democratic Party. Yet, somehow, even with all the vehement partisanship that characterized our nation almost from its beginnings, America always muddled through. So what's the difference today? Part of the answer to that question is the increase we have experienced in polarization.

In its strictest sense, polarization is a phrase used by political scientists simply to describe how far apart members of Congress are politically. They use legislative votes to measure it. Others use it to denote how far apart the electorate is from itself—how far apart rank-and-file Democrats are on the issues from Republicans. The term also is employed by veteran political observers to explain how much, or how little, political compromise takes place in Washington, D.C., or in state capitals. Some non-academics use the term to describe the uncivil discourse that is common in modern politics, and on the airwaves and Internet. In its broadest sense, the term refers to all these things, each of which are interlocking and mutually reinforcing. Some have pointed to the rise of the Tea Party as evidence that our politics have become polarized.

In recent years, Tea Party conservatives have relentlessly taken aim at the federal government on the grounds that it has grown so large and unwieldy that even the most committed Federalist at the original Constitutional Convention wouldn't recognize it. In that complaint they are on solid ground. When the Tea Party position gets shaky is when it is used to attack Republican members of Congress for daring to compromise with Democrats. People who use the word "compromise" as a dirty word don't know their U.S. history. One of those historically challenged critics is Jim DeMint, the South Carolina Republican who had the most conservative voting record in the chamber when he served the U.S. Senate. Here is how he put it while exhorting conservatives to make no accommodation with liberals: "I can guarantee you the [Super Bowl] coaches are not telling their players to go out on the field and cooperate and compromise with the other team," he said. "There is a reason for that; the other team has an opposite goal—they are there to beat you."[10]

DeMint's declaration is a blunt description of the zero-sum politics practiced by today's absolutists. It's the verbal equivalent of the tug-of-war scenario I used in my television ads in Kansas. But I was mocking the politicians who endlessly and fruitlessly pull at their partisan rope. Jim DeMint and his like-minded rebels are serious. They never get tired of invoking the Constitution to justify their intransigence. But they are as far from the spirit of the founders as it is possible to get. Every delegate in Philadelphia at the Constitutional Convention made concessions to get that deal done. Our Constitution was one big compromise: between North and South, between urban and agrarian, between slave-owning states and abolitionists. It's not too much to say that the foundational spirit of America is the spirit of compromise.

Some might agree with DeMint and insist that sometimes it is better *not* to compromise—and point to the Constitutional Convention to make this point. Papering over the differences on slavery only forestalled resolution of this great moral dilemma, ensuring that untold millions lived in bondage and forcing the question to be resolved on the battlefields of the Civil War at great loss of life. It's a fair point, and not a new one. Nineteenth century abolitionist firebrand William Lloyd Garrison celebrated Independence Day in 1854 by burning a copy of the Constitution, which he labeled "a covenant with death and an agreement with Hell!"[11] Similarly, certain conservatives would claim that when the constitution failed to recognize an explicit right to state nullification of federal laws a great wrong was committed.

In our time, Jim DeMint represents a movement, heavily imbued with Christian evangelical beliefs, that believes compromising on such issues as abortion, gay marriage, and gun control is also making a deal with the devil. And certainly those who support the opposite social values feel equally committed to their moral stance. The same is true for those who celebrate the free market and those who favor democratic socialism. My point here is that partisanship is not always merely tribal—especially not to partisans who prevail on their pet issue—and it's certainly not always cynical. Millions of Americans, left and right, are ideological. They have gravitated toward the Democratic and Republican Parties for rational reasons. I would argue that hyper-partisanship is dangerous because it prevents people from examining arguments of the other side. I would also argue that campaign consultants and political professionals stoke partisan impulses—weaponize them, as it were—for very temporary political advantage.

Jim DeMint was only one senator, but he wielded more influence beyond South Carolina's borders and across the Capitol grounds into the House of Representatives. When John Boehner took over as Speaker of the House after the 2010 midterms, the Ohio Republican noticed to his dismay that freshmen Republicans elected with Tea Party support were keeping their distance from him. There were four such members in the South Carolina delegation alone, and they wouldn't take Boehner's calls.[12] The reason, he soon learned, was that if they acted too cozy with the GOP leadership—or, God forbid, dealt with Democrats—they feared that DeMint would run someone even more conservative against them in the primary. This wasn't an idle threat. Remember Dan Kahan's hypothetical about the South Carolina barber who felt peer pressure to deny climate change? Kahan used that illustration deliberately. It wasn't a hypothetical example; it was a real-life case study example. Only he wasn't a barber. He was a congressman from South Carolina named Bob Inglis, who ran afoul of DeMint for suggesting that their fellow evangelical Christians should use more temperate language when talking about their opponents and steer clear of a fight to pass a constitutional amendment forbidding same-sex marriage. Inglis also suggested that Republicans should heed the opinions of the National Academy of Science on the issue of climate change.

Although Inglis had helped get DeMint started in politics and hosted a Bible study group in his home attended by DeMint and his wife, these stances put him on a collision course with the senator. In the Republican primary, DeMint backed a political newcomer named Trey Gowdy—he would become one of the freshmen who shunned Boehner—against Inglis, who lost handily.

"Tea-party Republicans were elected to go to Washington and save the country—not be co-opted by the club," DeMint wrote in *The Wall Street Journal* the day the 2010 midterms ended. "So put on your boxing gloves. The fight begins today."[13]

In 2012, DeMint took his take-no-prisoners crusade national, leaving the Senate to become president of the Heritage Foundation, a conservative think tank. This, too, was a sign of the times—and not a good one. Three decades earlier, Heritage had been staffed by the best and the brightest Republican minds in the country. During the 1980 campaign that brought Ronald Reagan to office, the Heritage Foundation produced a twenty-volume report called *Mandate for Leadership* that formed a blueprint of the "Reagan Revolution." The new president presented copies of a condensed version (it was still one thousand pages long) to members of his cabinet with the tacit understanding that they would begin pushing its tenets. "All of a sudden," Democratic senator Daniel Patrick Moynihan noted with both alarm and admiration even before Reagan won in 1980, "the GOP has become the party of ideas."[14] Heritage is also the think tank that gave us the individual and employer mandates that formed the foundation of so-called Romney-Care in Massachusetts and were later used in creating the Affordable Care Act.

Under DeMint, Heritage has morphed into a different animal. It's now a fundraising magnet that stakes out extreme and partisan policy positions—and it threatens Republicans who don't obey its dictates. As president, Ronald Reagan would tell his aides to try to get 80 percent of what they wanted in a negotiation. Jim DeMint finds that attitude wimpy and defeatist. He spent the 2013–2014 election cycle—the one in which I ran in Kansas—touring the country demanding total victory. His specific demand was to make congressional Republicans and GOP candidates sign a pledge to "defund" ObamaCare.

"Republicans are afraid," he said. "And if they are, they need to be replaced."[15] DeMint put his money where his mouth was, or at least

Heritage's money. Its overtly political arm, Heritage Action, spent half a million dollars attacking Republicans who didn't go along with DeMint.

HOW DID WE GET HERE?

So America's political parties have become more polarized. But what about the voters themselves—have they followed suit? Answering this question is tricky. In 2014, the Pew Research Center produced a report based on a massive survey of ten thousand Americans. The title of this study told the story: *Political Polarization in the American Public: How Increasing Ideological Uniformity and Partisan Apathy Affects Politics, Compromise, and Everyday Life.* "Republicans and Democrats are more divided along ideological lines—and partisan antipathy is deeper and more extensive—than at any point in the last two decades," it began. "These trends manifest themselves in myriad ways, both in politics and in everyday life."[16]

That seems obvious, but for more than two decades, Morris Fiorina, a thoughtful professor at Stanford University, has offered a counternarrative. In books, articles, and lectures, he has maintained that the "culture wars" narrative pitting Republicans against Democrats is overblown. Fiorina believes that the culture wars construct accurately describes the divisions among party activists and intellectual elites, but does not accurately reflect the attitudes on policy issues held by the vast middle of the electorate. And he's right. Evidence shows that a large plurality of Americans holds more moderate views than the bases of the two major political parties—and has done so consistently for more than four decades.

Fiorina points to the third sentence in that 2014 Pew study to underscore his point: "And a new survey of 10,000 adults nationwide finds that these divisions are greatest among those *who are the most engaged and active in the political process.*"

"What has happened in the United States is not polarization, but sorting," Fiorina declares. "Prior to the 1980s the Republican Party had a significant liberal wing and the Democrats a significant conservative wing. People of my vintage can remember liberal Republicans like Gov. Nelson Rockefeller of New York and senators like Jake Javits of New York, Hugh Scott of Pennsylvania, Charles Percy of Illinois, and Mark Hatfield of Oregon. No more. Similarly, the Democratic Party contained a slew of conservative Southern governors, senators and representatives."[17] Fiorina notes that in the 1950s and 1960s, the greatest support—and the greatest opposition—to civil rights legislation in Congress took place within the Democratic Party. Fiorina adds that in 1970, one would have been hard-pressed to say which party was more pro-choice on the issue of abortion.

The Stanford professor is right, but with two important caveats. First, although there is indeed a difference between sorting and polarization, what we've learned is that sorting inevitably *leads* to polarization. The combination of these two factors, sorting and polarization, creates a sort of chemical compound—I call it hyper-partisanship—that gridlocks our government. The second point is that hyper-partisanship is a toxic stew not easily confined to politics. There is evidence that it has leeched out from politics into the wider culture.

Let's take these two points in order: How does the combination of partisan sorting and polarization lead to a political stalemate? Here's Fiorina himself on that very point: "In the terminology of political science, our single-member, simple-plurality electoral system manufactures majorities," he writes. "But the fact that the winners in two-party competition get more votes or seats than the losers by no means guarantees that the winners' positions are those actually favored by a majority of the voters, only that those positions are likely to be preferred to those of the losers."

As an example, Fiorina cites the issue of abortion. "The 2012 Republican platform plank stated essentially: never, no exceptions. The

Democratic platform plank stated the opposite: any time, for any reason," he adds. "How many Americans would want a government in which either a powerful Democratic or Republican government was able to enact its abortion platform plank? Given public opinion on the issue, 75 to 80 percent would answer in the negative." Fiorina continues: "Unleashing the majority would unleash a policy with nothing approximating majority support among voters. Abortion may be an extreme issue, but public-opinion data suggest that on other issues as well—immigration, deficit reduction, environmental and energy issues—majorities of Americans would prefer something between the polar programs advocated by the bases of the two parties. This has contributed to the voter backlash observed in recent episodes of unified control of government."

REFORM'S UNINTENDED CONSEQUENCES

It wasn't supposed to be this way. After World War II, the best political minds in the country assured us it that a little more polarization might actually help elected officials govern more effectively. They have been proven wrong. But let's go back in time to 1950. That year, the American Political Science Association published the results of a blue-ribbon study called "Toward a More Responsible Two-Party System."

The political scientists behind the study believed that European-style democracy was superior to our own in one essential way: The political parties on the other side of the Atlantic were organized along coherent ideological lines. Britain and France didn't have our equivalent of northeastern liberal Republicans, or libertarian western Republicans, or socially conservative Catholic Democrats—let alone Southern Democrats. This had been a pet peeve of Franklin Roosevelt's. Frustrated by

Southern Democrats who blocked New Deal legislation, FDR groused to White House speechwriter Sam Rosenman, "We ought to have two real parties: one liberal and the other conservative."[18]

Academics also fretted over this, in a classic case of never being too careful what you wish for. Six-and-a-half decades later, the academics' fantasy has become a reality. Our only two major political parties are now truly ideologically coherent. If you're a conservative today, you are a Republican. If you're a liberal, you're a Democrat. (If you're moderate, a definition that seems to fit a plurality of Americans, you're out of luck.) So if the political parties are "responsible" today (a word the academics used in 1950 the way we'd use the word "responsive" today), we must ask: to whom are they being responsible? The answer is that they are beholden to the special interest groups that fund them, as well as the ideologues on their fringes.

"We finally got ideological purity, and it's a disaster for the country," observes Senator Angus King of Maine. "We have ideological gridlock. You can't solve problems this way."[19]

As we discussed in Chapter 5, the process of self-segregation by party—Bill Bishop's "big sort"—is a big part of what's happening, as is gerrymandering. Other factors contribute to our extreme politics, including the following:

- Declining regionalism as a source of political identity. Conservative Southern Democrats, liberal Republicans from New England, economic libertarians from California, border state moderates—all these archetypes have become endangered species.
- The 1994 Republican takeover of Congress, which ended the status quo of Democratic control and encouraged both parties to view each election cycle as potentially disastrous, effectively nationalizing every election by making them about the battle for control between Democrats and Republicans.

- The 1998 Senate trial of Bill Clinton, which alienated most voters. Two-thirds of Americans opposed impeachment, leaving the majority wondering why Congress wasn't heeding their wishes.
- The 2000 presidential election recount in Florida, and the accompanying 5-4 Supreme Court decision, which put a man in the White House who'd lost the popular vote and created the perception among many voters, particularly Democrats, that our system is rigged.
- Fact-free talk radio and shout-fest cable shows that cheapen political discourse and garner ratings and attention through extremist and vitriolic rhetoric.
- Internet misinformation and Balkanization, which also devalue civility as each side talks among themselves in ever-escalating venom directed at the opposing side.

The Internet is an especially potent medium in taking hyper-partisanship out of its politics sphere and into everyday American life. Futurist Esther Dyson says that the Internet fosters "virtual communities" of like-minded souls. When they connect, say with other people who share a passion for Hungarian folk music, that's a positive thing. When it enables Americans to segregate themselves into partisan cyber-ghettos where they spend their days reinforcing their preexisting political views while demonizing those with whom they disagree, well, that's not so good.

The group of us being marginalized is not a small one. We are, by some measurements, a plurality of the citizenry. I've already mentioned that 43 percent of Americans described themselves as Independent. There are other metrics, too. On issue after issue, voters steer a centrist ground between the two major parties when presented with policy options. And though moderates of either party are largely extinct in Congress, fully 35 percent of Americans self-describe as moderate.[20]

The year John F. Kennedy was elected president, a tiny minority of Americans—4 percent of Democrats and 5 percent of Republicans—told

pollsters that they would be "displeased" if their child married someone from the opposite political party. Fifty years later, one-third of
Democrats and half the Republicans said they would be "somewhat" or
"very" unhappy at the prospect of their child marrying someone from
the rival political party. Think about that. In a nation in which gay marriage is the law of the land, an African-American family lives in the
White House, and two women have run for president, partisanship is
our newest form of prejudice.[21]

As we increasingly live in like-minded communities, walled off by distance and partisan affiliation, we have fewer and fewer people in our lives
from the "other" political party. Unfortunately, fewer and fewer of us live
in communities where we are exposed to the opposite party anymore. Like
Dan Kahan's fictional South Carolina barber, those people who live among
us but don't share the same partisan leanings as the "in-group" often keep
their political leanings hidden for fear of being ostracized. Much of the
media doesn't help bridge this gap. As I'll discuss in Chapter 9, the media
reinforces these prejudices. Many members of the Fourth Estate—and
entire news organizations—have all but abandoned their civic obligation
to report the news and give both sides. This divide manifests itself on every
conceivable policy issue.

Asked to evaluate key details of George W. Bush's proposed Social Security reforms, a majority of Americans expressed widespread support—
unless the pollster identified it as Bush's plan. Then the bottom fell out
among Democrats. In his successor's era, the same dynamic was present regarding many key features of the Affordable Care Act—until the
person conducting the survey mentioned Obama's name. Then support
plummeted among Republicans.

This desire to shun anything identified with the opposing party has
led to a divergence on a variety of bedrock values. At the end of Ronald
Reagan's era as president, according to a Pew Research poll, 86 percent of
Republicans and 93 percent of Democrats answered affirmatively when

asked whether "there needs to be stricter laws and regulations to protect the environment." That consensus is gone. The sentiments of Democrats have remained the same, but today only 47 percent of Republicans still support that statement. We have completely politicized the issue of clean air and clean water—along with almost everything else. Moreover, Americans from both parties don't merely believe they have better ideas; they find the other parties' positions truly threatening.[22]

Here is a table from the Pew foundation's landmark study on polarization that illustrates the depth of the mutual mistrust.

Beyond Dislike: Viewing the Other Party as a 'Threat to the Nation's Well-Being'

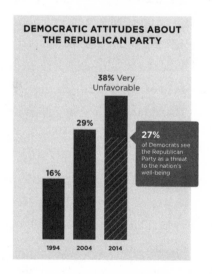

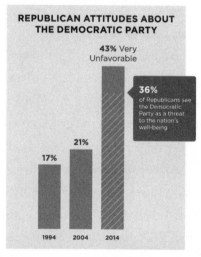

Source: 2014 Political Polarization in the American Public, Pew Research Center

We live in an era not just of political polarization, but also a kind of social self-segregation that manifests itself not only in Democratic and Republican neighborhoods, but in Democratic and Republican churches, Democratic and Republican restaurants, and even television programming that identifies itself as either Republican or Democrat. That becomes a real problem when the country must pull together—or face a crisis.

Today, even war and peace are viewed through a partisan political prism. This is a new development, and an ominous one. Consider the following questions, and the tables of answers:

> Looking back, do you think the United States did the right thing in taking military action in Iraq or should the U.S. have stayed out?

	DEMOCRAT	REPUBLICAN
RIGHT THING	19%	71%
STAYED OUT	76%	25%

Contrast those findings with polls taken by the Gallup Organization during the Vietnam and Korean wars.[23]

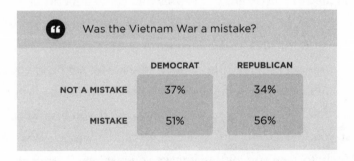

> Was the Vietnam War a mistake?

	DEMOCRAT	REPUBLICAN
NOT A MISTAKE	37%	34%
MISTAKE	51%	56%

> Was the Korean War a mistake?

	DEMOCRAT	REPUBLICAN
NOT A MISTAKE	45%	37%
MISTAKE	43%	55%

These charts show that for all intents and purposes, the citizens of the United States now believe that whether a war is good or bad depends on who sits in the Oval Office. It's tantamount to having "Democratic Party wars" and "Republican Party wars." What this suggests is that we have less in common with the Greatest Generation of World War II and afterward than we do with Americans of the mid-nineteenth century—those who fought a Civil War.

Republican and Democratic efforts at divisiveness have been exceedingly successful, if we can really use the word "success" to describe the efforts of the professional political class to demonize half of the country. According to Emory University political scientists Alan I. Abramowitz and Steven Webster, Americans are exhibiting levels of party loyalty in the voting booth not seen in six decades. Frighteningly, what is animating these party-line voters is not necessarily support for their party, but hostility to the opposition party. Abramowitz and Webster call this phenomenon "negative partisanship," and predict it will continue well beyond the 2016 elections. "A growing number of Americans have been voting against the opposing party rather than for their own party," they wrote in an April 2015 academic paper.[24]

In an essay examining the Emory study, *Vox* editor-in-chief Ezra Klein amplified on their findings. "It's worth saying that a bit more clearly: You're more likely to vote Democratic if you hate Republicans than if you love Democrats, and vice versa," he wrote. "What parties need to do to keep you loyal isn't make you inspired. Rather, they need to make you scared."

"Politics isn't about who you love," Klein summarized. "It's about who you fear."[25]

One of the most obvious tactics that both sides use to make voters fear the other is to paint their opponent as being extreme on a particular issue. In my Senate campaign I encountered such fearmongering over a range of issues. On the issue of abortion, I was painted as someone who supports late-term abortion on demand for any reason. Now, I want you to think about that for a second. Do you actually know *anyone* who supports late-term abortion on demand for any reason? I don't. Unfortunately, in the context of political advertising, campaigns generally wouldn't be able to create fear if they told the truth.

We've been at this point before in our country's history. During the height of the Civil Rights movement, a time that divided our country in two, Robert F. Kennedy delivered a speech in Cleveland. Coming just two months before Kennedy's assassination, his words have an eerie ring of relevance for today:

> When you teach a man to hate and fear his brother, when you teach that he is a lesser man because of his color or his beliefs or the policies he pursues, when you teach that those who differ from you threaten your freedom or your job or your family, then you also learn to confront others not as fellow citizens but as enemies . . .
>
> We learn . . . to look at our brothers as aliens, men with whom we share a city, but not a community, men bound to us in common dwelling, but not in common effort. We learn to share only a common fear—only a common desire to retreat from each other—only a common impulse to meet disagreement with force. For all this there are no final answers.

Kennedy's words serve as a warning, that we can't allow our politics to continue down the path advocated by those who divide us to serve their political purposes. We can't, as a country, devolve to the point where we view those who disagree with us as enemies. Otherwise we will live in fortresses of fear and anger, and just stop talking to those we don't agree with—the way Sybil's high school classmate did.

The plurality of Americans who are truly Independent need to work to break the partisan stranglehold on our politics. We need to appeal to likeminded Americans in both parties, who are holding on to the memory of a party that has long since left them, to join with us in reforming our politics. Together we represent a silent, but strong majority in America. We need to collectively reject the labels and the false choices and the bitterly negative politics of division that defines good versus evil based solely on a partisan imprint. We need to implore our fellow citizens to think for themselves and recognize that we will never meet our potential as a country if our mode of conveyance is a Republican elephant or a Democratic donkey. We need the Independent's life raft.

PART III

REINFORCING

the

DUOPOLY

———— ★★★ ————

CHAPTER 8

The Triumph of Crony Capitalism

HOW SPECIAL INTERESTS
GET THEIR PIECE OF THE $4 TRILLION
U.S. GOVERNMENT PIE

———— ★ ★ ★ ————

SEVENTY-FIVE YEARS BEFORE I ran for the Senate in Kansas, in 1939, Hollywood produced two classic movies that still resonate with American audiences.

One of them, *Mr. Smith Goes to Washington*, was overtly about U.S. politics. Jefferson Smith, played by James Stewart, is appointed by the governor of an unnamed western state (it was Montana in the original novel) to fill a vacancy in the U.S. Senate. In Washington, he ends up fighting a lonely but ultimately victorious battle against entrenched interests and corruption. Famed director Frank Capra intended the movie to underscore the fragility of democracy at a time when dictatorships were marching across Europe and to remind Americans just how much our democratic system of government is dependent on elected officials who put the nation's well-being above their own interests.

The other film, *The Wizard of Oz*, is set in my state of Kansas. Ostensibly, it's a timeless tale about home and hearth. Dorothy Gale, the teenage protagonist played by Judy Garland, is caught in a fearsome Midwestern tornado only to learn—along with the Scarecrow, the Cowardly Lion and the Tin Man—that the power to prevail in life can be found within each of us. Both those movies have a turning point where an ordinary person decides to rise to the occasion. Today, we need that kind of wisdom, courage, and heart on a national scale. As I see it, we can either try to preserve a broken political system that does not serve the people of this country and that is steadily allowing the greatness of America to slip away, or we can embrace a new and more courageous kind of politics.

"Pay no attention to that man behind the curtain," the phony wizard told Dorothy. That's essentially what leading Republican and Democratic Party politicians tell the American people every day. We need to tear that curtain away.

What we have now is an environment in which Democrats and Republicans allow powerful special interests to rig the system for their own benefit at the expense of the nation's well-being. What we need is a new politics where citizen leaders, like Frank Capra's "Mr. Smith," can challenge the special interests and once again put the people in charge of their government and their country. What we demand are elected officials independent of the two major political parties. As this chapter will show, our two parties are so corrupted by crony capitalism that only Independent, unbeholden officeholders can change the game.

CASH, CRONYISM, AND QUID PRO QUO

Congress today is sorely lacking in Mr. Smiths. Rather, the two houses of our national legislature seem to be occupied mainly by people with three types of agendas.

The first are the true ideologues who emerge from ideologically

With Hubert Humphrey and my family at home in Mankato, Minnesota. I'm holding my sister, Jackie, in the lower left hand corner of the photo.

Being sworn in as President of Boys Nation.

Being informed that I had to make a presentation to President Reagan five minutes before the event. In the White House Briefing Room.

Presenting President Reagan with the Boys Nation legislation.

With reporters on launch day.

In Winfield with Dave Seaton, Chairman of the Winfield Courier.

Walking with Sybil in the Fourth of July parade in Lenexa.

With my dog, Lucy, before the Fourth of July parade in Lenexa.

The Orman for Senate parade truck with my mother-in-law, Seana, at the wheel.

Sybil gathering signatures in the rain at a race. Sybil gathered roughly five hundred signatures herself.

My sister, Michelle, setting up to gather signatures in the hot sun.

At our bus tour kick-off event in Shawnee.

Making dinner at a Salina rescue mission.

With the core bus tour team in Salina.

Sybil and our bus tour team in McPherson. Notice our parade horse standing in the back row.

Sharing a light moment with Sybil after the McPherson Triathlon.

Meeting with voters and community leaders in Colby.

Like father, like son. Talking with voters in Hutchinson.

Working at Youthville in Dodge City as part of our public service bus tour.

Handing out a balloon on a parade route. Regardless of how many balloons we had, we invariably ran out by the middle of every parade.

Walking in the Tiblow Days Parade in Bonner Springs.

Walking with former Army Ranger Jade Lane in a parade in Manhattan.

Getting a voter's signature in Abilene to get on the ballot.

My field director, Aaron Estabrook, organizing our signatures.

The day we announced that we had the signatures to get on the ballot in front of the state capitol in Topeka.

Being interviewed at WIBW radio in Topeka.

Talking about predatory lending targeting military personnel in Manhattan.

Being interviewed by Kasie Hunt before appearing in front of the Heartland Retired Teachers Association in Wichita.

With Sybil before a K–State football game.

With Steve and Barb Morris at the Women for Kansas rally in Wichita.

The audience at the State Fair debate. I was grateful to see so many people wearing our campaign t-shirts.

With Senator Roberts on the State Fair debate stage.

With Sybil before the Chamber of Commerce debate in Overland Park. Sybil was carrying the campaign buttons that she made by hand to save money.

With Dana Bash and other members of the media after the Chamber of Commerce debate in Overland Park.

With supporters after the Wichita debate. My mother-in-law, Seana, is in a campaign t-shirt, taking a picture with her cell phone.

Talking with voters at my dad's furniture store in Stanley. I think my dad spent more time campaigning than he did selling furniture.

At a town hall meeting with the Heartland Retired Teachers Association in Wichita.

Talking with students at Washburn University in Topeka.

Meeting with voters in our Wichita field office.

Talking about higher education affordability at the University of Kansas. About one hundred students came to learn about our plan and share their thoughts.

Sybil leading an early voting rally sponsored by Women For Kansas in Wichita.

With Coach Gregg Marshall and good friend Dave Johnson before a Royals' World Series game.

Giving my closing argument speech in the warehouse of Combat Brands in Lenexa.

Preparing to be interviewed by Chuck Todd who was traveling the country to cover multiple races during the last month of the election.

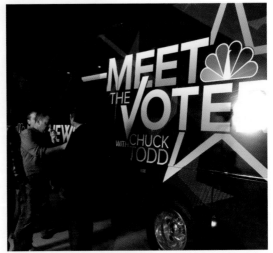

Walking with Sybil to the podium before my concession speech. I couldn't have asked for a more dedicated partner.

Imogen at home after spending a couple of weeks in the ICU.

My beautiful daughter, Imogen. Thankfully, she looks like her mother.

Imogen's first Christmas.

charged primaries because they really do belong to the right or left political fringes of American political discourse.

Some of these folks also fit into a second, larger category: career politicians who never worked much in the private sector, and never really wanted to. These officeholders are the political lifers, who'll take the salary and (very generous) government pension, because they lack the talent to do anything else. They talk a lot about facilitating the public good, but when it comes down to it, they usually take whatever path is necessary to win the next election.

The third kind of elected official views public service as a stepping stone to a seven-figure job lobbying their former colleagues, generally to the detriment of the vast majority of Americans, including their former constituents. It's these second and third types of legislators I want to focus on in this chapter. They are the ones at the heart of what is rightly called "crony capitalism."

Its most literal definition is a system in which cushy jobs, contracts, and insider business deals are doled out to the family and friends of government officials. It has existed since long before the United States was a country and goes by various names in different parts of the world: *"guanxi"* in China, *"keiretsu"* in Japan, *"chaebol"* in Korea, *"semibankirshchina"* in Russia.

American political lexicographer William Safire traced the first use of the term in the United States to 1946 when a fellow *New York Times* columnist, Arthur Krock, lamented that New Deal Democrats and conservative Republicans alike had recoiled from a feature of the cliquish Missourians in Harry Truman's administration who practiced "government by crony."[1]

As our government has grown larger, crony capitalism has taken on a life of its own. The practices have found their way into the tax code, subsidies for businesses, and government support for a whole range of private sector activities. Also referred to as "corporate welfare," it has been decried by politicians on both the right and the left. Unfortunately, many of those same politicians have determined that they can benefit from that same system of cronyism, through campaign cash and the lobbying careers that follow their public service. It's a vicious cycle that does a huge disservice to the American people.

One of the first positions I staked out in my first Senate campaign was a lifetime ban on lobbying for members of Congress. It's also the reason my campaign refused to accept direct contributions from PACs or lobbyists. Despite a one-year prohibition on lobbying for departing House members (and two years for former senators), most departing members of Congress—and a greater portion of their staff—move directly from Capitol Hill to lobbying positions when they leave office. This number is four times as high a percentage as it was in the 1980s, and two-and-a-half times as much as in 1998.[2] Ask yourself a question: Do you think those members are thinking about how to enrich their campaign coffers or enhance their future lobbying careers while considering legislation that affects the very interests from whom they will be seeking cash or a lobbying job? To ask that question is to answer it.

As for those on the other side—the corporations, unions, associations, and other special interests who retain the lobbyists and contribute money to the politicians—does any of us believe for an instant that they are stupid and like to waste money? Or do we believe that when a special interest spends $2.5 billion lobbying over a fifteen-year period, as the pharmaceutical industry has done, that they get what they are paying for?[3] Big Pharma racks up some $200 million a year in lobbying costs, while forking over another $20 million in campaign contributions. You better believe they're getting their money's worth. The prohibition on Medicare's ability to negotiate prescription drug prices alone is generating roughly $25 billion a year in excess profits for the drug industry. That's an astounding return on their investment. The fortune they spend on politicians represents a meager 1 percent of what they get in return.

Exhibit A of the quid pro quo that dominates Washington is the rise and fall of House Speaker J. Dennis Hastert. For nearly a decade, he was the number three person in the government in the White House succession—after only the president and vice president. Now he is a convicted felon.

The political fallout and loss of House seats during Bill Clinton's impeachment resulted in the unlikely 1999 elevation of rumpled, obscure, and seemingly harmless Illinois congressman Denny Hastert to become the fifty-first Speaker. Hastert's appearance proved misleading. He wasn't harmless at all, in either his personal or professional life. His reign lasted eight years, and before it ended America's two-party dysfunction had been codified by a parliamentary gimmick called "The Hastert Rule." The rule applied only to the Republican majority in the House and required that a majority of the Republican members of the House approve of a bill before it was debated on the House floor. The Hastert Rule overtly discouraged cooperation between the Republican majority and Democratic minority in the House, because even if a bill would pass the House with a combination of Democrat and Republican support it wouldn't see the light of day without a *majority* of Republicans agreeing to it.

When a sex abuse scandal unfolded eight years after he left office and details of Hastert's personal and financial life were laid bare, it revealed more than hypocrisy. It exposed the corruption that lies at the heart of government gridlock.

Denny Hastert's fall from grace was sudden and shocking. The story broke on May 28, 2015: The former House Speaker was being indicted on federal charges pertaining to hush money paid to a former student at Yorkville High School in the Illinois town where he taught and coached wrestling five decades earlier. The federal indictment neither identified the student nor specified what Hastert was trying to keep secret, other than to describe it as "past misconduct."[4] It quickly emerged that the misconduct concerned sexual molestation—and that there was likely more than one victim. The statute of limitations having long since expired for those crimes, prosecutors didn't dwell on those details. They focused instead on the surreptitious banking practices Hastert employed to funnel cash to the former student, methods that circumvented money laundering statutes designed to thwart drug dealers, and on the misleading statements he made about the money to FBI agents. Both are felonies under federal law.

An astonishing amount of payoff money was involved. Hastert, who eventually pleaded guilty, had agreed to give his victim $3.5 million in cash—and had paid nearly half this amount when he was arrested. How, people wondered, could a former schoolteacher and public servant cobble together that kind of money?[5] The answer to that question opened a door into an entirely separate kind of corruption.[6] Hastert was the poster boy for an institutional debasement so deep it undermines democracy itself.

When Dennis Hastert arrived in Washington in 1987, his estimated net worth was $300,000. When he left office two decades later, the best estimations of his holdings were around $7 million. (Congressional financial disclosure forms show only a range, so it's impossible to know a precise amount.) It's certainly feasible to make savvy investments in real estate and other ventures—even on the salary of a congressman who keeps a home in Washington and one back in the district. But the source of Dennis Hastert's success invited suspicion even while he was still in office. The *Chicago Tribune* reported in 2006 that Hastert made a $2 million profit on farmland in his district that he and some partners had purchased only three years earlier. One big factor in the increased value in the land was a proposed federally funded highway that Hastert had put his political muscle behind.[7]

But it was *after* he left Congress that Hastert's portfolio really grew—when he became a Washington lobbyist. He began by hanging out a shingle, Hastert & Associates, which worked on various schemes ranging from an effort to bring Formula One racing to Chicago to getting a California golf tournament to move to the Middle East. Hastert also hooked up with a Washington-based lobbying outfit called Dickstein Shapiro, where his major clients included shipping giant Maersk Inc., FirstLine Transportation Security, ServiceMaster, two energy companies, and Lorillard, a giant tobacco company. Lorillard alone paid Dickstein Shapiro $7.9 million in just a three-year period from 2011 until 2014. To be fair, Hastert also earned some money through non-lobbying ventures. He served on various corporate boards, gave paid speeches to corporations, and continued to buy and sell real estate. Hastert also received a taxpayer-funded government pension in excess of $100,000 a year. Through all these activities, Hastert was able to pay $3.5 million in *after-tax* hush money.[8]

So what do clients get for all this dough?

"Either these lobbyists are hoodwinking their clients, or they really are able to open doors that people with lesser experience at the highest levels of Congress cannot open," says University of North Carolina political science professor Frank Baumgartner.

I'm betting it's the latter, not the former, but either way what Hastert's experience shows—and he's hardly alone—is that there is tremendous incentive while these members are in Congress to vote the way various special interests want them to vote. That incentive is personal wealth.

And how many members of Congress-turned-lobbyists are we talking about exactly? According to the Center for Responsive Politics, 427 former members of Congress are now lobbying their 535 onetime colleagues in the House and Senate. Their numbers are growing. In 1974, about 3 percent of former members of Congress became lobbyists after leaving office. Today, that number is about 50 percent.[9] After the 2010 midterm elections in which 118 members left Congress, either because they retired or because they lost elections, the Center for Responsive Politics found that 36 percent went to lobbying firms and another 22 percent went to work for lobbying firms' clients themselves—58 percent in total. There's more, too: between 2007, when Congress supposedly tightened its ethics rules, and 2014, some 1,600 House or Senate staffers registered to lobby within a year after leaving Congress.[10]

A handful of members don't go that route. Owing to their reputations for reform politics or personal probity, a rare handful aren't even offered the temptation. The mirror image of Dennis Hastert is another Dennis—Dennis Kucinich. The onetime mayor of Cleveland, presidential candidate, and eight-term Democratic member of the House in the Ohio delegation, Kucinich never considered lobbying. "My 'Not-for-Sale' sign came with my birth certificate," he explained in 2015.[11]

Long before Donald Trump shook the 2016 presidential primary season, Americans expressed a wistful desire for a successful business leader to take control of government's levers of power. A big part of that desire was driven by the belief that people who had already made enough money on their own wouldn't be tempted to do the bidding of special interests. That was the initial appeal of Ross Perot, and before him of Chrysler Motors chief Lee Iacocca. It was a large part of Michael Bloomberg's ability to leap from the world of commerce directly into the mayor's job in New York. It was what I tried to do in 2014.

My own father had a more basic question. When it came to Congress, he always wondered, only half in jest, why someone would spend millions of dollars auditioning for a job that paid $174,000 a year. In his mind, the math didn't add up. When my dad asked me that, I'd give the traditional good-government answer: that very little of the money they were spending to earn the job was theirs—and that the candidates' intention was to have a positive impact on our country and our world. While I still believe that many of the folks in Congress entered politics with the best intentions, based on the behavior of the longest-serving members, I'm beginning to think my father was right all along.

GOVERNMENT MALPRACTICE

Crony capitalism, and the personal greed that lies at the heart of it, has introduced a whole additional layer of dysfunction to American politics. In the past thirty years, as Republicans have gotten more conservative and Democrats more liberal, compromise has become more difficult—a natural result when ideologues are put in charge of policy. But if that dynamic was all that was wrong with our politics, it might be manageable. Instead, the money that flows into campaign coffers—and, after retirement, into politicians' personal bank accounts—warps the system further. The upshot is often a disconcerting gap between politicians' stated philosophies and their actions.

Consider the example of a federal agency created with bipartisan support by Congress during the presidency of George H. W. Bush called the Agency for Health Care Policy and Research. Its mission was straightforward: the improvement of health-care services in this country by developing evidence-based research on the best clinical practices and imparting that knowledge to physicians besieged by contradictory data.

While we may indeed perform evidence-based research on pharmaceuticals, for medical procedures we have less stringent requirements, which was why the president and Congress agreed to establish the agency in the first place. Previously, such slack standards had led, for instance, to a decision in the mid-1980s to treat stage IV breast cancer with high dose chemotherapy, followed by bone marrow transplant, instead of normal dose chemotherapy, which was the prior standard of care. Insurance companies had initially balked at this regimen—the new treatment was roughly four times as expensive as the old one—but after losing several lawsuits and having the Susan B. Komen Foundation put its heft behind the cause, the insurance companies relented. They greenlighted the new treatment and raised premiums accordingly. All these actions had been taken in the belief that cost was no object when it came to providing the best possible care for cancer patients.

The problem was it wasn't the best possible care. Ten years later, after multiple clinical trials were completed, it was determined that the new treatment was actually killing patients. Mortality rates for the new treatment were the same after five years, but substantially *higher* after two years. As we went back to the old treatment protocol and all the bone marrow transplant centers that had sprung up to provide the new treatment shut down, we learned a valuable lesson about health care.[12] The Agency for Health Care Policy and Research was intended to address these expensive mistakes.

As part of that mandate, in 1993 AHCPR assembled a task force of twenty-three experts on lower back pain. Back surgeries were one of those rapidly increasing medical procedures contributing to spiraling health care costs. But were these operations necessary and effective? Or were they often unnecessary—and perhaps even harmful? This was the question the AHCPR panel was tasked with determining. After reviewing the available evidence, the AHCPR panel concluded that surgery for lower back pain should be considered a last resort and that doctors would better serve their patients by trying non-surgical treatments first. This recommendation quickly became an economic issue, not merely a medical question, however, when the people with financial incentives

to propound back surgery galvanized politically. For the physicians per-
forming these operations, the obvious issue was whether AHCPR's recommendations would jeopardize government reimbursements. "If the
study showed that a surgery was no better than nonsurgical remedies, or
only about as good, there was a chance that Medicare would stop reim-
bursing for it," noted Shannon Brownlee, author of *Overtreated: Why
Too Much Medicine Is Making Us Sicker and Poorer.* "If Medicare made a
back surgery provisional, private insurers were likely to follow."[13]

Letters from worried surgeons poured into Congress. Although some
of the mail was spontaneous, most of the opposition was well organized.
The back surgeons' professional association, the North American Spine
Society, challenged the scientific methods used in the review and tapped
its lobbyists to convey that concern to Congress. Neil Kahanovitz, a past
president of the North American Spine Society, formed another group,
the Center for Patient Advocacy, which took aim at the very existence
of the AHCPR. In another line of attack, Sofamor Danek Group Inc., a
large manufacturer of pedicle screws used in back fusion surgeries, sued
the agency in federal court.

Consciously playing on Republicans' stated desire for leaner government and their reflexive antipathy for federal regulations, opponents found a willing audience on Capitol Hill after the GOP's 1995
takeover of Congress. House Budget Committee Chairman John Kasich
put AHCPR on a "hit list" of 140 targeted federal programs. Under
the stewardship of recently installed Speaker Newt Gingrich, House
Republicans dubbed AHCPR the "Agency for High Cost Publications
and Research," and voted to eliminate its funding.

AHCPR wasn't without allies on Capitol Hill. In the other legislative chamber, Republican moderates teamed up with Senate Democrats
to save it. But the assault took its toll. The agency sustained a 21 percent
budget cut, saw its mission curtailed to the status of a "clearinghouse"

for data produced by others, and had the word "policy" purged from its name. Renamed the Agency for Healthcare Research and Quality, it became, as House Republicans intended, toothless.

But did these small-government fiscal conservatives really save taxpayers money, as they boasted? Quite the contrary: Neutering the AHCPR, and cutting its budget by $32 million annually, empowered the spinal surgery industry to essentially ignore the back panel's recommendations, which has cost Americans tens of billions of dollars. Meanwhile, the number of spinal fusion surgeries in the United States has increased by five-fold in that twenty-year span, from 100,000 to almost 500,000. This number represents half of all such procedures done in the entire world. The cost to Medicare and the value to the industry of this increase is likely measured in the tens of billions of dollars over the past twenty years. Not bad for a $3 million lobbying investment. When it came to support and reimbursement of spinal surgery, the ultimate diagnosis was government malpractice—an all-too-common disorder in Washington.

HYPOCRISY, A SHARED VALUE

The Democrats in Congress are just as hypocritical when campaign cash is involved. A great example of this concerns the taxes paid by the hated hedge fund and private equity managers. I say "hated" because every four years like clockwork, prominent Democrats begin pounding them—along with venture capitalists and partners in private equity firms—for using federal loopholes that put them in preferred tax brackets.

"There's something wrong when hedge fund managers pay lower tax rates than nurses or the truckers that I saw on I-80 as I was driving here," Mrs. Clinton told a small group of roundtable participants in Monticello, Iowa, as she campaigned in April 2015.[14]

Bernie Sanders, who emerged as Clinton's main opponent in the Democratic primaries, also employed the comparison between hedge fund managers' tax rates and "truck drivers and nurses." Later, Sanders added "firemen and police officers" to the mix. Although the IRS rules are arcane, the underlying argument is pretty basic: Working-class Americans are getting hosed by Wall Street.

By 2015, Republicans were chiming in with similar rhetoric. Jeb Bush called for doing away with the loophole.[15] Donald Trump joined the fray with his typical rhetorical flourish. "The hedge fund guys," Trump said, "are getting away with murder."[16]

What they are criticizing is a rather complex part of the U.S. tax code, one which has grown in significance in recent years. Explained simply, what they are talking about is an IRS regulation known as "carried interest." It allows investment managers to classify their performance bonuses as "capital gains," which are taxed at a lower rate than ordinary income.

"It's a pure scam," says former secretary of labor Robert B. Reich. "They get the tax break even though they invest other people's money rather than risk their own. The loophole has no economic justification."[17]

The carried interest provision costs the U.S. Treasury a lot of money. Most estimates are $11 billion annually, although the Real Estate Roundtable, one of the industry groups that has lobbied successfully to retain the system, believes it's as high as $13 billion.[18]

Hillary Clinton's remarks in her 2015–2016 campaign about hedge funds were not new. She made the same comments, almost word-for-word, eight years earlier in her primary fight against then-senator Barack Obama. Campaigning in the summer of 2007, she called carried interest a "glaring inequity."

"It offends our values as a nation," she added while talking to voters in Keane, New Hampshire, "when an investment manager making fifty million can pay a lower tax rate on her earned income than a teacher making fifty thousand pays on her income." By then Obama and John Edwards, a third Democrat seeking their party's nomination, had issued similar challenges. Bold talk, but in Clinton's case—and almost every Democrat then in the Senate—that's all it was: just talk.

A month earlier, in June 2007, Senators Max Baucus of Montana and Charles Grassley of Iowa proposed legislation to close the loophole on private equity managers. Baucus, a Democrat, was chairing the Senate Finance Committee. Grassley was the ranking Republican on the committee. Both men had been galvanized into action by the excesses of Wall Street CEO Stephen Schwarzman, co-founder of a private equity company called the Blackstone Group. In February of 2007, Schwarzman threw himself a sixtieth birthday party worthy of the Gilded Age. Held at the Park Avenue Armory, it featured entertainers Martin Short and Rod Stewart, as well as singer Patti LaBelle, who led the Abyssinian Baptist Church choir in a version of "He's Got the Whole World in His Hands." For guests too obtuse to understand that this number was sung as an ode to Schwarzman, a giant portrait of the CEO was imported from his home to the venue.[19]

A month later, Blackstone's lawyers filed papers with the Securities and Exchange Commission with the intention of taking the firm public, a move *The Wall Street Journal* estimated was worth $7.5 billion to Schwarzman and his partners. This came less than four months after he complained to the *Financial Times* that the Sarbanes-Oxley financial reform law enacted in 2002 was hindering companies from going public.[20]

To Baucus and Grassley, this move was more alarming than an over-the-top CEO birthday party. It showed that private equity managers wanted it both ways when it came to tax policy: They wanted all the advantages of a U.S.-backed corporate entity, but not the tax responsibilities that go along with it. The upshot was their measure, officially known as Senate Bill 1624, and unofficially known on Capitol Hill as "the Blackstone bill." In supporting the measure, Grassley was bucking the Republican leadership in the Senate. As it turns out, so was Baucus. The leadership of both parties discouraged senators from signing on to it. Barack Obama and Baucus's fellow Montanan, populist Democratic Jon Tester, were the only two co-sponsors, and it died quietly without coming to a vote in the committee.

Liberals put the blame on Republicans. Chuck Grassley, they said, didn't have the support of his own party.[21] This was true, but as a rationale for inaction, it was only half the story. After Baucus inherited the Finance Committee chairmanship from Grassley in 2007, prominent Senate Democrats—ranging from John Kerry[22] to Chuck Schumer—publicly undercut the legislation.[23]

Hillary Clinton merely steered clear of it, even while touting its principles on the campaign trail. The Democrats' excuse became impossible to swallow after the 2008 election that left them in control of both houses of Congress and with one of Grassley's four co-sponsors in the White House. A companion bill was passed in the House of Representatives, but again failed to get traction in the Senate. Why?

It's easy to surmise that campaign contributions had much to do with it. Don't take my word for it. Listen to Robert Reich, who served in Bill Clinton's cabinet:

"To find the real reason Democrats didn't close the loophole, follow the money," he wrote in December 2014. "Wall Street is one of the Democratic party's biggest contributors. The Street donated $49.1 million to Democrats in 2010, according to the nonpartisan Center for Responsive Politics. Hedge-fund managers alone accounted for $5.88 million of the total. Schumer and a few other influential Democrats were among the industry's major beneficiaries."

"Wall Street," Reich concluded, "has continued to be generous to Democrats (as well as to Republicans)."[24]

Hypocrisy, it seems, is a shared value among Democrats and Republicans on Capitol Hill.

THE LEGISLATOR-INDUSTRIAL COMPLEX

Harvard professor Larry Lessig has a name for elected officials who rationalize away their own philosophical views or tailor their policy votes to fit their funders: "shape-shifters," he calls them. "They constantly adjust their views," he says, "in light of what they know will help them to raise money."

I confronted this temptation during my own Senate run. A number of my friends stepped up to support my campaign financially. One of them, Bernie Cahill, worked with his business partner, Will Ward, to host two fundraisers in Los Angeles. The second of these events occurred right after *The Hill* newspaper reported that my opponent was raising over $100,000 a day from lobbyists in Washington, D.C. While our events in Los Angeles were successful, Bernie and Will wanted to do more, particularly in light of *The Hill* story showing how much money was being arrayed against my campaign. Bernie started reaching out to more of his friends and acquaintances, making an argument for my candidacy. One of them owned a large stake in a for-profit university. Bernie called me to ask about my position on for-profit education. He suggested that if I came down on the side of for-profit education, it could be worth as much as $100,000 to the campaign in bundled donations from supporters of the for-profit education industry. In Bernie's mind, those particular donations would at least offset one day of Pat Roberts's fundraising on K Street.[25]

Having spent time researching higher education, I understood why the industry was looking for friends in Washington. Their track record on student loan default rates was abysmal. The Obama administration was putting pressure on for-profit schools by threatening to cut them off from federal student loan money over their high default rates. Most for-profit institutions would find that cutoff to be tantamount to a death sentence: They relied that heavily on government-guaranteed student loans.

I believe in the free market. I believe that when companies provide a service that consumers value, it generally makes sense for the government to allow the marketplace to work unfettered. In this instance, however, where significant government money was involved and consumers were being misled, the administration's proposed reforms were not unreasonable. With over $1.2 trillion in outstanding student loan debt, the student loan debt situation has been referred to as a crisis. Most people view the problem as a byproduct of the rising cost of higher education. That's only partly true. Another factor is the increasing number of students who take on debt to start a degree program and then drop out before getting that degree. As a result, they incur much of the cost of getting a degree without getting the related benefits.

This problem is particularly acute with for-profit institutions. They spend inordinate amounts of money recruiting students, in many cases without regard for the individual's ability to succeed academically at their institution. At some of these schools it appears that the only real requirement for admission is a student's ability to qualify for government-guaranteed loans. I wasn't about to taint my ability to stand up for students and hold for-profit institutions accountable in exchange for any amount of money in my campaign coffers. I had to tell Bernie that I couldn't in good conscience accept his offer of bundled donations from the for-profit education industry.

Unfortunately, turning down campaign cash doesn't seem to be the norm on Capitol Hill. The best example of this phenomenon might be the ninety members of Congress who voted in favor of the 2008 Wall Street bailout, but then turned around and voted *against* the financial reforms enacted by lawmakers who wanted to make sure it didn't happen again. (Sixty-nine of these members were in the House—sixty Republicans and nine Democrats. The twenty-one senators were all Republicans.)[26]

Think about that for a moment: When corrupt or incompetent business practices cause banks and other financial institutions to go bankrupt, these politicians want the taxpayers to pick up the tab. At the same time, they want these institutions to have free rein to do it all again. Such a double standard is called privatizing profits and socializing losses. It conforms to no known political ideology. What it does conform to is access to campaign cash—and possibly post-congressional employment.

"When you examine campaign contribution data, it's really no surprise that these particular lawmakers voted to mortgage our economic future to Big Finance," said Zach Carter, who writes about political money for *The Huffington Post*, in 2010. "This election cycle, they've raked in over $48.8 million from the financial establishment."[27]

Sometimes, these politicians are refreshingly candid. After the 2014 election in which the U.S. Chamber of Commerce flooded Kansas—and many other states—with campaign contributions on behalf of Republicans, one of those beneficiaries of Chamber largesse gave as succinct a summary of the state of American politics as it's possible to provide. On a late February 2015 conference call, a newly elected Republican, Dan Sullivan of Alaska, blurted out the truth. "Without your support," he said, "I think it's very doubtful I'd be sitting here as *your* U.S. senator, talking to you right now."[28]

As the 2016 presidential election got underway, a conservative author, Peter Schweizer, wrote a book entitled *Clinton Cash*. The book described the intermingled and intertwined connection between the Clintons'

campaign finances, their foundation fundraising, and their personal for-
tunes. He was dismissed by Democratic Party loyalists as a partisan, but
Schweizer actually has a history of documenting grotesque—and quite
bipartisan—abuses. In 2011, he wrote a book titled, *Throw Them All
Out: How Politicians and Their Friends Get Rich off Insider Stock Tips, Land
Deals, and Cronyism That Would Send the Rest of Us to Prison.* Two years
later he followed up with *Extortion: How Politicians Extract Your Money,
Buy Votes, and Line Their Own Pockets.* Along the way he concluded that
crony capitalism is a moral crisis in this country. "We've got to change
the incentive structure that exists in Washington, and that incentive
structure is driven by cronyism, where the state and private sector inter-
sect," he explained. "If I were to define crony-capitalism, I really use the
term cronyism because I don't think that it speaks of capitalism per se,
but cronyism is essentially where economic decisions in terms of who
accumulates wealth and who doesn't, is not based on merit, it's not based
on economic prowess or success or meeting needs in the marketplace. It's
based on political connections and relationships whereby you are able to
either manipulate the state to your advantage, and to the disadvantage of
your competitors."[29]

The current crop of presidential candidates decry what they call
"crony capitalism" while practicing it themselves. Republicans pointed
out the Obama administration's disastrous $535 million government loan
to Solyndra, a solar company that went belly-up taking 1,100 jobs and all
that taxpayer money with it. But cronyism relating to "green" projects of
dubious worth (not to mention other dubious projects of all colors and
stripes) transcends party boundaries. Although Governor Scott Walker
of Wisconsin vowed while running for president to rid Washington of
"special interests," one of his senior aides back in Wisconsin lobbied for
a state-backed $500,000 loan to a Walker donor on a sketchy scheme
to do a green energy retrofit of several local banks. On a much bigger

scale, Walker backed a plan to use $250 million of Wisconsin taxpayers' funds for a new basketball arena in Milwaukee. One of the owners of the Milwaukee Bucks, the pro basketball team that would benefit from the stadium, is John Hammes, who was the finance co-chairman of Walker's presidential campaign.

Likewise, one of Marco Rubio's early financial supporters was Miami-based sugar industry mogul Pepe Fanjul. Like Rubio, Fanjul is a conservative Cuban-American Republican from Florida. These similarities make Fanjul's support seem innocent enough. Rubio's longstanding support for government subsidies and import protections for the sugar industry, however, reveals a corrupt bargain that has helped keep the Fanjul family very wealthy while costing American consumers billions of dollars a year in higher prices for sugar, candy, and sweets. It is particularly corrupt in light of Rubio's election to the Senate, in which he described himself as a fiscal conservative and decried the evils of the government's support of private industry.

How long do we keep giving these politicians the benefit of the doubt? Crony capitalism not only hurts our politics, it hurts our economy. A Gallup Poll in September 2015 showed that 69 percent of the public thinks Congress is "focused on the needs of special interests rather than the needs of their constituents." Half of the respondents in the poll said they consider U.S. lawmakers "corrupt." That kind of widespread disgust is how you get to a historically low 14 percent approval rating.[30]

Voters historically cut members of Congress some slack regarding the desire to cater to their constituents, but according to researchers at Princeton University and Northwestern University, the public is giving Congress *too much* credit for weighing voters' desires. In a study completed in 2014, Princeton politics professor Martin Gilens and Northwestern political scientist Benjamin Page examined congressional action on 1,779 policy issues. Their conclusion was astounding. "When the preference of economic elites and the stands of organized interests are controlled for," they wrote, "the preferences of the average American appear to have only a miniscule, near-zero, statistically non-significant impact upon public policy."[31]

Beyond fueling the public's sour perceptions of our elected leaders, crony capitalism is a drag on the U.S. economy, many economists believe. The American Enterprise Institute, a free market-leaning think tank, details how this is happening. For starters, the government has become a more dominant player in the economy. In the mid-1960s, total federal, state, and local government spending made up about one-fourth of GDP. Today that ratio exceeds one-third. As elected officials have made more and more of the decisions that drive our economy, bureaucrats have produced a geometrically increasing body of regulations.

With considerably more of the economic action being determined by government, elective office has become more precious to special interest groups, which have bid the cost of running for office up to astronomical levels. The year George W. Bush and Al Gore ran for president, $3 billion was spent on all federal elections—including the Bush-Gore race. The 2016 presidential contest alone will have likely cost $5 billion before it ends. The cost of running for Senate has become mind-boggling: $54 million spent in Kentucky in 2014; $45 million in Georgia; $40 million in Minnesota; $38 million in Louisiana. This doesn't even take into account money spent by outside groups on these races. The average Senate candidate has to raise $14,000 every weekday for six years just to compete. That's a lot of time asking for money from people who expect something in return, which explains the AEI's third factor in the rise of crony capitalism: the huge increase in money spent on lobbying activity—more than $3.2 billion annually.

Let that figure wash over you for a moment. While some of those dollars are clearly spent lobbying the administration and various federal agencies, much of it is directed at Congress: $3.2 billion represents an expenditure of $5.6 million for every member of the House and Senate.

The moneyed interests controlling our elections are competing for the right to slice up a $4 trillion federal budget pie. In that context, spending $5 billion on congressional races and another $5 billion on the presidency seems like a sound investment for the great cabal of people seeking to profit from power. Over the last five years, our judicial branch gave special interests the tools they needed to spend unlimited sums campaigning. In a series of rulings—*Citizens United, Speechnow.org,* and *McCutcheon*—the Supreme Court and lower federal courts sided with the plaintiffs against the Federal Election Commission in rolling back campaign finance laws. *Citizens United* allowed companies and unions to spend unlimited independent expenditures on campaign-related activities. The *Speechnow* verdict allowed PACs that didn't make contributions to candidates to accept unlimited funds from unions, corporations, and individuals—thereby giving rise to the term super PAC. Finally, the *McCutcheon* decision removed restrictions on how much total money individuals could give to candidates during an election cycle.

While the Supreme Court left in place various rules that prevent campaigns from coordinating with these big money behemoths, candidates have worked out imaginative ways to skirt those rules. Jeb Bush was able to solicit donations in excess of a million dollars from individuals on behalf of his super PAC, which is well in excess of what that law allows a federal candidate to do. How did get away with this? He contended during the whole period of time that he was not a candidate—despite numerous instances where he slipped up and acknowledged he was running for president. No one who was paying attention believed this ruse. They weren't really expected to. It wasn't supposed to fool voters; it was designed to give cover to the Federal Election Commission, an agency equally split between Democratic and Republican appointees.

I would like nothing more than to see *Citizens United* and the associated verdicts overturned. I think the ability for individuals, corporations, and unions to spend unlimited sums attempting to affect the outcome of elections is incredibly damaging to our country. With that said, I will admit to being relieved when three super PACs started spending money to assist my candidacy. My colleagues at the Common Sense Coalition led the formation of two of the super PACs, while Larry Lessig's May-Day PAC also started spending on my behalf. Seeing the array of forces aligned against me was daunting. By the time our race was over, almost 50 PACs, super PACs, and 501(c)4s had lined up to spend money against my candidacy. Having a way to rebalance the scales was heartening. Unlike Jeb Bush and Hillary Clinton, however, I drew the line at engaging in any fundraising activity on behalf of the super PACs. In fact, I cut off all contact with anyone who was associated with those entities until after the election.

In his 1961 farewell address as president, Dwight Eisenhower famously warned his countrymen of a growing "military industrial complex." Eisenhower, a career U.S. Army officer, was specifically concerned about how, when the nation had a large standing military, defense contractors who stood to profit from its growth could engage in the "acquisition of influence." Eisenhower's warning was prescient; America now spends almost as much as the rest of the world combined on the military.

Yet as surprising as this statistic might be, our spending on national defense (now almost $650 billion annually) is dwarfed by what America spends on health care. In the public and private sector combined, we now spend almost $3 trillion annually on keeping ourselves alive and healthy. While the yearly growth rate has slowed in recent years from double digits to less than 5 percent, health-care costs have increased more than one hundred-fold since 1960 and will more than double in size again between now and 2025.[32] In 2015, health-care industry players spent almost a half a billion dollars on lobbying. Much of this money was spent to ensure that the way Medicare operates is financially advantageous to various interest groups within the industry. While Eisenhower decried the potential ill-effects of a military industrial complex, I'm far more concerned about the impact of a medical industrial complex.

We also have a tax code that's a veritable buffet of special interests giveaways. In 2010, as Congress was focused on getting rid of "earmarks," which are tailored expenditures for a specific program or geographically sensitive project, it was estimated that we spent less than $20 billion annually on these expenditures. According to the Joint Committee on Taxation, we spend over $1 trillion every year through tax loopholes that essentially drive behavior by giving a financial incentive to Americans to act in a certain way or otherwise use the tax code to pick winners and losers.[33] In other words, we spend fifty times the amount on tax breaks, many for narrow political interests, than we did on earmarks. But because they're hidden in the dark corners and mysterious passageways of the tax code, there is no tax break equivalent of Alaska's famous "Bridge to Nowhere" to rally popular outrage.

What all these dollars add up to is a gigantic feeding trough between Congress and special interests that has grown ever more colossal since Dwight Eisenhower's presidency. Call it the "legislator-industrial complex." Eisenhower himself would have understood: In the first draft of his farewell address he wrote, "military-industrial-*congressional* complex." (Ike ultimately decided to take the word out, telling his brother, Milton Eisenhower, "It was more than enough to take on the military and private industry. I couldn't take on the Congress as well.")[34]

As with much of what originates in Washington, there's a basic irony embedded in the legislator-industrial complex. The very court rulings that allowed super PACs such as "End Spending Now" to exist guarantee that their goal of ending spending will never be accomplished. That organization actually spent money against me in my 2014 race—but not with the goal of supporting a candidate who truly wanted to curtail spending and reign in crony capitalism. They opposed me so as to ensure that a candidate who received significant financial support from the pharmaceutical, health-care, financial, and numerous other industries could get reelected and maintain the status quo.

As if there weren't enough ways for elected officials to fall into the thrall of special interests, there's one final tool at their disposal: leadership PACs. These are operated by political candidates themselves and, therefore, are subject to strict limits on how much any one individual or political action committee can donate (currently $5,400 every two years). Unlike political campaign committees, however, there are almost no rules on what a leadership PAC can spend its money on. Want to hire your mistress to videotape you at campaign events, as John Edwards did?[35] Use your leadership PAC. Want to put your kid on the payroll? Feel free. Viewed this way, these contributions seem little less than legalized bribes: 99 percent of the money contributed to leadership PACs over the last twenty years has come from special interests. That's right: Individuals account for just 1 percent of the donations. In 2014, over $60 million was contributed by special interests to these political slush funds.

In *Mr. Smith Goes to Washington*, Jimmy Stewart's idealistic senator naïvely tries to thwart the political machine by proposing a boys' camp on a tract of land back home—and he even comes up with a way to pay for it that won't cost the taxpayers a dime. The corrupt political bosses had another idea: construct an unnecessary dam on the land, through which they will profit personally. Like much of Frank Capra's work, the film operates on two levels. While it celebrates the cooperative spirit and public works programs associated with the New Deal, it simultaneously exalts the rugged individualism of the solitary American hero. But if the political message of *Mr. Smith Goes to Washington* doesn't easily lend itself to partisan pigeonholing, there's a good reason for that: Neither did the film's director.

Katharine Hepburn, a lifelong progressive, considered Capra "quite liberal." *Variety* magazine termed a Capra protagonist in *Mr. Deeds Goes to Town* "quasi-communistic."[36] Left-leaning actors and screenwriters who worked with him—some of whom were actual Communists—assumed as much. Well-known playwright Robert Riskin, who collaborated often with Capra, was a Democrat devoted to Franklin Roosevelt. As it turns out, Capra himself was a registered Republican who opposed the New Deal—and never once voted for Roosevelt. But he hired men who did, and he worked well with them—because besides being a gifted artist, Frank Capra was a problem solver. He was independent-minded, as were the heroes he put on the big screen, and he recognized that in the end, the best politicians are those with integrity.

"There's no place out there for graft, or greed, or lies, or compromise with human liberties," Jimmy Stewart says at the end of *Mr. Smith Goes to Washington*. "And, if that's what the grownups have done with this world that was given to them, then we'd better get those boys' camps started fast and see what the kids can do.

"And it's not too late," he adds. "Great principles don't get lost once they come to light. They're right here; you just have to see them again!"

Those words, "It's not too late," must be our mantra as Independents.

CHAPTER 9

The Misinformation Age

THE WAY THE MEDIA REINFORCES
THE FALSE CHOICES OF THE
TWO-PARTY SYSTEM

——— ★ ★ ★ ———

IN THE WEEKS BEFORE the 2014 midterm elections, the three leading cable television news networks ran 838 segments on the Ebola scare. While CNN anchor Ashleigh Banfield was discussing the issue, the network ran a banner with the words, "Ebola: The ISIS of biological agents?"[1]

Before the epidemic had run its course, it had taken several thousand lives in West Africa, but only four in the United States—so why was it such a huge story here? When western health workers using modern precautions contract an exotic and deadly disease and come back to the United States for treatment, that is certainly news. But why in the four weeks leading up to Election Day, did CNN, Fox News, and MSNBC become so obsessed with this story? And why, in the two weeks *after* the 2014 elections, did those three news organizations run only forty-three Ebola stories?

It wasn't that the Ebola virus was miraculously cured on the Wednesday following Election Day. In fact, the rate of growth of confirmed

Ebola infections continued to accelerate well into December of 2014. So why would Fox News and CNN abruptly end their Ebola coverage? More importantly, why did they run so many stories about Ebola in the first place?

The answer to those questions helps explain why Americans hold the press, like Congress, in such low esteem. Public contempt for the two institutions seems to be linked, which makes sense: The failings of both the media and our legislature have taken their toll—on each other. The gradual decline of the U.S. media into its current condition has made it harder for everyone—journalists, candidates, elected officials—to make sense of the constant stream of information being fed to us. Often the information is purposefully misleading and intended to accomplish a political objective. As a result, I've often said we are no longer living in the information age, but rather, the misinformation age.

Today, the media is a hodgepodge of competing formats and philosophies: mainstream print publications that claim to be objective; digital outlets that span the spectrum; cable and network television; satellite and old-line radio programming—much of it dominated by bombastic right-wing talk radio hosts—and social media platforms that seem to be driving it all. It has made it nearly impossible for voters and consumers of political news to separate fact from fiction, reporting from opinion, sense from sensationalism, real news from click-bait, and genuine media from "Frankenstein" creations.

Existing within that thicket of competing platforms are two different traditions: mainstream journalism and partisan organs. Unfortunately, driven by financial pressures and decades of hyper-partisanship, the distinction between the mainstream media and partisan media is blurring. This especially disadvantages Independents, who are caught up in a partisan-driven media environment that only reinforces the belief that politics is nothing more than a contest between two tired old political parties.

AN UNEASY BARGAIN

For most of the twentieth century, it was said of America's daily news-papers that reporters were liberal, while their publishers were conser-vative. The notion was that straight news reporting generally favored the underdog, while the editorial page—the opinion pages that were the publisher's purview—defended the status quo. This dichotomy provided a rough justice, or at least journalists told themselves it did.

This was the bargain journalists made with themselves, and the public more or less accepted. Then things began to change.

First, as old family-run fiefdoms were sold off to newspaper chains, the editorial pages became less conservative and more homogenized. Then the "great sorting" that led to polarization in party politics rip-pled through newsrooms too. When the U.S. Senate included liberal Republicans and conservative Democrats, the ideologies of reporters and editors didn't equate to strictly partisan leanings. But when liberals and conservatives completed the process of aligning themselves with the Democratic and Republican parties, it also altered the equilibrium inside newsrooms.

Crusading reporters and editors were no longer just liberals on the side of the underdogs. Because of the changing landscape outside jour-nalism, they were now perceived to be—or were—liberal *Democrats*. This upset the uneasy bargain.

Conservative readers noticed and began to drift away. One of the places they ended up—by the millions—was in Rush Limbaugh's radio audience, soaking up his daily screed denouncing Democrats and liber-als. Limbaugh's fans proudly called themselves "ditto-heads." Objecting to what they perceive as the casual liberalism permeating mainstream media, they were saying that they agreed with everything that came out of Limbaugh's mouth.

While traditional media's loss of subscribers and viewers to talk radio was real, it wasn't a danger to their business model. At the dawn of the twenty-first century, however, technological innovation was. Craigslist was wiping out newspapers' classified advertising revenues, while big retailers and other traditional advertisers were figuring out how to use the Internet to target customers more directly. The Internet was also able to deliver news in real time. This eliminated the need to read the morning newspaper and perpetuated the continuous news cycle that CNN had pioneered in the late 1980s. It also led to a proliferation of online news outlets. To add insult to injury, some of these outlets were news aggregators who gathered up links to the costly reporting done by traditional journalists and leveraged it by repackaging it on their sites. Cable news networks were also affected by the instant communication and vast choices of the Internet.

In the last fifteen to twenty years, traditional media outlets found that their revenue streams eroded along with their newspaper circulations or their TV audiences. This created an existential problem for the mainstream press. In time, every major news organization pursued an online presence, complete with websites, social media pages, Twitter feeds, and smartphone apps. Traditional media companies also behaved like many businesses do when they are under financial strain by laying off staff, including investigative reporters. Financial pressures forced editors to pressure their remaining writers for stories that would increase circulation, ratings, and online "clicks." In this environment, sensationalism and superficiality reign supreme. Thoughtful examination of issues and true investigative journalism became less financially feasible given the limited resources available and the competition for attention from viewers and readers.

If all this wasn't bad enough, another threat arose: the proliferation of partisan media outlets. With active voters sorting themselves along partisan lines and growing less receptive to information that contradicted their beliefs, there was an increasing audience (and greater profits) for news that was tailored to specific political beliefs. MSNBC and Fox News, with their demographically charged political programming, were following a trail pioneered by conservative talk radio. Dozens of Internet sites and social media outlets dedicated to either Democratic or Republican points of view popped up as well.

Caught in the crossfire were nonpartisan voters and Independent candidates. When I ran for office, I was attacked by conservative media outlets worried I would deprive a Republican incumbent of his seat in the Senate. (If I'd been running against a Democratic incumbent, I would have gotten it from the other direction.) At the same time, the Democratic Party's media proponents didn't defend me: I wasn't one of their own. I believe there are still two kinds of journalism in this country: the mainstream establishment media and partisan media. Yet when I ran for office I found that when it comes to covering the ideas and aspirations of candidates who don't fit into the dominant Democrat-Republican paradigm, it can be a distinction without a difference.

MAINSTREAM MEDIA AND THE CLICK-BAIT MENTALITY

American journalism has always been a business, but it's never been *only* a business. Its practitioners consider their profession a calling, with a mission that goes beyond consideration for the bottom line. In a 1925 address to newspaper publishers, Calvin Coolidge tipped his cap to this ethos. The line usually quoted from that speech is "The business of America is business." But in the context of the speech itself Coolidge actually was making the opposite point about journalism. "The chief ideal of the American people is idealism," he said. "No newspaper can be a success which fails to appeal to that element of our national life. I could not truly criticize the vast importance of the counting room, but my ultimate faith I would place in the high idealism of the editorial room of the American newspaper."[2]

We think of freedom of the press as a byproduct of the American Revolution, but the relationship between the press and the nation's founding was symbiotic. Colonial newspapers agitated for disunion with Britain, and when the Declaration of Independence was signed on July 4, 1776, Philadelphia's broadsheets, including Benjamin Franklin's old paper, the *Pennsylvania Gazette*, published it on their front pages. George Washington had the Declaration read to his troops in New York defending the city against the British. After independence was won, freedom of the press was enshrined in the Bill of Rights.

"Were it left to me to decide whether we should have a government without newspapers, or newspapers without a government," Thomas Jefferson wrote the year the Constitution was signed, "I should not hesitate a moment to prefer the latter."

The timing of his remark is significant: Jefferson hadn't yet been president in 1787. By his sixth year in the White House, he held a less romanticized view. "Nothing can now be believed which is seen in a newspaper," Jefferson complained. "Truth itself becomes suspicious by being put into that polluted vehicle." The "polluted" news organs he was referring to were party newspapers, specifically the house organs of the anti-Jefferson Federalist Party. Yet Jefferson never wavered in his commitment to journalistic freedom. When his successor, James Madison, was president, Jefferson wrote from Monticello to a friend that although he deplored the "putrid state into which the newspapers have passed, and the malignity, the vulgarity and mendacious spirit of those who write them," he saw no alternative. "It is however an evil for which there is no remedy," Jefferson explained. "Our liberty depends on the freedom of the press, and that cannot be limited without being lost."[3]

Notwithstanding the mutiny by Republican presidential candidates following the October 28, 2015, CNBC debate, American politicians and elected officials, irrespective of their vexation about their own treatment by the media, have mostly accepted Jefferson's vision. Politicians may decry what the media say about them, but they view the press as an American institution and a bothersome necessity. Newspaper and broadcast correspondents—and now Internet journalists—are granted front-row seats to the workings of government and politics. Because they serve as politicians' inevitable conduits to the citizenry, they have reserved seats in the congressional press galleries, a dedicated White House briefing room, and access to nearly every trial courtroom in the nation, from county courthouses to the U.S. Supreme Court. Reporters also enjoy access at political conventions, campaign events, and candidate debates.

If there's a bargain implicit in all this access and in the protections of the First Amendment it is that the Fourth Estate must act in a manner befitting what its practitioners claim it is to be: not just another way to make money but a vital American institution. What I'm saying—and this sentiment doesn't come easy to a businessman—is that the special status granted the media carries with it an obligation to sacrifice some profits in the name of civic responsibility.

As they try to adhere to their best principles, it won't ever be easy for the media to forego a single cent. Today's currency in journalism's Digital Age is clicks. The more times people click on a web-based story to open it, the greater the amount of money, via ads, that flows to that news organization. Headlines were always supposed to be catchy, but the wit of yesteryear has been replaced by a willingness simply to mislead readers into clicking on stories, often at the expense of the reputation of others. That's why we see publications such as *The Hill* newspaper in Washington writing a headline implying that Elizabeth Warren snubbed the Pope (actually, she initially offered to her granddaughter her seat at the Pope's address to Congress),[4] or penning another one suggesting that John McCain refused to let Ted Cruz speak at a Senate Foreign Relations Committee hearing (he didn't).[5]

"Click-bait" is endemic and toxic. When Sarah Palin showed up at the 2010 Belmont Stakes in a white blouse that made her look curvy, one blogger wondered aloud if she'd had breast implants.[6] Here is a partial list of the publications that thought this newsworthy: *People* magazine, the *Daily Mail*, the *Telegraph*, *Village Voice*, *New York Daily News*, and *The Huffington Post*, which ran several stories on this made-up story, which wouldn't even be legitimate news had it been true. Some publications offered the thin justification that because the blogosphere was full of talk about this matter, it was their journalistic obligation to report it. Instead of foregoing even a cent of profits in favor of pursuing larger civic purpose, these journalists were scraping money off the table to publish something they knew to be false. Click-bait sensationalism now infects all of mainstream media, even the most stately and institutional elements of it, and not just when they are talking about tabloid presences like Palin but also the serious stuff of citizenship.

During my Senate campaign I did encounter notable exceptions to the click-bait mentality in the national media. Molly Ball of *The Atlantic* wrote a long and thoughtful piece about my campaign.[7] Kelly O'Donnell, from NBC News, did a tough, but fair interview with me in the warehouse of Combat Brands. She challenged me on the issues, discussed control of the Senate (but didn't dwell on it), and asked me how I planned to have an impact in the current environment in Washington. When my media director tried to end the interview, O'Donnell made it clear that she had more questions and expected to be able to ask them so that she could present her viewers with a complete picture of me as a candidate. I admired her commitment to her job, even if it made me late for my next event.[8]

There were others like O'Donnell—honest professionals who understood their obligations as reporters. With the attention focused on control of the Senate, however, it was difficult for reporters to get out of the blue/red partisan construct that dominated their stories. Even non-ideological reporters tipped their hand. CNN's Dana Bash ambushed Sybil at our campaign headquarters. Bash had been frustrated by our campaign's unwillingness to allow her to do a one-on-one interview with me, so she went searching for me at our office in Shawnee, Kansas. While I wasn't there, Sybil was. Bash wanted to get Sybil on camera and assured her that she would reserve any substantive questions for me. When Sybil consented, the first thing Bash asked her was, "Which party is Greg going to caucus with?"

While I'm troubled by the relaxing of journalistic standards in pursuit of clicks and viewership, mainstream media's adoption of the blue/red paradigm creates a bigger dilemma for Independent campaigns. Media attention is incredibly valuable, but it can also be harmful. We need only look at Donald Trump to understand how valuable it can be. Despite the candidate's deep pockets, the Trump campaign spent far less money than his rival Republican presidential candidates in 2015. Why? Because, as we have all seen, the media gave him all the free airtime he wanted.

While I didn't generate one percent of the amount of media attention Trump has garnered, I got a lot of coverage for a first-time candidate. One of our media consultants, a veteran of over twenty years in the industry, mentioned that we received more notice than most of his candidates do over decades. It can be exciting when a first-time contender for public office creates enough buzz that reporters from the national media markets come calling. In my case, that anticipation faded as it became clear that media interest had very little to do with the choice that voters faced in Kansas and everything to do with who held the levers of power in Washington.

By mid-September, we decided to stop doing most national interviews because participating in them simply furthered the way the media was framing the race—that it was all about control of the U.S. Senate instead of the relative qualities of the two candidates. This made sense from the national media's point of view—Pat Roberts's possible defeat was what brought the reporters to Kansas in the first place—but it also played into Roberts's hands, because that was exactly how he was describing the race. By tacitly accepting the Republican narrative, the media was doing what in *Star Trek* would be known as violating "the prime directive," which is interfering with the normal course of human events.

Foregoing free media went against my instincts. Yet while I wanted the opportunity to share the campaign's vision with as many voters as possible, I wasn't going to unwittingly participate in a campaign ad for my opponent. In a historically Republican state like Kansas, if the race was solely about Democrats versus Republicans, success would be incredibly difficult. George Will, as I noted in this book's opening argument, illustrated the problem when he wrote that upgrading the "intellectual voltage" in the United States Senate—as he said my election would do—was less important than making sure one more Republican was reelected to Congress's upper chamber.

It's true that George Will is an opinion columnist and a conservative intellectual, so he's not necessarily being inconsistent. But it's also true that much of the establishment media, including political reporters who claim they have no ideological axe to grind, have bought into the "red state"-"blue state" paradigm. In the process, they've given tacit approval—if not overt support—to the hyper-partisanship and "permanent campaign" mentality that plagues American politics and has made it a zero sum game with no orientation toward problem solving.

So it seems fair to ask whether today's Fourth Estate justifies Jefferson's vision and Coolidge's faith. Its practitioners certainly say they do. When the professionalism of Fox News anchor Megyn Kelly was impugned by Trump after the first Republican presidential debate of 2015, Kelly vowed to "continue doing my job without fear or favor"[10]— consciously borrowing iconic language used by *The New York Times* publisher Adolph S. Ochs in an April 18, 1896, editorial explaining how he intended to run the media property he'd acquired: "To give the news impartially, without fear or favor, regardless of party, sect, or interests involved." Kelly saw her calling as a noble one, of the kind whose tenets are inscribed on bronze plaques in public places.

The *Times* still pays homage to Adolph Ochs, whose marble bust is enshrined in the company's new headquarters at 620 Eighth Avenue in New York City. Tellingly, the old inscription that once accompanied the bust—the promise to deliver the news "impartially"—is no longer on display. Perhaps that was a simple oversight, a building designer's artistic decision. But what an irony that a Fox News journalist is the one quoting Adolph Ochs today.

THE TOXICITY OF PARTISAN MEDIA

Two weeks before Election Day 2014, *Rolling Stone* magazine produced a piece on Kansas politics. Mostly, the article was a spirited hit piece on Kansas governor Sam Brownback. But *Rolling Stone*, which makes no pretense toward objectivity, operates from a playbook that is easy to read:

Liberal Democrats = good.

Conservative Republicans = bad.

Governor Brownback and Senator Roberts, predictably, didn't come off well in the story, but how would such a media outlet treat an unaligned Senate candidate? Independents don't figure in this binary world view, so the *Rolling Stone* writer never troubled himself to call me:

He simply quoted an anonymous Kansas political insider as saying, "This Orman guy seems to be a slightly sleazy businessman."[11]

Having thick skin is helpful in politics, but a hit-and-run slur like that would bother any candidate. Here was a writer I've never met talking to a source who I can only assume doesn't even know me, dismissing my entire career with an ugly little smear that no one who knows me well professionally would ever use. It wasn't personal, I'm sure. It illustrates the straitjacket partisan journalists put on themselves. But if Republicans are bad and Democrats are good, where do Independents fit in? We don't know, but apparently "businessman" is a trigger word for leftist journalists, meaning that they can loosely throw around terms such as "sleazy businessman" without giving it much thought.

I believe that my frustration in this regard is shared by those who enter politics from the world of business. Most members of the U.S. Senate have limited, if any, private sector experience. The mainstream journalists who cover them often stumble when reporting on issues relating to business and economics. Michael Bloomberg was so frustrated by what he viewed as economic illiteracy among political journalists that he started a news organization that bears his name. Professional business-people also function in a world whose rules and practices don't always translate clearly into the political realm.

One problem for candidates who come from the private sector is that lawsuits have become part of the landscape in business. Allegations contained in lawsuits are often untrue. In fact, the court system is one of the few places in the public sphere in the United States (the floor of Congress is another) where someone cannot be sued for libel. In other words, you can make almost any allegation you want in a lawsuit with impunity. As such, legitimate journalists take allegations in lawsuits with a large grain of salt—until they are proven in court. Even then, given the political aspirations of some judges and law clerks and the talents of the respective lawyers involved, lawsuits and other litigation materials should be read by journalists with a healthy dose of skepticism. Good journalists still call the parties involved and try to understand the facts independent of what was presented in a court file.

As you may have guessed, I have had some experience with scurrilous reporting of legal matters—experience that I think points to a recurring problem in how the media reports legal and private issues of people in public life and often makes them subject to partisan assault. *The Wichita Eagle*, Kansas's largest newspaper, ran a story with the headline "Greg Orman Once Sued Actress Debbie Reynolds Over $1 Million Loan to Museum."[12] While it wasn't clear to me that this was newsworthy, I understood that my legal involvement with an icon of Hollywood might be interesting to readers.

The backstory here is rather simple. Over four decades, Debbie Reynolds had accumulated one of the world's most impressive collections of Hollywood memorabilia. It was her vision to build a museum to showcase the material. Her son, Todd Fisher, approached me about providing a six-month bridge loan so that he could complete the architectural work while they were lining up permanent financing. The permanent financing, however, never came through. I gave Todd more time to find a new location, but after five years and another false start, I finally gave up hope that the museum would come together. Todd wasn't yet convinced of that and didn't initially want to sell any of the memorabilia to repay the loan. Todd never really disputed that his organization owed me the money. He contested the litigation largely to buy time.

In this case, *Eagle* reporter Bryan Lowry did it right. He went the extra step of calling Todd Fisher and, to his credit, he put Todd's quotes in the story:

Todd Fisher says that he has known Orman for 20 years and that Kansas would be lucky to have him representing it.

"We did get into litigation with Greg however this was done strictly as a business decision. In the end he and I have always settled our issues in person amicably, we remain friends to this day," Fisher said in an email.

"I feel Washington and Kansas would be lucky to have someone as qualified as Greg representing (the) state."

Needless to say, this is not how the partisan press handled the story—or other business stories about me.

"Federal Judge Berates Kansas Senate Candidate Greg Orman in Boxing Equipment Lawsuit."[13]

This was a headline on the home page of Breitbart News, a right-wing online news outfit. Actually, I wasn't in the courtroom at the time this lawsuit was being discussed, so the visual of me being berated by some judge is invented. If Breitbart was interested they would have found a real news story in this deal—one relating to how many jobs I saved in Kansas, where a local company was being foreclosed upon by its creditors. The lawsuit was from a competitor of that business that wanted to see it closed so that they could buy up the assets cheaply.

This example illustrates how the ideological right and the ideological left sometimes meet up with each other on the far side of the moon. *Rolling Stone*'s default position when it came to me was that businessmen were "sleazy." For Breitbart, a right-wing online outlet, the default position is that we are "greedy." Here is how that piece on the boxing manufacturing lawsuit ended:

It also brings to public attention questions concerning the role of private equity investment firms. For Democratic critics, a Republican private equity investor like Mitt Romney was characterized as a selfish "vulture capitalist." It remains to be seen if Democratic and independent voters in Kansas will now give Orman a pass, or if they will start to look at him in the same negative light as they did Mitt Romney in 2012.

The author's tone is almost hopeful that Kansas voters will view me in a "negative light." That's so blatant it's barely journalism at all. Usually partisan journalists are subtler. After one of the debates in my campaign, a national reporter asked me a question that was a verbatim Pat Roberts talking point. When I asked him what organization he represented, he said he was from the *Washington Examiner*. I told him I'd written a couple of op-eds for his paper, which surprised him. That, in turn, surprised me: An East Coast daily newspaper had dispatched a reporter to Kansas who hadn't bothered with the minimal amount of background research— even to check his own paper's clip files. It might not have mattered. It was clear that the article he intended to write didn't really require much preparation. I think it was probably already written—if not on paper, then in his head. Speaking to me was merely a formality intended to give his story the appearance of legitimacy. He recounted how I put forth more detailed policy positions than Senator Roberts and had many positions that were pro-business but that, in the end, I was clearly a partisan Democrat. His substantiation for this last point was a recycled litany of attacks from the Roberts campaign.

Apologists for the partisan media—some of whom are in the mainstream media—like to point out that the newspapers in Thomas Jefferson's day were essentially political party organs. Being called "sleazy" by a Federalist newspaper would have been notable only for its restraint. Perhaps the better course, they say, would just have every journalist, mainstream or partisan, own up to their biases and objectives. That way, inquiring readers could analyze the news they are receiving and synthesize it into something akin to truth. This is a flawed idea. There are many facets of colonial American life we do not wish to replicate, including slavery and disenfranchisement of a majority of the adult population—including all women. The U.S. has evolved during the two centuries after our founding, the media along with it. To surrender to a partisan media retrenchment would not be progress. It would be a relapse into a mentality that never served America well. Here are some of the reasons that partisan media is toxic for America:

- A partisan media ecosystem makes it difficult for voters to make informed decisions. And an informed electorate is the underlying rationale for the one person, one vote system of democracy. Instead of searching for truth, partisans spin the facts in furtherance of pre-determined outcomes. They don't write journalism; they put out propaganda.

- Partisan journalism limits the dialogue to two competing points of view. The truth often lies in the middle between Democrats and Republicans, meaning that in an utterly partisan, red/blue environment, the truth often goes unmentioned.

- Similarly, the best policy solution may lie outside the parameters of the two parties altogether—but does not merit consideration by a partisan press devoted to winning the argument.

- The two parties are well-organized, well-resourced, and well-established. Layering a partisan press on top of that system creates an environment in which the sheer volume of what the two parties put out drowns Independents and other rational voices out of the media.

- A partisan press contributes to the demonization of the other side. Incivility debases our campaigns and governing process. It makes campaigns less enlightening and makes legislative compromise more difficult once the elections are over.

But preventing compromise is the very result that ideological pur- ists in the media desire. On the left, some of the most powerful voices are on the Internet, and sites such as Daily Kos. On the right, the most incendiary voices are on talk radio, a medium in which Limbaugh and his imitators sound the tom-toms daily on a relentless drumbeat of issues, urging their listeners to call Republican members of Congress to account. The fury they gin up obscures a wide array of subjects rang- ing from prominent national issues such as immigration reform and the Common Core educational standards to subjects like the Export- Import Bank and the debt ceiling.

In a lengthy examination of hyper-partisan radio hosts for the Shoren- stein Center, journalist Jackie Calmes says that these radio stars are the *de facto* captains of the Republican Party.[14]

"If leaders of the Republican Party are not setting its agenda, who is?" she wrote. "As many of them concede, it is conservative media—not just talk-show celebrities Rush Limbaugh, Sean Hannity, Mark Levin and Laura Ingraham, but also lesser-known talkers like Steve Deace, and an expanding web of 'news' sites and social media outlets with financial and ideological alliances with far-right anti-government, anti-establishment groups like Heritage Action, Americans for Prosperity, Club for Growth and FreedomWorks. Once allied with but now increasingly hostile to the Republican hierarchy, conservative media is shaping the party's agenda in ways that are impeding Republicans' ability to govern and to win presi- dential elections."

The loud, raucous voices of left and right are also making it hard for Independents to be heard through the din, and for voters, regardless of their leanings, to evaluate what's real and what is make-believe. And as Jackie Calmes describes, partisan media also blur the very lines between journalism and activism—and they do it deliberately.[15] Which brings us to the newest monster creation of hyper-partisanship.

THE RISE OF FRANKENSTEIN MEDIA

One of the more misleading headlines relating to my old lawsuit against Debbie Reynolds and her son was posted by America Rising. It read: "Kansas Dem Once Sued Princess Leia's Mom."

This was a reference to Debbie Reynolds' other child, Carrie Fisher. The item was accompanied by an embedded video of Gene Kelley dancing with his umbrella in *Singin' in the Rain*, the 1952 musical that made Debbie Reynolds a movie star. "Kansas Senate candidate Greg Orman once sued *Singin' in the Rain* star Debbie Reynolds," it began. "It's unlikely that sentence has ever been written about any other Senate candidate in American history."

The snide tone is a hint of what is going on here, as is that inaccurate description, "Dem," in the headline. Mislabeling me as a Democrat was not a journalistic error; it was a campaign tactic. Although this post pops up in any online search that includes my name and that of Debbie Reynolds, America Rising is not a journalism entity. It's a political action committee devoted to promoting Republicans and trashing their opponents. America Rising is the same group that paid "trackers" to follow Sybil and me to every public event and videotape everything I said. They also showed up at our volunteer events and recorded all the license plates of cars that were in our parking lot. They were effectively an extension of the Roberts campaign's opposition research team. Increasingly, a political party's opposition research team will unearth information about their opponent that it thinks is damaging or that proves a narrative it's trying to sell. At a minimum, the information is taken out of context and twisted into the worst possible light. Often it is just dishonest.

Opposition research teams start by trying to shop the information to mainstream media outlets in the hopes that the story will get picked up. If mainstream news outlets don't take the bait, the opposition teams find a way to recycle the trash. They send it to advocacy groups that fashion the research into a press release—or they slip it to some quasi news organization that is really a partisan organ, such as America Rising. Those fake news organizations turn the item into a Frankenstein, a monster of their own creation, fashioning it into a seemingly credible news story complete with a catchy headline. The campaign media teams then re-post these stories on their websites and Facebook pages, email blast them with links to the stories themselves to their email lists, and forward them to the mainstream media outlets with the hopes that now that the story has broken, legitimate news outlets will pick it up and run with it. Even when they don't, the smear serves a purpose: It's out there in the ether, passed around by volunteers and partisan activists, planting the seed of a poisonous narrative in the minds of their faithful. Many voters aren't aware that these "news" sites are biased. The net result is that credibility is conferred on a story that a reputable news outlet wouldn't touch.

During my campaign, I'd frequently receive emails from friends and acquaintances with the simple subject line "Is this true?" The body of the email would contain the latest scurrilous or inaccurate rumor being peddled by the opposition. At least my friends had the good sense to ask.

The most egregious of these Frankenstein headlines end up in attack ads on television. With an ominous narrator bellowing allegations against a candidate, the headlines are splashed across the screen to add an aura of credibility to the attack. The accompanying video is generally a grainy shot of one's political opponent, often shown in slow motion.

The typical Internet practices of mainstream journalism also allowed voters to pass on their most biased invective, which they get from the two parties. Slow to react to the new challenge, mainstream media overreacted by opening up its pages to "comment" sections following most stories on their site. In that format, profanity and vitriol—not to mention partisan character assassination—became the norm. This is not progress either. Twenty years ago, if you wanted to have your views publicized, you penned a letter to the editor, complete with your name and address, found a stamp, and mailed it. The required effort had the practical effect of allowing newspaper editors to screen out inflammatory and harebrained personal attacks. Now all you need is access to the Internet, and thirty seconds in which to peck out an ugly screed. Most news outlets will publish it, literally sight unseen. As a result, the sensationalism and dishonesty of the Frankenstein Media often make their way into the mainstream media through the backdoor of the comment sections.

"SENATOR SMITH," MEDIA RESPONSIBILITY, AND THE INDEPENDENT CITIZEN

After my campaign was over, I received a note from Patrick Caddell, the pollster, campaign operative, and political commentator. Caddell made his name in politics working for Jimmy Carter. In the intervening years he has sworn off politics, only to reemerge in the thick of election years, taking swipes at both parties, as a dependable maverick. At this point in his career, neither Democrats nor Republicans will claim him—and the media struggles to define him—but that's fitting: Pat is the very epitome of an Independent.

In 1983, he conjured up a prototype of a Democratic presidential candidate voters would support. This mythical candidate, dubbed "Senator Smith" as a tip of the hat to Frank Capra, was a moderate Democratic U.S. senator in his forties. Senator Smith was bold enough to break with party tradition and speak for a new generation. He also possessed the charisma that would bolster a Kennedyesque call for patriotic sacrifice.[16] Senator Smith would be compassionate but also be honest about liberal programs that had failed. Caddell independently conducted a poll to test the potential of Senator Smith against the formidable Democratic frontrunner, former vice president Walter Mondale, and Ohio senator John Glenn, the former astronaut. In his testing, the hypothetical Senator Smith was a handy winner.

Caddell first approached Senator Joe Biden in hopes of persuading him to run against Mondale and Reagan. Biden ultimately declined to run. But Gary Hart, an upstart Kansan then serving as Colorado's junior senator, who had worked with Caddell in both the McGovern campaign and his own Senate election, saw his chance and decided to run on the Senator Smith themes concocted by Caddell. He lost the nomination to former vice president Walter Mondale, but he made his mark in the way that Caddell wanted.

Four years later, Joe Biden decided to run as Senator Smith—as would Hart, a second time. Caddell's two candidates revealed character flaws and came up short, but what struck the veteran strategist was how snarky the political coverage of "Senator Smith" had become. He was also dismayed at the zeal with which political journalists played "gotcha" on personal issues while giving short shrift to the public policy proposals of the various candidates.

"In establishing a system of checks and balances, the founders exempted one institution, the press," Caddell wrote to me. "They did so not out of fondness (for they felt anything but), but for a higher purpose. They believed that there could be no free government without a free press to protect the people from the excesses and oppression of government." He continued, "They never intended a press that would see itself in the role of the defender and advocate of partisan government. They never intended a press that believed that institutionally they had a right to tell people not only who they must vote for, but also decide which truth should be told and which truth should be withheld from the American people."

The idealist in me wants to appeal to the better angels of journalists' natures—and remind them of their sacred role in our democracy. I realize, however, that such an impulse is naïve. Journalists either already recognize their vital role in the democratic enterprise, or they view journalism as a means to a partisan end.

Which brings us back to the hysterical obsession with Ebola on the part of the U.S. media, especially cable news. What was going on with that?

For starters, we have to recognize that Fox News, which aired 281 segments on Ebola leading up to the 2014 elections (and ten afterward), was carrying water for the Republican Party. With control of Congress on the line, GOP candidates seized on the Ebola issue to demonstrate the Obama administration's supposedly ineffectual response to the potential spread of the virus in America. Fox News obliged Republicans by faithfully adhering to that storyline. Knowing that many Republican voters tend to prioritize national security, Fox also likely deduced that the perception of a national security scare would inspire Republicans to go to the polls. Fox's coverage, in turn, galvanized MSNBC into action—in defense of the Democrats. CNN, which ran the most stories on Ebola—335 of them—well, they were apparently in it for the ratings.

At some point, it was all too much for another American with the surname Smith, this one a real person. This was Shepard Smith, one of Fox News Channel's most popular anchors. "You should have no concerns about Ebola," he told his audience in exasperated tones one day. "None. I promise." Then, in words that could be a much broader indictment of modern political news coverage—and not only on his network—Smith added: "Do not listen to the hysterical voices on the radio and the television or read the fear-provoking words online. The people who say and write hysterical things are being very irresponsible."[17]

Rather than entreating the media to forego the absolute pursuit of profit and partisanship and embrace instead a more generous view of their First Amendment responsibility, I want to speak to you, the independent-minded citizen, voter, and consumer of political media. First, I want to encourage your greater awareness of how much of what you read, see, and hear is political misinformation intended to dupe you into supporting one side or the other in an ongoing tug of war between crony politicians. Here are some rules of the road:

- Exercise common sense. If something sounds too sensational, it probably is.
- Don't just read headlines; they are usually click-bait. Read the articles, too.
- Look for weasel words in headlines, such as "accused" or "potential." They are a red flag regarding what follows.
- Challenge the assumptions made by reporters or commentators.
- When possible, find the original sources cited a press account. Often, they are only a click or two away.
- Consider the publication or individual reporter. Do the writer's stories have a discernible angle? Are other stories overly partisan—or consistent in their slant?
- Make a point of identifying reporters and news organizations that put a premium on facts rather than snark, partisanship, rumor, or sensationalism. Develop your own rigorous roster of trusted sources.
- Understand that journalism is a business, and a fragile business at that, one that pursues profit as much as truth—or even more than truth.
- If the site you're reading is a news aggregator, ask if it's trying to lull you into a false sense of objectivity by including a few "straight" articles that have nothing to do with elections.
- During political campaigns, read the candidates' own websites. While each one obviously promotes its own candidate, it will often include information on policy positions that might help you evaluate the truth and worth of that candidate's claims. If that candidate is an Independent, you'll find material not filtered through the partisan media ecosystem.
- Read and watch multiple sources of news. In other words, resist the habit of watching just MSNBC or Fox News—or even CNN.

Sorting fact from fiction requires more of you—more of us all. It can feel like a daunting task to have to vet every political fact and story you see on a screen or read in a newspaper or website, but the more you do it, the more you'll sharpen your political acumen, access the real truth and possibilities of American civic life, and hone your own Independent instincts.

CHAPTER 10

Rigging the Game

HOW THE POLITICAL DUOPOLY
AVOIDS ACCOUNTABILITY AND ENSURES
ITS CONTINUED DOMINANCE OVER
THE AMERICAN PUBLIC

——— ★ ★ ★ ———

BASEBALL IS CALLED THE National Pastime, although football and basketball may have surpassed baseball in popularity. What all three games have in common—and why Americans love spectator sports—is that the athletic competition at the professional level is exciting, unpredictable, and fair. By "fair" I mean that the rules are the same for everybody and everyone can compete. At their best, organized sports are the closest thing we have to a pure meritocracy. That's why so many fans were rooting in the 2015 World Series for the Kansas City Royals, my hometown team.

The Royals appeared in the World Series in 2014 and 2015, losing the first time and winning the second. It was their first championship in thirty years, a drought partly due to the economics of Major League Baseball. Because there is no salary cap in the big leagues, large-market teams enjoy a big advantage over small-market franchises. The revenue disparities give teams from cities such as Chicago, Los Angeles, and New

York a greater ability to pay for top talent than teams from places like Kansas City.

Private sector competition is one of the most inventive aspects of our national character. Franklin D. Roosevelt called this national trait "American ingenuity." FDR would have loved the Kansas City Royals. Their financial disadvantages prompted them to take a creative approach to the game. Today's trends favor hulking power pitchers who amass strikeouts, as well as free-swinging sluggers who hit home runs. The Royals' brand of baseball was a hybrid of old-school offense and cutting edge defense. Their hitters struck out fewer times than any other team, scoring runs by putting the ball in play while running the bases with flair. On defense, their superb fielding was built around team speed in the outfield, sure-handed infielders, and aggressive shifts that relied on advance metrics that helped them make better game-time decisions. On their team, relievers, not starters, anchored the pitching staff. There was an economic method to this madness: Relief pitchers are generally paid less—just as singles hitters are more affordable than home run hitters.

The Kansas City Royals won the World Series over the New York Mets despite significant financial disadvantages because they adapted their game to the realities of their situation, and they played with passion. In an environment like baseball, where the rules are the same for every team, anybody can win the World Series—even the teams for whom the odds are the longest.

The rules, however, aren't the same for our politics where we allow the dominant party in a state to write the rules to their own advantage.

OUR POLITICAL DUOPOLY

Americans abhor cheating in the marketplace. We cherish fairness. These are values still shared by Democrats and Republicans—and Independents.

It's why monopolies have been illegal in the U.S. since the late nineteenth century, or, in the case of natural monopolies, like electric utilities, heavily regulated. With few exceptions, however, monopolies are less of an issue today. Duopolies are another story.

A duopoly is present when two companies dominate a marketplace. I've used that term throughout this book to describe the chokehold that Republicans and Democrats exert on our politics. In some ways, duopolies can be worse than monopolies. Although they create the illusion of competition, duopolies compete against one another while working together to suppress outside competition. They define the parameters of the game—and then rig the rules of that game to keep others out.

My private sector experience has left me attuned to how duopolies bar entry to would-be competitors. Legally prohibited from colluding directly, two all-encompassing, competitive entities work together to erect barriers that protect the duopoly. After years of consolidation in the global beer industry, for example, two multinational conglomerates, Anheuser-Busch InBev and MillerCoors, control 70 percent of the U.S. beer market. This may have been a good deal for the companies involved, as they were able to improve profits by achieving economies of scale, but it didn't take long for consumers to get a bad taste in their mouths: A study by the American Antitrust Institute showed that beer prices began rising faster than the consumer price index.[1] Meanwhile, although American beer drinkers are enjoying a craft beer renaissance, smaller brewers have reported difficulty in getting their products into stores, bars, and restaurants because the duopoly has quietly pressured beer distributors to sell only their brands.

Taking their cue from the political world, private sector duopolies also look to the government for help suppressing competition. Why wouldn't they? It's exactly how Republicans and Democrats behave. In city after city, the response by the dominant local taxi cab company to Uber, the popular new ride-sharing company, was to lobby city or airport authorities to change existing rules to ban ride sharing, require background checks on drivers, impose onerous insurance requirements—anything to prevent competition.

Cable companies are another interesting case study in anti-competitive behavior. Cable companies generally provide two services to consumers: content, through their video offerings, and Internet access across their cables. On the Internet access side of their business, they enjoy duopolies in some jurisdictions (and monopolies in others). They responded to competition on the content side of their business by trying to leverage their duopoly power on the Internet access side of the business. They attempted to charge newer content providers such as Netflix based on the amount of bandwidth their services demanded—notwithstanding the fact that the cable industry's customers were already paying for their service based on the amount of bandwidth made available to them. In effect, they were attempting to charge both content providers and consumers for the same thing. This strategy was basically a ruse designed to marginalize competitors by driving consumers to their own video offerings.

In these cases, the advocates of the newer business model fought back—to the benefit of consumers. But when Democrats and Republicans do this, we have little recourse. Occasionally, courts will step in to challenge the political duopoly and reset the terms of play, but the judiciary is reluctant to get involved in political disputes like this. State attorney generals are invariably elected Republicans or Democrats, usually with further political ambition. They often benefit from the rule rigging that's taking place. In fact, when a concerned citizen decides to challenge an election law, the government generally steps in to defend the law as written—effectively protecting the entrenched duopoly with taxpayer money. The Federal Election Commission, created in the aftermath of Watergate, is tasked with monitoring political practices, but it is a toothless organization that codifies the duopoly's advantages.

Why does the FEC. operate this way? Here's a hint: It's made up of three Republicans and three Democrats.

RIGGING THE SECRET BALLOT

Squeezing out Independents is a conscious strategy of the duopoly. While publicly, Democrats and Republicans tend to be dismissive of Independents in an effort to reinforce their popular narrative that Independents can't win elections and your vote for them is "wasted," at every opportunity they seek to rig the rules to protect their duopoly. Throughout our country's history, with every reform that is intended to improve our governance and elections, Republicans and Democrats alike have used their power to enact legislation to turn these good government reforms into shields that serve to protect their grip on power. The fact that we allow the dominant players of the game to also write the rules of the game as we go along has never been a more destructive feature of our democracy. Nonaligned voters—43 percent of all Americans—are now being disenfranchised by two parties, who each represent less than a third of our citizens.

Gerrymandering, that scandalous invention of the early nineteenth century, isn't the only way partisans have rigged the rules around voting. The "secret ballot," considered a hallmark of American democracy, also created more opportunities for the ruling duopoly to disenfranchise voters. The secret ballot is actually not an American notion. It's an idea imported from Australia as a mid-nineteenth-century reform. Before the advent of the anonymous ballot, voters received party ballots, which were printed with the names of all of a particular party's candidates for each office. They were generally distinguishable based on the color of the ballot, and they were usually cast in public. Anonymous ballots were a solution to the practice of ruffians who worked for the political machine and intimidated citizens into casting the "right" colored ballot. The secret ballot had obvious benefits, including privacy and safety, so by the late nineteenth century the new method had made its way across the oceans to Great Britain and ultimately the United States.[2]

One consequence unanticipated by the reformers was a steep drop in voter participation. Another was that minor parties, often regional or local in their appeal, had flourished under the old system. Major parties often included minor party candidates on their slates and vice-versa. The effects of these ad-hoc alliances were two-fold. A broader array of ideologies and political philosophies were represented by elected officials, particularly in municipal and state government. The ruling political party had a vested interest in taking the concerns of the minor parties into consideration. In effect, it gave minor parties a voice.

The Australian ballot made it easy for the duopoly to manipulate how candidates' names and their political affiliations were presented on written ballots to the voters.[3] Minor parties now found themselves unable to ally themselves with major party slates on an ad-hoc basis because ballots were printed ahead of time, with the names and party affiliations of the candidates. To counter this development, minor parties and third parties—mainly in the West and the Midwest—created "fusion" tickets during the last decade of the nineteenth century in which a single name would be listed as the nominee of both the Democratic Party and the Progressive or Populist Parties.

In state after state this stratagem worked with stunning success. In 1896 in Kansas, for instance, Populists and Democrats formed fusion tickets all over the state, sweeping their candidates into office. Republicans ceded control of the state legislature and the governor's mansion, lost six of eight congressional races, and watched as Democrat William Jennings Bryan carried Kansas over winning GOP presidential candidate William McKinley.[4]

Two years later, Republicans out-organized the Democrats and recouped most of their losses. Concluding that they didn't want to have to deal in third parties or Independents again, the Republican legislature rammed through laws outlawing fusion tickets. In effect, the law said that more than one party couldn't nominate the same candidate. The Populist Party attempted to challenge the law in front of the Kansas Supreme Court. At the time, the Court was made up of seven elected judges—four of whom were Republicans running for reelection. They immediately recused themselves from hearing the case, which left the Court without a quorum. It was, therefore, unable to hear the challenge to the law, which stands to this day.[5]

As a result, a reform that was intended to lead to better elections, the secret ballot, ultimately was used to disenfranchise voters who didn't support the dominant party in the state. By putting power in the hands of politicians to determine how that secret ballot was designed, once again we put the fox in charge of the hen house.

Most other states took similar steps, all of them calculated to restore either the Democrats—or, more often, Republicans—to primacy. This occurred even in reform-minded California, where the Progressives broke Republican dominance and with it the massive power that the Southern Pacific Railroad exerted over the state. But although legendary Progressive reformer Hiram Johnson brought the railroads to heel, the two-party system proved much harder to vanquish. California's legislature also succeeded in outlawing fusion tickets, replacing them with "cross-filing," a system that stripped ballots of party labels—but which allowed candidates to run in both Republican and Democratic Party primaries. Cross-filing gave the illusion of weakening party control, but it actually kept Republicans dominant over Democrats, while utterly undermining Independents for the next fifty years.

When future Supreme Court Chief Justice Earl Warren was elected governor of California in 1946, for example, he and most of the winning statewide officeholders—along with half the congressional delegation— won the primaries in both parties. Cross-filing was finally eliminated in 1959, but anti-fusion statutes are still on the books in most states in the union, including California and Kansas.

PRIMARIES—THE ONLY ELECTIONS THAT MATTER

Because of gerrymandered districts, party primaries have become the most important stage of the electoral process in most congressional districts. This is where the real action is—the election that determines who will represent the 700,000 Americans who live in each congressional district. Polarization of the electorates in Democratic "blue" states and Republican "red" states means that, increasingly, the primaries in statewide elections—including for governor and senator—are also the contests that matter most as well. The duopoly is forever tinkering with this system to solidify their primacy: In a majority of states, Independents are barred from full participation in the primaries.[6]

Seventeen states, including Kansas and the District of Columbia, use a strictly closed primary. (The others are Connecticut, Colorado, Iowa, New Jersey, New York, Delaware, Florida, Kentucky, Maine, Maryland, Nevada, New Mexico, Oregon, Pennsylvania, and Wyoming.) Voters must formally join one of the two political parties at some point before the primary in order to cast votes. Other states have a hodgepodge of rules and regulations. In Idaho, Oklahoma, South Dakota, and Utah, the Republican primary is closed, while the Democrats in those states hold either an open or a "semi-closed" primary.

Being an Independent in these places is tantamount to disenfranchisement, as Pennsylvania newspaper editorial editor Matt Zencey reminds his readers each year in a column dedicated to explaining how unfair the voting laws are to the state's Independents. "Tuesday is Primary Election Day," he wrote in 2014, "and every year when it rolls around, I'm reminded of this unpleasant fact: Tax-paying Pennsylvanians who don't belong to a political party are forced to help pay for an election in which they are not allowed vote."[7]

In neighboring New Jersey, the closed primary is under legal challenge. Governor Chris Christie's administration has responded by asserting in court that a "voter who feels disenfranchised because of a regulation that conditions participation in primary elections on party membership should simply join the party." The state's legal brief also asserted that no previous court has made a finding that unaffiliated voters have a fundamental right to participate in primary elections "even when those elections are an integral part of the electoral process."[8]

Yes, Independent voters *could* join the Democratic or Republican Parties, but this is precisely what we've decided not to do, and for good reason. Independents reject the duopoly's obedience to special interest and its superficial storyline, which is that there are only two possible public policy choices. Moreover, if party primaries are a private political endeavor, as courts have ruled, why does the state administer the primary elections—and why do taxpayers pay for the process of holding them?

THE SCANDAL OF POLITICAL PARTY FINANCING

Speaking of financing elections, in 1970 a burglary took place in Minnesota at the home of a well-known political operative named Fred Gates—on the day of his funeral while his family was in church. Fred Gates was Hubert Humphrey's closest political aide and confidant, going back to his days as mayor of Minneapolis. They were really more like best friends. When Hubert took the oath of office as vice president, Fred Gates held the Humphrey family Bible. Fred was also my grandfather.

The robbers stole Fred's wall safe, which undoubtedly contained sensitive papers, while leaving behind easily accessible jewelry. Coming as it did while Richard Nixon's "plumbers" were beginning the activities that would land them in prison, Humphrey himself suspected political intrigue as the motive for the break-in at Fred Gates' home. A decade later, the prominent Minneapolis-based investigative journalist Don Shelby cracked the case. The burglars, it seems, didn't care about political memos. They were interested in the $250,000 in cash Fred Gates kept in the safe. The money was unspent political donations, presumably for Hubert.

At the time, when the local CBS affiliate, WCCO, aired Don Shelby's reports—a weeklong series of broadcasts—there was a palpable sense of disgust at how much money was in my grandfather's safe. But that's how political donations were made until the excesses of the 1972 Nixon reelection campaign changed how business was done. Donors contributed anonymously to campaigns—often in cash. The image of $2 million in cash being donated by one man, Chicago financier W. Clement Stone, to Richard Nixon's reelection campaign—would end that practice. But the Watergate-era reforms would all benefit the duopoly.

Limits on campaign contributions were enacted: $1,000 for each primary for federal office and another $1,000 for a general election. Political action committees were limited to $5,000. But the political parties themselves could receive up to $25,000—provided they were a "major" party. Practically speaking, this meant Republicans or Democrats. For minor parties, the limit was $5,000. So even at the height of their reform zeal as Watergate was unfolding, Washington policy makers were careful to protect the duopoly—giving themselves a fundraising limit that was five times as large as minor parties (and infinitely larger than Independents who don't have a party to spend on their behalf).

This practice has continued unabated for the last four decades, and it's become even more obscene than it was in the days of briefcases loaded with wads of hundred-dollar bills. In fact, rigging the game through political party financing was recently further reinforced in the law.

The very symbol of dysfunction in modern Washington is the last-minute funding of the government by emergency appropriations, instead of the regular budget process. In Washington jargon, business as usual is Congress passing "continuing resolutions" (also known as a CR) and "omnibus" spending bills just in the nick of time to keep the government operational. Sometimes they miss deadlines, leading to government shutdowns. Facing this possibility in the lame-duck session of the 113th Congress in 2014, Senate Democrats met behind closed doors with House Republicans to forge a $1.1 trillion spending bill that was part CR and part omnibus bill. This process produced a new jargon word: "CRomnibus." The ensuing legislation also had the dubious distinction of codifying the corrupt ethics of the duopoly into a brazen new campaign finance law so grotesque it would have embarrassed the political bagmen of my grandfather's generation.

No longer are U.S. citizens limited to contributing a mere $97,200 annually to the Republican Party and the Democratic Party. The new limit was set at $777,600. (It had an inflation adjuster, so as of this writing in 2016, the figure is $834,000.) Those numbers are not typos. This limit is in addition to the amounts they can give to a Democratic or Republican candidate. Guess how much an American can legally donate to an Independent candidate running for federal office? The answer is $5,400 every two years. Only a Washington politician could justify such a disparity.

Defenders of the duopoly will note that Independent candidates can still have unlimited dollars spent on their behalf through super PACs or other independent expenditure organizations. The difference is that the major parties can coordinate with their candidates through hybrid ads

(ads supporting both the party and the candidate), thereby making party expenditures much more effective.

Not to be outdone by the corrupt bargain negotiated between John Boehner and Harry Reid at the end of the 113th Congress, the current Senate majority leader, Mitch McConnell, added another rider to the must-pass spending bill of 2015 eliminating altogether the caps on how much a party can spend in a coordinated fashion with its candidates. The goal of this rider is to re-establish the major parties as the most efficient spender of high dollar donations, giving them an advantage over super PACs in the race for high dollar donations. A coalition of liberal Democrats, who want more limits on campaign spending, and Tea Party Republicans, who have historically been targeted for defeat by the establishment Republicans who control the national party, came together to defeat the provision.

HOW PARTIES SHUT DOWN INDEPENDENT VOICES

Rigging the rules around political party rules and financing not only helps Democrats and Republicans get elected, but it also insulates them from any real accountability to voters. It's no wonder that four-fifths of Americans tell pollsters it's important to have Independents run for political office. More than 60 percent say they'd consider voting for an Independent for president. But the duopoly makes that a difficult proposition, and one way they keep it that way is by making it exceedingly difficult for a third-party candidate or an Independent to participate in presidential elections.

In the era of modern politics, only Ross Perot managed to appear on stage with the Republican and Democratic nominees. That happened the first time he ran, in 1992, but not 1996. No one else has accomplished it,* and the duopoly erected formal structures designed to prevent it from happening again. The gatekeeper is the Commission on Presidential Debates, an organization that was formed in 1988 when the League of Women Voters ended their formal sponsorship of the presidential debates. In pulling out, the League president, Nancy Neuman, noted, "It has become clear to us that the candidates' organizations aim to add debates to their list of campaign-trail charades devoid of substance, spontaneity and honest answers to tough questions. The League has no intention of becoming an accessory to the hoodwinking of the American public."[9]

The League's withdrawal was actually just fine with the ruling duopoly, as it allowed the major parties to take over the management of all presidential debates. The Commission on Presidential Debates claims to be "nonpartisan." In reality, they are no such thing—they are bipartisan. Although those words are often used interchangeably, they shouldn't be. A *nonpartisan* Commission would be oriented toward opening up the process. A *bipartisan* Commission exists to perpetuate the duopoly. The current organization is the latter. It was created by Republicans and Democrats and is staffed by Republicans and Democrats.

In 2012, some 67 million Americans tuned in to watch the first debate between Mitt Romney and Barack Obama.[10] This is more than half the total number of voters in the 2012 election. If an Independent is ever to be a viable presidential candidate, he or she simply must have access to that stage. But the duopoly stands in the way.

The 2016 rules for debates set by the commission require that a

---

*   In 1980, third-party candidate John Anderson was invited to participate in a three-way debate with incumbent President Jimmy Carter and Republican challenger Ronald Reagan. Carter refused to participate if Anderson were present, so Reagan debated him alone. Anderson bowed out of the second scheduled debate, preserving the power of the Duopoly: Carter and Reagan debated alone.

candidate have more than 15 percent support in at least five national polls in mid-September. Although this threshold sounds reasonable, it's actually so effective a barrier to entry that no candidate from outside the duopoly can reasonably hope to achieve it. (To appear in the first Republican or Democratic primary debate of the 2016 campaign, a candidate merely had to achieve 1 percent in the polls.) It's a classic Catch-22: Independent candidates can certainly attain that level of support—Ross Perot surpassed that percentage of the vote in November of 1992—*but only if they are allowed in the debates.* It's a little-remembered historical fact that even Ross Perot didn't meet the 15 percent benchmark: He was only invited to the 1992 debates at the request of the Bush and Clinton campaigns, each of which feared a backlash if they didn't open up the process. Research shows that to achieve 15 percent support in September, a candidate who competes outside the major party primaries would need to achieve 80 percent national name identification. For someone like Donald Trump, this might not be so difficult. For a relatively unknown candidate to achieve this, he or she would have to spend an estimated $250 million. The upshot, and it's not unintentional, is that the 15 percent rule locks out anyone but the nominees of the two major parties.

The CPD is distorting the marketplace of ideas in our political system, perpetuating the status quo by protecting the major parties from real, unfettered competition. Americans don't like the product we're getting, but thanks to rigged rules like this, we're stuck with it.

I wrote about this problem in the *Concord Monitor* in 2015, explaining my support for an effort called Change the Rule that is attempting to modify the presidential debate rules to make them genuinely nonpartisan.

> My career has been in business, and so markets and competition are what I know. In the free market economy, we believe in the power of competition to bring the best value to consumers. As

a result, innovative upstarts often supplant stodgy companies that are set in their ways. This principle of economic freedom and valuing competition has made the lives of Americans better, improved our economy, and rewarded innovators.

When it comes to our politics, however, we've forgotten that lesson. It's no surprise that Washington's approval ratings are so low. As the two parties work to entrench themselves, they become less responsive to the needs of voters. The fact is that the system through which we select our political leaders is not defined by free and fair competition, but by a firmly entrenched Duopoly.

"ASSISTING" THE VOTERS

The easiest way to rig elections is by keeping off the ballot the names of citizens who might win. This is how military dictatorships and tyrants do it in places like Burma, Turkey, and Russia. Although they'd be horrified at being compared to Vladimir Putin or Third World juntas, Republicans and Democrats do precisely the same thing in the United States.

To qualify for the 2012 presidential ballot in California, as an example, Americans Elect, the organization that was trying to nominate a presidential ticket outside of the party process, had to spend millions of dollars employing some 1,500 people to gather signatures. They gathered 1.62 million in all. For their trouble, Americans Elect was the subject of letters of complaint to the Internal Revenue Service on the part of ranking members of the duopoly who demanded to know all of the organization's contributors. This is a classic example of the "heads I win, tails you lose" approach employed by Democrats and Republicans. Americans Elect had to gather all those signatures precisely because it was an independent group, not a political party, but then the parties tried to force it to comply with rules the parties have set up to keep outsiders out.

In Kansas, the arbiter for ballot access-related issues is Secretary of State Kris Kobach, a very conservative—and very partisan—Republican. In 2011 he tried to invalidate some 32,000 signatures submitted by Americans Elect on the grounds that sixty-four of them were misdated. This was a thin rationale, considering that Americans Elect filed twice as many signatures as would be required to form as a political party in Kansas.

Kobach was running in 2014 himself, seeking a second term. In the GOP primary, former Lawrence school board member Scott Morgan called him "a partisan hack."[11] In response, Kansas's secretary of state called Morgan a Democrat in Republican's clothing. He would say that. To a defender of the faith—i.e., an active member of the duopoly— there are only two choices. That's why when I ran for the Senate the state's ruling Republicans kept calling me a closet Democrat. If I'd run for office on the same platform as an Independent in Minnesota, the state of my birth, which is far more Democratic, the ruling elites would have called me a closet Republican.

Three months after I threw a scare into the status quo by doing better than initially expected in the Senate contest, Kobach, who had won his race, proposed two election-related bills designed to make it more difficult for Independents in the future. Such a response, coming more than a century after Kansas had eliminated fusion tickets after the last threat to his party's dominance, was predictable. The first proposed law would have made the death of a candidate the only way a primary winner's name could be removed from the ballot. His other bill sought to bring back straight-ticket party voting in which voters check a single box with the name of a political party to cast a vote for every member of that party on the ballot. The goal here was to get low information voters to reflexively support one party and never have the opportunity to vote for an Independent candidate.

"I think it will improve participation in races down the ballot and it's a matter of voter convenience too," Kobach explained. "It's just another way of assisting the voter."[12] He said these things with a straight face, just as Michigan Democrats who were simultaneously making similar proposals were also claiming that party-line ballots are all about good government. What it's really about, of course, is maintaining the control of one major party or the other—and preventing Independents from ever being viable.

Elected officials who really cared about American democracy wouldn't always be gaming the system this way. Their reflexive response to an electoral scare wouldn't be to ask, "How do I change the rules to prevent my party or our candidates from ever having to be held accountable again?" It would be to look in the mirror and ask themselves pointed questions: "What are voters looking for that we're not providing? What am I doing wrong? What is my political party doing wrong? How do we respond to what the people clearly want? Do we need more competent candidates? Where do we find real public servants? In short, how do we provide better public service?"

Which brings us back to the Kansas City Royals. Many sportswriters viewed the 2015 World Series as a morality play. That's overstating things, as the Mets' power-pitching and hitting style is still likely to be baseball's future. But even casual fans appreciated that despite their small payroll, the Royals had a fair chance to compete on the field. Next year may belong to the Mets, or another large-market team. But engage with me for a moment in a second thought experiment:

What if the winners of the pennant in each league were allowed to change one rule every year—and apply it only to themselves? The slap-hitting Kansas City Royals might decide that they get four outs each inning, while everyone else still gets three. The lead-footed New York Mets might want to add a tenth fielder when the other team was hitting, while their opponents still had only nine. If the Royals and Mets met again in 2016—and the chances are good, with those skewed rules in place—they could come up with another rule change. And remember: Their competitors couldn't use the new rule, only the winners of the pennant.

The inevitable result would be that the Royals and the Mets would meet in the World Series every year. It wouldn't be fair, and it wouldn't make for good baseball. Fans would sour on the game. That's what Republicans and Democrats have done to U.S. politics—and in the same way: by shamelessly rigging the rules of competition. We wouldn't stand for it in our professional sports, and we certainly shouldn't in our politics.

PART IV

An

INDEPENDENT
SOLUTION

★★★

CHAPTER 11

It's Not Rocket Science

AN INDEPENDENT APPROACH TO ACHIEVING COMMON GROUND ON GUNS, ABORTION, IMMIGRATION, AND A WHOLE LOT OF OTHER ISSUES

——— ★ ★ ★ ———

ON MAY 23, 2015, Sybil gave birth to our daughter, Imogen. She was six weeks premature and spent just over two weeks in the intensive care unit. Our baby was attached to various monitors to track her breathing, heart rate, and oxygen levels. She went through multiple IVs to deliver fluids and was fed through a tube in her nose. Blood samples were taken from her heel every few hours.

Knowing ahead of time that she was arriving early, the doctor who delivered Imogen warned us that she might need to be rushed directly to the ICU. Sybil might not even be able to hold her daughter after giving birth to her. Thankfully, our baby was born alert and stable. Sybil held her for almost 45 minutes before I went with my tiny daughter up to the ICU.

As I watched her lie helpless, attached to various tubes and wires, I realized how much she needed her parents to protect her and care for her and make sure she felt loved and accepted. The previous year, I had spent the campaign talking about the need to protect our children and grandchildren's future. I spoke of the moral obligation we have to leave our kids with a country that's in better shape than the one we inherited. I referred to it as the sacred social contract that is the very foundation of the American Idea. While I believed that to my core when I said it, the meaning of those words intensified as I watched my little girl in the incubator.

"Surely our elected leaders have to be intelligent enough to understand that politics is about more than just winning and losing," I thought to myself. "It's not a game."

I touched on this in the closing speech of the campaign when I said:

> At its heart we face a choice not just between two candidates, but between two different views of America. One view comes from the politicians in Washington as they look at the rest of us. In that America, they believe that elections are nothing but contests for political power and privilege . . . a game to be won or lost between the two political parties. They share an inherent assumption that nothing could benefit America more than the perpetuation of their rule.
>
> There is another view, one that I and many Kansans share. And that view is that both parties have made a mess. Democrats and Republicans have created the very gridlock, the paralysis that prevents our nation from moving forward.
>
> In that view, Americans see a great nation, but a broken system. Those of us in the Heartland looking back toward those who've made the mess, we desperately want to shout, "Stop the fighting! Stop the games! Solve problems! This isn't about your personal power or prestige. It's about the rest of us."

Maybe our leaders in Washington, D.C., have just concluded that we've passed the point of no return, so they're going to gather up as many of the spoils for themselves and their patrons even if it means eating our children's seed corn. If so, whether they admit it to themselves or not, this is tantamount to giving up on America.

Our leaders insult the intelligence of the average voter every time they run a negative ad that they know to be false or every time they engage in political theater and hold show votes to create the illusion of representation. They take voters for granted every time they avoid a critical vote because it poses some political risk to them. The disdain with which they obviously hold voters must bring with it a healthy skepticism about the future of those same Americans.

Their blatant pursuit of self-interest has also robbed America of political leaders with the moral authority to ask more of our citizens. How can leaders, so clearly invested exclusively in their own futures, ask Americans to sacrifice for our country? Back when our country worked, when the ruling elites of both parties joined together to tackle our country's challenges, our leaders had the moral authority to ask Americans for their time, their contribution, their patriotism. Today, a president who issued John F. Kennedy's memorable challenge, "Ask not what your country can do for you, ask what you can do for your country," would be scoffed at.

It doesn't have to be this way. In spite of what our leaders tell us, we can come together—by thinking and acting with an open and Independent mind. And it's easier than we think.

SHARING COMMON GROUND

In Chapter 7, we discussed at length how Democrats and Republicans work to divide voters. We examined how deliberate divisiveness created an environment of fear that pits neighbor against neighbor simply on the basis of party identification. While this attempt to divide has proven to be an effective electoral strategy for the vast majority of incumbents who now live in safe districts, the American people aren't nearly as far apart on the issues as campaign rhetoric would imply.

The evidence that we actually share more common ground is more than anecdotal. Stanford University political scientist Morris Fiorina has spent a good part of his long academic career documenting how Americans' political attitudes are more temperate than their political leaders. "In the aggregate, the American electorate has changed little in the past generation," he says. "Political independents and ideological moderates in the American electorate have not declined in numbers, let alone disappeared. Indeed, their numbers continue to exceed those of partisans and ideologues on either side."[1]

The Pew Research Center has conducted surveys on forty-two attitude, value, and policy subjects in the years since Ronald Reagan was in the White House, and they have reached a reassuring conclusion: "The way that the public thinks about poverty, opportunity, business, unions, religion, civic duty, foreign affairs and many other subjects is, to a large extent, the same today as in 1987. The values that unified Americans 25 years ago remain areas of consensus today . . . "[2]

I saw this reflected clearly as I traveled through Kansas in 2014: Voters from across the political spectrum came to our town hall meetings and other events and were able to speak to each other respectfully and constructively. We need to tap into that shared sense of purpose—that desire by most Americans, regardless of ideology or party affiliation, to leave a better America to our children. If we can move past the divisive rhetoric, we can work to reform our dysfunctional politics and rebuild the American Idea.

BELIEVING IN SHARED AMERICAN VALUES

As Kansas is, so is America. Interacting with Kansans on the campaign trail, I reaffirmed my belief that most Americans are well-intentioned people. While they often disagree on policy, and, in some cases, were blinded by pure partisanship, they genuinely cared about America. What they shared was far greater than what divided them. Most Kansans are pre-occupied with the same basic concerns. How will they support their families? Will they be able to send their children to college? Will they have security in their lives, their homes, their retirements? Will their children be safe and happy and able to lead productive lives?

A large majority of Kansans also share the same core principles. They believe we have an obligation as a country to provide equal opportunities to every American. This doesn't mean that they think outcomes should be the same. Most of them believe that success should be a function of your willingness to work hard, take risks, and persevere—not a function of who your parents are, or the politicians you know. They also believe in accountability—the notion that actions have consequences and that if we insulate American companies and individuals from the consequences of their bad behavior, we guarantee more bad behavior. This didn't mean they lacked compassion; rather, they didn't want our country repeatedly bailing out institutions and individuals who weren't willing to alter their destructive habits.

They also believe that the institutions that we are counting on as a country to serve us with ethics and integrity are broken, possibly irreparably. They don't believe they're hearing the truth from either our elected officials or the media, and they believe that truth is indispensable for our democracy to work.

In that same vein, they believe that corruption is killing us as a country. While many feel powerless to fight back, they have come to the reluctant realization that large companies, lobbyists, and career politicians are colluding to rob our treasury and to write rules to perpetuate their advantages. The Kansans I talked to still believe America has a special place in the world. By virtue of our heritage and stature, most Americans recognize that the world looks to us for leadership and direction—and that without that leadership, the world is a less safe place.

Finally, most of the people that I met on the campaign trail believe that it is immoral to saddle future generations with the sorts of obligations we are leaving behind. They believe that all Americans have a shared financial responsibility to put our country back on firm footing.

These beliefs were almost universal. It didn't matter whether I was talking to a liberal Democrat, conservative Republican, or an irascible Independent. Kansans, and I believe Americans in general, overwhelmingly shared a view about the United States' place in the world, and the obligations and opportunities that are presented to every citizen.

GUNS, ABORTION, AND IMMIGRATION

Most of the people I interacted with were also, believe it or not, able to find common ground on many of the issues. Perhaps voters flocking to hear an Independent candidate speak are more open-minded in this way. Also, this doesn't mean they agreed on every aspect of every issue. They were able, however, to discuss issues rationally and civilly—and they agreed on so much substance that they opened a path to making fundamental changes to policy.

As we tried to come to any sort of consensus in our discussions, I found that I needed to start every conversation by trying to understand where people were coming from and pointing out to the assembled audience the areas where they agreed with each other. I acted as kind of a facilitator. It started with listening carefully, a trait not associated with modern political campaigning. Generally, how people phrased their questions told me a lot about their position on the issue—and how much partisan programming had been drummed into them. If someone asked me my position on "the Second Amendment," for example, I knew they were more supportive of gun ownership rights than those who asked about "gun control."

Even on some of the most complex issues—immigration, guns, and abortion—the Kansans I met on the campaign trail were able to find agreement. On immigration reform, most Kansans I met believe that we need to enhance border security and require that businesses truly verify the employment eligibility of every new worker. They also generally believe that the country should create a mechanism for undocumented workers to stay in America. Very few people (though there were some) want the federal government to pursue a policy of mass deportation of the undocumented—except for those among them who had committed crimes.

Together, we were able to talk through a plan that required increased vigilance on the border along with implementation of the e-Verify system to ensure that employers weren't improperly employing undocumented workers. At the same time, I proposed that if an undocumented worker registered with the U.S. Immigration and Customs Enforcement Agency (ICE), paid a small fine or performed community service as an acknowledgment that our laws were broken, and paid taxes, they could stay in America and work.

While not everyone loved this resolution, after thinking about it, even many of the most ideologically rigid Kansans conceded that this was better than the current dysfunctional system that Congress and the president have been unwilling to fix. The e-Verify system provided comfort to those concerned about a permissive immigration system creating new incentives for further illegal migration. At the same time, labor leaders, who initially didn't welcome the additional competition for jobs, reluctantly conceded that requiring newly registered workers to pay taxes and be covered by our labor laws created a more level playing field for existing workers than the current system does. Even some who advocated for deportation acknowledged that registering undocumented workers with Immigration and Customs Enforcement and fully implementing the e-Verify system was better than the current system of limited enforcement actions and the turn-a-blind-eye approach in many "sanctuary cities," where local officials have essentially forbidden their police forces from cooperating with federal immigration authorities—or even, in some cases, following federal law.

I saw similar common ground on the issue of guns. Many skeptical gun owners attended my town hall meetings. They usually had an edge in their voices when they asked me about my position—no doubt a byproduct of the busy NRA activity on behalf of my opponent. But after talking through the issue, I found that many gun owners, even many ardent Second Amendment supporters, were comfortable with the notion of expanding background checks to include arms bought at gun shows. I'd explain that I myself owned more than one gun and, as a result, had to go through a federal background check. I noted that the process generally took no more than a minute and had never prevented me from exercising my constitutional rights. Generally, the same person that asked the question nodded his head in agreement.

But my campaign platform also drew the line in terms of what constituted the "arms" Americans have a right to keep and bear. Most gun owners, acknowledging that when the Framers wrote the Constitution Americans owned muzzle-loaded rifles, were willing to discuss what they had in mind when they wrote it. While we didn't always come to a consensus, I never encountered anyone who thought it made sense for private citizens to own guided missiles. That was a start.

Even on the issue of abortion we found a path forward, and much more of it than the two major political parties would lead you to believe exists. Few, if any, issues are as politically charged as abortion—particularly among Democratic and Republican primary voters. And while I met a lot of pro-life voters and a lot of pro-choice voters on the campaign trail, I didn't meet a single "pro-abortion" voter. Most Americans are more nuanced on this issue than we acknowledge, with a lot of pro-lifers believing that there need to be exceptions (in the case of rape or incest, or to protect the life of the mother) and a lot of pro-choice voters believing there need to be limits (no late-term abortions except to protect the mother).

My own position on the issue was far more complex than Kansans for Life wanted voters to believe. Many of the one-on-one phone calls or meetings that I had with pro-life friends of Sybil's were about this particular issue. They heard lots of rhetoric aimed at me that was troubling to them, and they cared enough about both this issue and their friendship with Sybil to want to speak with me about it directly. I assured them that my position wasn't as callous as Kansans for Life had suggested (Orman favors "late-term abortion on demand," they said), but that I didn't want society to return to a time when women put their own lives in jeopardy by having the procedure in back alleys or other unsanitary venues.

When Bill Clinton ran for president he dealt with this issue by saying that abortion in this country should be "safe, legal, and rare." A conservative critic might maintain that he didn't do anything in office to fulfill the last portion of that three-word promise, but Clinton's instincts were sound. He was where most of the people are—and where they are still. I think an overwhelming majority of Americans agree with the idea that fewer abortions would be a good thing. This shared belief allowed us to have some really constructive conversations on the campaign trail about an issue that few politicians ever seem willing to address without immediately reverting to campaign talking points.

We were able to talk about reducing the number of elective abortions by addressing their root cause: unwanted pregnancies. Most Kansans seemed willing to acknowledge that education, contraception usage, and economic factors were key contributors to the problem. While some wanted to talk exclusively about abstinence-only education, as a general rule, Kansans were open-minded about the measures that we could take to help avoid unwanted pregnancies in the first place and drive down the abortion rate.

These conversations led to a lot of talk about potential solutions. A 2009 initiative in our neighboring state of Colorado had demonstrated the effectiveness of a thoughtful approach to addressing unwanted pregnancies. The program provided free long-term birth control to young women who opted in to it. While most young women use some form of birth control, the methods they were using, while cheaper in terms of up-front cost, also proved to be less reliable. Partly as a result of the program, over the past six years, teen pregnancy rates dropped by 40 percent and abortions dropped by 35 percent in Colorado.[3] I haven't seen an economic analysis of the Colorado program, but one can only assume, based on other data about the uphill battle faced by single teen mothers and their kids, that it ultimately leads to lower levels of poverty, less dependency, and lower crime rates, and that ultimately it will pay for itself many times over.

I chose to highlight these three issues for a reason: They're among the most contentious issues we deal with as Americans. They are at the core of the issues that divide us politically. They are used as litmus test issues in partisan primaries, they get included in most scoring models that are developed to target voters, and they consume a disproportionate amount of campaign mail and are the subject of countless misleading and outright dishonest campaign ads. These issues get all this attention because the two major political parties never stop talking about them—they use them as a tactic to gin up their respective bases—and because the media loves conflict. Yet, as I learned on the campaign trail in Kansas, voters from across the political spectrum were able to come together and move forward toward solutions.

MOVING FROM CAMPAIGN-DRIVEN GRIDLOCK TO REAL SOLUTIONS

If we can find common ground on guns, abortion, and immigration, surely we can find common ground on other important issues as well. On the issue of income inequality, as an example, I have found very few people (even extremely wealthy Americans) who aren't troubled by the lack of income gains made by average Americans over the last two decades. While they sometimes have different perspectives on the root cause of this stagnation, they are almost universally concerned about the calcifying effects of having a permanent underclass, coupled with the overwhelming concentration of wealth in America.

When I spoke in Kansas about the New American Paradox—it's harder than ever for the average American to get ahead, but paradoxically easier to do nothing with your life—Kansans were open to discussing both sides of the phenomenon. We talked about a range of solutions for addressing it. Providing summer learning programs for children in Title I schools, so as to help low-income kids close the achievement gap with high-income kids, was a corner-stone of our approach. With roughly eight million kids in kindergarten through eighth grade in Title I schools, we could pay for this investment if we changed the law in another area—simply making Medicare pay what Medicaid pays for its one hundred most-prescribed drugs.

My campaign also spoke about injecting accountability into our college education funding system. Today, we provide over $100 billion per year in support to make vocational and college education more affordable.[4] Unfortunately, all that support hasn't led to affordability—it's led to inflation. We proposed holding colleges and universities accountable for tuition increases and requiring them to limit increases to the rate of inflation in the general economy if they wanted federal dollars flowing to their institutions. Some Kansans thought that sounded an awful lot like more government involvement in the private sector. After discussing the issue, however, they realized that we should indeed ensure that strings are attached to federal aid to higher education. If a college wanted to raise tuition and fees by more than the rate of inflation, I wasn't proposing to prevent them from doing that. I was, however, requiring that every institution that benefited from taxpayer dollars intended to make higher education more affordable should have to help us accomplish that very goal.

These were just a couple of the many initiatives we discussed that would give American children the key to social mobility: some form of advanced education beyond high school. American businesses are clamoring for more workers with the know-how that colleges and technical programs provide. The high-tech industry regularly advocates for more H1-B visas to bring in high-skilled employees from overseas. My contention is that we can generate those workers from inside our borders if we adjust our policies to prepare students for higher education and then impose some accountability to ensure the dollars we spend to help them afford higher education actually accomplish that goal. Kansans from across the spectrum were open to these ideas and believed they helped accomplish the ideal of creating opportunities for all Americans.

By the same token, we spoke a lot about re-aligning programs for the poor to ensure that they were promoting upward mobility and accountability. Programs that were promoting dependency, I suggested, needed to be dramatically altered or eliminated. Pat Roberts himself gave me a thumbs-up after I said those words at the debate at the Kansas State Fair.

One program in clear need of reform is the Social Security Disability Insurance program. While President Bill Clinton may have "ended welfare as we know it" by signing a welfare reform bill, in part he just shifted the burden to other government programs. In 1996, about five million Americans were receiving SSDI payments each month. Today there are more than twice that many.[5] Clearly, there is significant fraud in the SSDI program. The popular news magazine *60 Minutes* did a program on this last year and described some towns where over 10 percent of the population was on SSDI. The local Walmarts in these towns staff up on the day the payments are made, knowing they will have an influx of customers.

The trust fund that pays for SSDI benefits will start running short on money next year. Republicans have made it clear that they will not support any shifting of funds to pay for it. As a result, average benefit levels are expected to fall by 20 percent. This blunt instrument will affect not only those that are defrauding the program, but also those who genuinely need it. When I discussed this issue on the campaign trail, even the most liberal Kansans realized that without an aggressive effort to root out abuse, we were going to hurt the very people this program was intended to help.

I was careful not to criticize the wealthy when I spoke of income inequality. I was clear that I thought some of the rhetoric around income inequality was not only an attempt to divide Americans, but was also damaging to the poor. Most of the people that I know who would be considered wealthy today got that way by taking risks, working hard, and putting themselves in a position to be successful. Instead of vilifying the "one percent" for having so much wealth, I think it would be more productive to examine the traits that helped them become successful. Viewing success through a jaundiced lens—assuming everyone who is wealthy cut corners, knew the right people, or cheated—makes it too easy to justify one's state in life as being predetermined. It becomes an excuse for failure instead of a blueprint for success. I've seen this lead to an epidemic of low expectations, where social stagnation becomes a self-fulfilling prophecy.

A more productive way of approaching this issue, in my view, entails creating more opportunities for lower income Americans to improve their lives as they confront the challenges presented by globalization. That's why we focused on investing in at-risk kids. With that said, there are a few structural advantages that benefit certain groups of Americans that should be addressed as part of a long-term, comprehensive program to address income inequality. While our tax code imposes the highest income tax rates on top wage earners, we need to examine the tax preferences for investing, which disproportionately benefit the top 1 percent. In terms of picking winners and losers, the tax code says that investing is more valuable than working. Warren Buffet has spoken out about this phenomenon, suggesting he pays a lower tax rate than his secretary.

The justification offered for having lower tax rates for capital gains is that it encourages the formation of new businesses. But are lower capital gains taxes truly a central incentive to entrepreneurship? Having started multiple businesses in my life, I can say with certainty that I never once considered the capital gains tax rate before I took the plunge. And while I've never met Bill Gates or Mark Zuckerberg, when they each weighed the pros and cons of dropping out of Harvard and starting Microsoft and Facebook respectively, I'd bet that the capital gains tax rate didn't factor into their thinking. Equalizing the tax rates between ordinary income and capital gains, carried interest income, and dividends would eliminate that perceived unfairness of taxing work at higher rates than investing.

Many people decry the rising disparity between CEO pay and that of rank and file employees in corporations. According to the Economic Policy Institute, the ratio has increased fifteen-fold over the past fifty years, from 20 to 1 to roughly 300 to 1.[6] In this regard, the United States has the highest CEO-to-average-employee pay ratio in the industrialized world. In 1993 when the government tried to address this with a law that could be easily bypassed, we heard cries of government interference in the legitimate decisions of business. As someone who has spent his life in the private sector, I understand that sentiment. I don't think the government should be telling companies what to pay their CEOs and other top executives. But I do think shareholders should.

Carl Icahn, one of America's most successful investors, has long suggested that there is more democracy in Russia than there is in the boardrooms of American public companies. A way to bridge the gap between those who are offended by high CEO pay and those who think it's none of the government's business is to empower shareholders. Today there's a movement called Say on Pay that's intended to give shareholders the opportunity to vote on executive compensation—but all the votes are non-binding and have no practical effect. What if we were to require such votes to be binding on the company and on the executives themselves? I'm not suggesting we require all shareholders to vote through a formal and expensive proxy contest, but rather requiring that six of the ten largest shareholders of a publicly held company approve executive compensation *in advance* of the company's being bound to pay it. When we discussed this proposal on the campaign trail, even the most ardent supporters of the free market acknowledged that empowering shareholders made sense.

And what about our federal debt? As I mentioned earlier, the overwhelming sentiment among the people I spoke to on the campaign trail was that it was immoral to pass on such a sizable debt burden to future generations. Over the last decade, multiple groups have put together their own solutions to this great challenge. In 2010, the Bipartisan Policy Center assembled a panel of nineteen experts to examine the problem.

Similarly, President Obama impaneled a commission of six Democratic elected officials and six Republican elected officials, as well as six private citizens, to come up with their own recommendations. While these two groups, the Domenici-Rivlin Debt Reduction Task Force and the National Commission on Fiscal Responsibility and Reform (also known as Simpson-Bowles), differed somewhat on the specifics of their proposals, their recommendations were aligned around the big picture. They both also included a combination of spending cuts, including reductions in entitlement spending, and revenue enhancements. Most of the revenue enhancements came from streamlining the tax code, while at the same time lowering overall rates. The appeal of this approach to revenue enhancement is that it lowers the tax compliance burden that most Americans pay to comply with an overly complex tax code. Some have estimated this regulatory burden to cost as much as a quarter of a trillion dollars annually.[7]

Obviously, none of the proposals has seen the light of day. Republicans recoiled at the notion of any revenue enhancement, while Democrats suggested that the caps on spending growth, particularly entitlement spending, were non-starters. Instead of working together and compromising, both sides embraced the status quo, which points to accelerating deficits at the end of the decade and an ocean of red ink all the way to the horizon. My experience running for the Senate in 2014 convinced me that Americans are more open to discussing solutions than our elected leaders.

Meanwhile, the 2016 campaign trail was full of more talk about free college, mass deportations, and vast new foreign policy commitments. What was missing—any serious discussion about addressing our almost $19 trillion national debt. Every first tier Republican candidate, however, had a tax cut plan that will lead to trillions of dollars in new debt.

I spoke a lot about controlling health-care costs, which is one of the keys to controlling our growing federal debt. I believe we have incentives aligned all wrong. While there have been some recent changes as a result of the Affordable Care Act, the law currently covers just a fraction of federal health-care spending, and as a whole the system still pays health-care providers on the basis of the number and type of procedures they perform, regardless of the outcome. The health-care industry is not structured to keep people alive and well. Worse yet, it's not even set up to reward successful patient outcomes. It's set up to keep people paying for health care whether it benefits them or not. Kansans intuitively realized that incentives matter. They also realized that we needed to start addressing some of these issues before they overwhelm our country's capacity to handle them.

A dialogue like the one our campaign had with the voters of Kansas would be nearly impossible for partisan candidates to undertake. Their party labels would get in the way, preventing them from really understanding what voters were saying, particularly if those voters were voicing opinions inconsistent with the prevailing party line. They would revert almost immediately to party talking points or engage in the ever-present town-hall filibuster in which a partisan candidate plays lip service to a voter by empathizing with the voter's question and then pivoting to an attack on his or her opponent.

Many voters would also find it difficult to engage in a constructive problem-solving dialogue with a candidate or officeholder of a party different from theirs. Their filters and conditioning would make it difficult for them to actively listen and seek out common ground. Independents are unique in this regard. As Michael Bloomberg commented when he renounced the duopoly, "As a political Independent, I will continue to work with those in all political parties to find common ground, to put partisanship aside and to achieve real solutions to the challenges we face."[8]

As I mentioned in Chapter 9, our campaign stopped doing most national press interviews in September, but that didn't stop the national and even international media from coming to campaign events. I always enjoyed interacting with the international media, which frankly were less aggressive than our own press and genuinely interested in what we were trying to accomplish. With the exception of a Japanese reporter who inquired what brand of suit I was wearing after Pat Roberts's comment at the Wichita debate, they generally asked relevant questions.

At one point, a reporter from Scandinavia (I don't recall which country) approached Sybil for an interview. Sybil accommodated the reporter and then asked why he was so interested in our race. His comment was telling. He said, "American politics is so interesting—there's so much fighting." He went on to say, "Back home, we agree about almost everything."

In a sense that reporter got it right about American politics. There is a lot of fighting. What he missed in his explanation, however, is that we actually *agree* about a whole lot in America. So why are our politics so divisive? Why is there so much fighting? Why can't we address a whole range of issues where we clearly have common ground and in many cases a strong consensus for change? Why do we allow a small minority of our country to dictate our policies and our path forward as a nation?

The answer to those questions is that it's a confluence of forces: declining voter participation in increasingly partisan primaries leading to more extreme politicians (as we saw in Chapter 5); an American electorate that's more responsive to negative campaigning and programmed to respond to certain messages even if they're untrue (Chapters 5, 6, & 7); powerful financial forces that profit from the status quo and have a vested interest in fomenting continued fighting and gridlock (Chapter 8); a news industry that's sorted itself along partisan lines and has financial incentives to prioritize incendiary commentary and candidates over rationality (Chapter 9); and elected officials who rig the rules to avoid real accountability, demonstrating that they care more about their own futures than the future of our country (Chapter 10).

After the campaign ended, Sybil and I took a short but much-needed vacation. It was hard for me to relax or really enjoy the time away with my wife. I was disappointed with the results of the election, but that wasn't the only thing troubling me. While I couldn't articulate it at the time, later on I was able to formulate what was a challenging and worrisome insight: "I really might not be able to do anything about what's happening to our country."

I had never felt that sort of powerlessness before in my life. I had been energized by my interactions with voters and heartened by the number of people who worked to help us challenge Washington. But as I considered all the forces aligned to thwart any challenge to the status quo, I felt overwhelmed. I realized what we were up against. Then, in May 2015, I looked at Imogen lying in the ICU, a bundle of precious new life entrusting her future to Sybil and to me.

Giving up was no longer an option for me. Nor is it an option for any of us who have high hopes for our next generation, or the generation after that. And we all need to work to enact our hope.

It's going to take a movement of millions of Americans, all of us dedicated to casting off the heavy collar of partisanship and thinking for ourselves, if we are going to accomplish the monumental task of reforming Washington and delivering our children a better nation than the one we inherited.

CHAPTER 12

The Independents' Difference

A COMMON SENSE APPROACH TO
TRANSFORMING WASHINGTON

———— ★ ★ ★ ————

ON ELECTION DAY 2012, Sergey Brin, a co-founder of Google, posted a plaintive entry on his blog. "I must confess, I am dreading today's elections," he wrote, ". . . because no matter what the outcome, our government will still be a giant bonfire of partisanship."

Brin continued, "So my plea to the victors—whoever they might be: Please withdraw from your respective parties and govern as independents in name and in spirit. It is probably the biggest contribution you can make to the country."[1]

Brin's wish was not heeded. Instead, polarization in American politics, already at a twenty-five-year high point, worsened markedly.

In his second term in office, Barack Obama negotiated a binding nuclear arms deal with Iran that no Republican in Congress favored. The administration refused to call it a treaty so as to avoid Senate review and refused to reveal the terms of the agreement until it was signed. The president unilaterally issued policy edicts regarding illegal immigrants that he'd conceded earlier that he lacked constitutional authority to make. He also circumvented Congress by issuing executive orders on gun sales that he'd previously tried to achieve through legislation, spiked the Keystone XL pipeline project (but waited until after the midterm elections to do it), and mocked Republicans who raised concerns about ISIS operatives infiltrating the country—even after a terrorist attack in San Bernardino in which one of the perpetrators was a recent immigrant from the Mideast.

For their part, Republicans not only attempted to thwart Obama's policy directives, which is understandable, they subjected the presidency to a steady barrage of disrespect, which is unforgivable. Forty-seven Republican senators wrote an open letter to Iran's leadership trying to undercut the deal; Republican leaders in the House invited Israeli Prime Minister Benjamin Netanyahu to address Congress without so much as notifying the State Department. Congressional Republicans continued to hold show votes on repealing ObamaCare. When that didn't work, they tried to defund it. When that gambit also failed, they temporarily shut down the federal government. They stalled confirmation of administration appointees, sniped constantly at the president's foreign policy, and—as we discussed earlier—tried to make a campaign issue out of how federal agencies responded to Ebola.

Twice in 2010, Senate Republican leader Mitch McConnell told *National Journal* magazine that his party's goal was to make sure Obama was a one-term president. When Republicans didn't get their wish, they did everything they could think of to undermine him.

All this is why we need independent-minded leaders on Capitol Hill. But it will take voters like you and me to bring that hope to life.

Independence does not necessarily mean belonging to a third party or sharing a particular political ideology. Independence is really a state of mind. It means approaching politics in a third way—not the zero-sum game of partisan politics where one side wins and one side loses. It means solving problems and approaching public service with a different attitude. And while political independence isn't an ideology, solving our problems from an Independent perspective will have a profound impact on the policies of our country. Most importantly, being an Independent means putting our country before any political party.

RESPONDING TO THE NAYSAYERS

Partisans, and many establishment journalists and academics, downplay the significance that 43 percent of Americans identify as politically Independent. The establishment's line of reasoning is that when push comes to shove most voters really do identify with either the Democrats or the Republicans. Their argument is essentially that the number of actual Independents is small, maybe really as little as 10 percent of the population, the rest of them being voters who suggest they are Independent, but really are Democrats or Republicans. They also assert that Independents lack a coherent collective political philosophy.

These observations miss the central point. Of course, most Independents, particularly those who are engaged in the political process, lean one way or the other when it comes to supporting candidates. What choice do they have? After all, they can only vote for the choices before them. That doesn't mean that they are happy with those choices. Independent candidates rarely run for office. For many Independent voters, then, elections are merely exercises in choosing the least bad option.

While millions of Independents find the Republican Party too far to the right and the Democratic Party too far to the left, being an Independent doesn't necessarily mean being a centrist. Yes, millions of political moderates yearn for a third option. What truly sets us Independents apart, however, is not ideological. What sets us apart is that we don't let the duopoly do our thinking for us. I have characterized my own ideology as fiscally responsible and socially tolerant—a description that I believe applies to most Independents. But our movement welcomes principled conservatives and principled liberals—and they need our movement as much as those in the middle.

Why do I say that? Because, as the 2016 presidential primaries revealed, each of the two main political parties offers nothing resembling a coherent political philosophy. As an example, what do libertarians and social conservatives have in common? Beyond possibly sharing a definition of what constitutes fairness, the answer is that they agree on very little, as was evident when Ted Cruz and Rand Paul were on the same stage. The defining tenet of libertarianism is a belief in the rights of the individual to make their own decisions and be left alone. Social conservatives, many of whom are devout Catholics or evangelical Protestants, believe in specific sets of rules for how to live—and many of them want to impose those rules on society. These are fundamentally opposing governing philosophies. Yet, the vast majority of libertarians and social conservatives support the Republican Party.

In the Democratic Party, one of the top two presidential contenders in 2016 was a candidate (Bernie Sanders) who promised primary voters that, as president, he'd break up the big banks. The other, Hillary Clinton, has collected, along with her husband, tens of millions of dollars in speaking fees from Wall Street financial institutions—and much more in campaign donations. While Clinton pivoted mid-campaign in an effort to co-opt much of Sanders's message, this was a conversion of convenience.

In other words, no matter how they portray themselves to voters, the two major parties have large internal disagreements on basic political values. In Chapter 5, we described at length how the two major parties often abandon their stated ideological principles when it suits them politically. I'd actually suggest that this is the difference between having a *brand* (what you've persuaded the world you stand for) and a true *ideology* (a consistency in thought and action). Democrats and Republicans are just brands.

The most significant distinction between the two major parties and political Independents when it comes to how they are organized is simple—Democrats and Republicans see themselves as members of a team. The original reasons are no more important than why some gang members are Crips and others Bloods. Or why some New Englanders root for the Yankees and others for the Red Sox. Once they've chosen their colors, they simply—and fiercely—support the politicians from their team. They've overlooked a whole range of policy differences and, in the end, behave based on what's in the best interests of their side. Having chosen a side, as author Jonathan Haidt has shown, they stop thinking for themselves, which is the same thing as saying they stop thinking. "Once people join a political team," Haidt says, "they see confirmation of their grand narrative everywhere and it's difficult—perhaps impossible—to convince them that they are wrong."[2]

Independents, on the other hand, choose not to organize the same way as the duopoly does. We also have not outsourced our thinking process to a partisan press or a party mentality. While they may not share perfect alignment on policy matters, I believe the vast majority of Independents, along with large number of voters from both major parties, share more than partisans realize.

WE THE PEOPLE: THE SHARED WORLD VIEW OF INDEPENDENTS

Independents hold in common a set of beliefs about America and our leaders.

We believe that our government is broken and is incapable, as currently configured, to help Americans improve their lives.

We believe that our elected leaders no longer tell us the truth and are guided instead by whatever they believe they need to say to get reelected or advance the cause of their team.

We believe that powerful interests control Washington, and that the interests of average Americans are no longer of primary importance to our leaders.

Increasingly, we view politicians from parties as tools of special interests and see the real battle as not being between Democrats and Republicans, but between mainstream America and the ruling political elites.

We also believe the two-party system has failed the country and that our politics needs to be rejuvenated with new citizen leaders who are not career politicians.

"Ordinary people," to use Ross Perot's phrase, intrinsically know that those who enter party politics right out of college as Capitol Hill staffers, work their way up the partisan ladder until they can run for an elective position office, and then stay in office as long as they can, are not what democracy's creators envisioned. One such ordinary American, Karen Cole Huttlinger, wrote *The New York Times* from her Keene Valley, New York, home on May 30, 1989, in response to a Tom Wicker column about corruption in the House of Representatives suggesting that Democrats' long grip on power in Congress (and the Republicans' enduring control of the White House) was a big part of what was wrong in Washington. Wicker, Huttlinger wrote, "seems to have identified only part of what causes corruption of power in government." She identified another problem. "Not only has one party held majority power too long," she wrote, "but the politicians have also served too long." She continued:

> The founders of our system envisioned citizens who would take a leave from their jobs and lives, 'lend' their experience to the business of government and then return to private life. Through career politicians we have allowed a culture of access, influence and self-interest to grow up. By banishing the 'career'

politician and returning to the citizen-politician concept, we can break the power-and-corruption cycle. Limit the number of terms an individual can serve. Develop a nominating and electoral process that encourages citizens to contribute a term of their lives to government. Corruption disclosures should be no surprise. Any pond will stagnate if fresh water doesn't circulate through it.

In his farewell address as president, Ronald Reagan spoke to this ideal. "Ours was the first revolution in the history of mankind that truly reversed the course of government with three little words: 'We the People,'" Reagan said. "'We the People' tell the government what to do; it doesn't tell us. 'We the People' are the driver; the government is the car. And we decide where it should go, and by what route, and how fast."[3]

COMMON INDEPENDENT PRINCIPLES

In addition to sharing a worldview, Independents generally share a set of principles that together constitute a governing philosophy through which we view political decisions:

1. We believe first and foremost in the sacred social contract that is the foundation of the American Idea—that we leave a better country for future generations. That belief confers upon every American an obligation to give more to our great nation than we have taken from it. Call it the John F. Kennedy inaugural challenge. This shared purpose and responsibility is at the heart of the American Idea. We cannot be the first generation of Americans to have failed this test. We believe, as a result, that it is immoral to burden future generations with unreasonable debt.

2. Independents put the interests of our country ahead of the interests of a political party—not the other way around. Aligned with neither major party, we are not obliged to march lockstep with the partisan thinking that drives them into opposite ideological corners—or with the special interests that financially support, and increasingly control, Republicans and Democrats.

3. Independents don't share a strict political ideology, but rather, we believe that common sense is indispensable in the problem-solving process. Independents view political issues the way those running a business seek to ensure its success: understanding all sides, embracing facts, identifying root causes, and ultimately trying to make logical decisions.

4. We believe that America is an exceptional nation, because of its founding principles: equality, freedom, self-government, and the opportunity for self-betterment. Independents don't want government to dictate outcomes or pick winners and losers through their policies. Instead, we believe that Americans who work hard and play by the rules should be able to improve their station in life. We consider social mobility one of the defining characteristics of American life and one that serves to rejuvenate and energize our nation. As a result, we favor government actions that encourage, rather than stifle, equal opportunity in America.

5. We think transparency and fairness are absolutely essential to having accountable government that serves the people of this country. We believe that a political process corrupted by special interests, a duopoly that avoids accountability, and a get-elected-at-all-costs ethic have rendered our government incapable of addressing the genuine needs of the American people. Only through reforms that increase accountability and transparency and alter the incentives of elected officials will we be able to fix America.

6. We believe our political discourse needs to be based on facts and the truth, not spin and lies. The absence of intellectual honesty in our political life, from politicians, the media, and outside political spending, has allowed our challenges to grow and corruption to take root.

These principles lead us to believe that the only way we can put our nation back on a sustainable path is first to reform our broken politics.

THE INDEPENDENT APPROACH

The biggest single factor that differentiates Independents from political partisans is that we aren't party drones who unthinkingly adhere to a party position on an issue just because it's branded by an elephant or a donkey. Or maybe more precisely, we don't oppose a policy position simply because it was thought up by the "other side." We recognize that political support shouldn't be reflexive, like rooting for your favorite college football team. We don't need to adhere to the duopoly's false-choice paradigm. Partisanship is not a disease, exactly, but it's a debilitating condition that impairs one's ability to reason. Independence is the cure.

Without sacred cows and the "third rails" of untouchable party positions, Independents can think about a problem objectively and creatively. The Independent approach to solving problems involves first seeking to understand all points of view around an issue. Independents don't automatically assume others have bad intentions. We don't vilify or demonize people for their points of view. In fact, we believe that diversity of thought is a powerful lever in problem solving. We embrace intellectual conflict as a way to get to the right answer.

Independents understand that the key to solving a problem is to understand its root cause. We realize that sometimes the solution to a problem isn't obvious or transparent or based on some quick sound-bite or piece of schoolyard logic. Actually solving a problem requires understanding more than just its symptoms.

Independents also aren't allergic to facts—we embrace them. We're willing to change our minds when new information indicates that our prior position was incorrect, or when realities change over time. This doesn't mean we lack conviction. It means we are committed to fact-based problem solving and don't behave like stubborn children by insisting we're right despite strong evidence to the contrary.

The ideology of an Independent is what I believe is the ideology of America: Common Sense.

President Theodore Roosevelt, in a pamphlet published in 1916, describes the qualities he believes are crucial for individuals and nations alike. "There are many qualities which we need in order to gain success," he wrote, "but the three above all—for the lack of which no brilliancy and no genius can atone—are Courage, Honesty and Common Sense."[4]

That last trait, common sense, runs through Roosevelt's presidential speeches and writings. It's a phrase that appears twenty-four times in his own collection of speeches.[5]

But we don't need to consult the first part of the twentieth century to find a prominent politician to make that point. "Any successful elected executive knows that real results are more important than partisan battles and that good ideas should take precedence over rigid adherence to any particular political ideology,"[6] said Mike Bloomberg, as he announced his independence from the two-party system.

AN INDEPENDENT AGENDA

Given the lack of progress in Washington, D.C., over the last two decades, there are clearly a number of issues we need to address, many of which have been touched on throughout this book. Washington's hyper-partisanship and gridlock make it unlikely that meaningful progress will occur on any of those issues, until we confront the root cause of the problem. Where do we begin? We start with genuine political reform that changes incentives and takes the "For Sale" sign off of our government.

I'd propose that Independents work toward reforming how members of Congress can make money once they leave government. We also need to push for reforming how federal campaigns in the country are bankrolled.

We need to start by imposing a lifetime ban on lobbying for members of Congress. Today, members, when they retire or lose their offices, are prohibited from lobbying their former colleagues for one year if they served in the House of Representatives and two years if they served in the Senate. The rationale for this is intuitive and simple: Congress shouldn't be a stepping-stone to a six- or seven-figure job lobbying your former colleagues. Altering this incentive to please a potential future employer should change the decisions that Congress makes and potentially alter the make-up of Congress altogether, as those who view the position as an interim step to lobbying will be discouraged from running for office.

We should also prohibit members of Congress from setting up leadership PACs. We discussed these vehicles in Chapter 8. They are nothing more than slush funds that members of Congress can use to spend on just about anything. Ninety-nine percent of the money for them comes from lobbyists and special interests. They represent a $60 million annual bribe from lobbyists to Congress.

Finally, we should eliminate the congressional pension system and replace it with a 401(k) to eliminate the incentive for people to stay in Congress for their entire working lives. I don't want to punish members of Congress or make it impossible for anyone other than the wealthy to serve. With $174,000 annual salary, along with generous perks and privileges, members of Congress will do just fine. They shouldn't, however, get the kind of benefit plan that has largely disappeared for average Americans. This is in some ways a symbolic gesture, as it will likely save the government very little money. But it sends a strong message that public service should intersect your life's path for a brief time, not consume it.

To create campaign finance reform, our first goal needs to be to have 100 percent transparency in all political spending. To paraphrase former Supreme Court justice Louis Brandeis, "Sunlight is the best disinfectant." All political spending should be reported during a campaign's cycle, regardless of the type of entity that does the donating. To the extent that spending is done through shell companies or other intermediate organizations, the ultimate financial donor needs to be revealed. In effect, we should impose the same requirements on super PACs and 501(c)4 dark money vehicles as we impose on the candidates and the campaigns themselves.

Some members of Congress have worked hard recently to make sure this reform doesn't happen. In the recently passed Omnibus Bill, a provision was put in to handcuff the Securities and Exchange Commission from requiring that public companies disclose their political spending. SEC requirements would have been one potential avenue to getting that information if the dark money organizations weren't going to disclose the information themselves. While Congress pays lip service to the notion of transparency, it hasn't followed through on those sentiments since the Supreme Court unleashed unlimited spending on the American electorate.

Next, we should alter the composition of the Federal Election Commission to add three nonpartisan members. The current FEC dynamic, with three Democrats and three Republicans, is just an invitation for members of the duopoly to violate campaign finance laws. While this measure wouldn't stop the duopoly from rigging the rules when it suits both parties (around the Commission on Presidential Debates, for example), it would significantly increase the likelihood that campaign finance violations would be prosecuted. Three nonpartisan members would energize the commission and likely improve compliance significantly. They would help make the limited laws that we have related to campaign finance significantly more impactful.

Finally, we should empower Americans to participate in the electoral process by giving them a $500 tax credit for making federal campaign donations. This is a position I've come to reluctantly, as I believe the tax code is overly complicated and should be thoroughly streamlined. Unfortunately, until we can take away the power of special interests, we'll never be able to truly control spending in Washington. Encouraging average Americans to participate in the financing of political campaigns could dilute the impact and influence of these dark money vehicles and restore some balance to politics.

While I would far prefer to change campaign finance laws to eliminate super PAC and 501(c)4 expenditures, doing so would require the Supreme Court to revisit a series of verdicts or a constitutional amendment. I hope this happens, but don't believe we should rely on the courts to change our system of campaign finance. The six changes I've suggested above can all be accomplished legislatively. As with any measures that require the consent of the victims (and believe me, many politicians in Washington would view themselves as victims if these changes were enacted), there will be significant opposition. But it would be hard for candidates from either party to publically oppose the changes without coming across as protecting our corrupt system, particularly if Independent Americans joined together to demand them.

These measures wouldn't create a better-functioning government overnight, but they would be a step toward removing corrupting influences from Washington and eliminating some of the perverse incentives of public service. I also believe that, as part of an Independent agenda for America, these initial reforms would send voters a strong message about what Independents really stand for.

ON THE LOOKOUT FOR GENUINE INDEPENDENTS

Over the past year, I've spoken with dozens of potential candidates who are considering running for public office as Independents. In races from state capitals to the presidency, more committed Americans are considering the Independent path to office. They realize that our government is trapped in a quagmire of partisan dysfunction and, while they want to serve their fellow citizens, they don't want to be subsumed by a poisonous environment.

The first challenge for many of these potential candidates is understanding how difficult it is to run a race as an Independent. They look at the support that a political party provides and see that path as an easier one. Some have even asked me if they could run as a Democrat or Republican, but present themselves to voters as an Independent. They see political Independence as a campaign slogan and not a state of mind governed by a set of beliefs. My obvious answer to that question is, "no, you can't run as a major party candidate and expect to go to Washington and behave as an Independent."

This does, however, raise the question, what does it take to be a successful Independent candidate? The best Independent candidates will have the qualities of any good candidate. They will have a track record of success in whatever area of life they pursued prior to public service. They won't have engaged in any "disqualifying" behavior in the past. They will have a clear vision for why they want to be in Washington, D.C., and that vision will have nothing to do with the perks and the privileges of the office. In short, Independent candidates need to be vetted just like any other candidate.

There are, however, two absolute requirements for Independent candidates. The first is that they be truly unaligned with either of the two major political parties. You can't be truly Independent and owe your election to a party. Being unbeholden to the duopoly allows Independents to tell the truth and embrace the best policy ideas regardless of who came up with them and to negotiate with all sides in search of the best solutions. Independents aren't concerned with "who" gets the credit, Republicans or Democrats; we're simply concerned with doing the right thing for the country.

The second requirement is that Independent candidates must be unencumbered by obligations to special interests. This means rejecting all direct contributions from lobbyists and political action committees. When a lobbyist or a PAC hands a candidate a check, they expect something in return. To be truly Independent a candidate can't feel an obligation to a special interest. "When you go to Washington these days, you can feel a sense of fear in the air, the fear to do anything or say anything that might affect the polls or give the other side the advantage or offend a special interest group," is how Mike Bloomberg described it. "The federal government isn't out front—it's cowering in the back of the room."[7] The most disturbing part of Bloomberg's comment about our current predicament is his observation of how fearful our country's elected leaders have become. Personal ambition, and the calculations and machinations that go along with it, have always been a part of our politics. But the cowering he describes is almost un-American.

I mentioned John F. Kennedy's inaugural address earlier, and how he challenged his fellow countrymen to go to the moon precisely because it was hard. Another part of that speech came to mind when I heard Mike Bloomberg's comments.

"We dare not forget today that we are the heirs of that first revolution," Kennedy said, invoking the founders of our country. "Let the word go forth from this time and place, to friend and foe alike, that the torch has been passed to a new generation of Americans," JFK added. "Let every nation know, whether it wishes us well or ill, that we shall pay any price, bear any burden, meet any hardship, support any friend, oppose any foe to assure the survival and the success of liberty."

That obligation, as JFK noted in his speech, begins here at home. Pay *any* price, the man said. Bear *any* burden . . . to assure the success of liberty. That's our legacy as Americans, and our responsibilities as citizens. If Democrats and Republicans have shirked their duty, a new generation of Independents must carry the torch.

Declare your Independence!

THINKING AND VOTING
LIKE AN INDEPENDENT

——— ★ ★ ★ ———

IN FEBRUARY 1861, ABRAHAM Lincoln left his home in Springfield and headed to Washington, D.C., to confront the greatest crisis ever to threaten the survival of America. His train stopped in towns along the way, where the president-elect made impromptu remarks. In Indianapolis he voiced a theme that echoed throughout his journey: "I, as already intimated, am but an accidental instrument, temporary, and to serve but for a limited time, but I appeal to you again to constantly bear in mind that with you, and not with politicians, not with presidents, not with office-seekers, but with you, is the question, 'Shall the Union and shall the liberties of this country be preserved to the latest generation?'"[1]

While I've been highly critical of the ruling elite and the special interests that keep them in power, this book really isn't about them. It's about us. It's about you and me and all the other Americans who care deeply about this country. Our elected officials in Washington only maintain their power because we allow them to. Either by virtue of our blind adherence to partisan politics or by our abdicating our responsibility to participate, we are tacitly turning over our country to this group of self-servants.

Changing this won't be easy. Wresting power away from those who have it is always difficult. The two ruling parties have dug themselves in deeply, rigging the rules, dividing the country in two, pitting one side against the other. The media has been complicit in this process, picking sides and ultimately buying into the dubious narrative of the entrenched duopoly, that anyone who doesn't conform to the red/blue paradigm is a spoiler, or dishonest, or just plain crazy. Fortified by the Supreme Court's *Citizens United* decision and other enabling court rulings, companies, industries, and individuals with an interest in preserving the status quo now have the tools at their disposal to buy our government.

Our elected leaders, thoroughly co-opted, behave as if they're allergic to courage and devoid of free thought. They have lost the moral authority to ask citizens for their service and sacrifice and merely ask them for their price. The ways they campaign—and how they vote once they are elected—are carefully calibrated to facilitate reelection, but undermine their ability to govern. In the process, they have divided over half our country into warring camps, with each side blind to the common ground that exists for those with the courage and the intelligence to look for it.

Sometimes one warring camp wins, and sometimes the other warring camp claims victory. In reaction to stagnation and incompetence, since 1992 voters have switched control of Congress from Democrats to Republicans and back again, twice. The White House has been occupied by a Democrat, a Republican, and then another Democrat. But no matter which side wins, we Americans lose. We haven't seen any fundamental change in the long-term direction of our country. Millions of people are living in limbo within our borders. Our entitlement-driven budget deficit continues to careen out of control. The national debt has reached historic highs. Wages haven't come close to keeping up with the cost of living for average Americans as child-care costs, higher education costs, and health-care costs have all skyrocketed.

My belief, supported by the last two decades, is that changing from Democrats to Republicans or vice-versa will do very little to improve the lives of Americans. We need to introduce real accountability into the electoral process and start electing Independents. The vision of an Independent America, an America that works again, is within our reach. We have the numbers. If we want to lift every American, preserve the middle class, and have another century of American leadership in the world, it is imperative that we accomplish that vision.

Yes, the challenge is daunting. But there has never been a better time to change America. With social media and other online tools, it's easier than ever to identify and organize like-minded people. And while Democrats and Republicans retain their organizational advantage, a coordinated, focused effort on the part of Independents and disillusioned Democrats and Republicans could indeed take hold.

The existing parties enjoy a clear financial advantage, but money isn't votes. Their cash can buy them airtime and campaign consultants to enable their misleading and reprehensible attacks, and they can perform all kinds of analysis to determine precisely what you want to hear or what words will move you to act or stay home or do whatever it is they want you to do. But they can't go into that voting booth with you. That's where our power is.

Forty-three percent of Americans profess to be politically Independent, but I believe our potential ranks are much larger. I'm convinced that the great majority of Americans, regardless of party or ideological affiliation, are united in their demand for a transformation of the nation's political life. Indeed, the last time there was such unanimity of opinion on the need to reassert the people's sovereignty we declared our independence from a monarchy.

It's time to declare our independence again: Independence from the corrupt politics as usual. Independence from a broken political system more interested in fighting each other in Washington, D.C., than working for the people of America. Independence from do-nothing partisanship. Independence from both political parties and their joint hold on our collective imagination and capacity to solve problems.

Bob Dole wasn't critically wounded in the mountains of Italy for the Republican Party. He bled there for America—driven by the belief that his sacrifice was necessary for our freedoms to be preserved for an America that endures and prevails. John McCain didn't sit in the Hanoi Hilton, broken in body but not in spirit, to secure a Republican majority in the Senate. John Kerry didn't risk his life running months of missions up the Mekong River Delta and earn three purple hearts to advance the cause of the Democratic Party.

They, and countless others on battlefields, gave of themselves out of a belief that this country was worth dying for, if need be. We honor veterans today in many ways: tipping our cap at sporting events, giving up our seats on airplanes, saying to them directly, "Thank you for your service." A more lasting way to show our gratitude is to work to once again ensure that our politics is worthy of their sacrifice.

OUR INTERESTS, OUR VOICES

I spoke at length in our campaign about how electing Independents could alter our nation's political discourse and governance. I decided to run for the Senate not just to win but to govern. I didn't want to campaign in a way that would have prevented me from having an impact if I was elected. I outlined our governing strategy on the campaign trail, and by the time the race wound to a close I could explain its rationale in a few sentences:

Today I am going to state the conviction that is the foundation of my candidacy. If elected, no matter how I vote to organize the Senate, I do not intend to be a silent soldier for either the Democrats or Republicans in the Senate. I am going to stand for a better way, a new course in the Senate, and work with Senators of any party who are willing to stand for commonsense real solutions to our problems. I will stand not with the partisans and the politicians but with the people of Kansas who say enough is enough.

I intend to appeal to others who have been elected as Independents and have been subsumed by the caucus system to join with me in creating a new balance of power that represents the interest and the voice of the American people.

It is my belief that beyond that there are also Senators in both parties who are frustrated and dismayed at being imprisoned in the caucus system who would welcome the opportunity to become part of a new problem-solving coalition in the Senate. And I am not going to Washington to speak Republican or Democrat. It is time to start speaking American.

My hope was that my election would have been a catalyst for more Independents to run and win in 2016. In the years ahead, I want that goal to be achieved. If for the past century Democrats and Republicans have been dedicated to getting reelected, then we Independents can be equally dedicated and equally rational in our pursuit of victory in the next decade.

Imagine for a moment what our country would be like if we did more than just elect one or two Independent senators. Imagine if we had a country where Independent voters and Independent elected officials held just as much sway in Washington as Republicans or Democrats. The way Washington is governed and the way candidates approached elections could change forever.

Imagine elections with more credible choices than simply the duopoly's cookie-cutter candidates. With more options, voters might actually gravitate to the Independent candidate. Our corrupt campaign finance system would be upended. Dark money organizations could no longer attack a single opponent in a race with a belief that they could build their candidate up just by knocking down the opposition; their targeted attack ads would have the unintended consequence of helping a third candidate. These organizations might actually have to start running positive ads, building up their preferred candidate. Fear and dishonest attacks wouldn't disappear from our political discourse, but they might fade a little bit, as the number of positive ads would increase. Imagine, finally, the most likely result of having credible Independent candidates: election campaigns that become more hopeful, uplifting, and issue-oriented. The duopoly's candidates and their super PAC supporters would be forced to follow our lead and to make more compelling arguments for their own candidacies instead of simply tearing down the "other" party.

The way Washington operates would change. Problem solving and solution seeking would prevail. Party politicians who genuinely want Washington to get back to work would be liberated to make policy. Those who simply want to engage in show votes and failure theater would find themselves actually having to account for their time in Washington, D.C. Independents could enforce a form of binding arbitration, one requiring Democrats and Republicans to present their best solution to a problem and agreeing to choose between them. The best ideas of the Republicans and the best ideas of the Democrats would no longer be buried in partisan graves. Independents would gravitate to those superior policy solutions, improve them, and get behind them. They would give the real thinkers in both parties the political support with the media and with voters to enact real legislation. Some of those solutions might be principled compromises between Democrats and

Republicans. Others might be ideas that the constrained thinking of partisan politics never imagined.

Most importantly, we'd be sending a message to partisan politicians everywhere that they can't go to Washington and simply hide behind their party label, they have to get something done. They have to start working for the American people again.

Our media would change as well. No longer would the talking heads simply have a Democrat and a Republican arguing in party-approved talking points on their shows. An Independent would be sitting alongside them, objectively pointing out the merits and the drawbacks of a particular proposal. Partisans wouldn't simply be arguing each other to a draw.

Could Independent candidates win elections in large enough numbers, and could they make a difference once in office? No, not if the two major parties have anything to say about it—and yes, if newly empowered, independent-minded voters have their way. Our adversaries have spent decades conditioning the electorate to believe that there are only two options when it comes to our politics. Independents or minor party candidates are portrayed as fringe players or spoilers—as if the only people who are competent to lead are Democrats or Republicans. The intent is to create a viability deficit—to make people believe that they are wasting their votes if they cast them for someone whose face isn't painted in tribal red or blue.

Americans are slowly, but surely, rejecting the major parties and open to new choices. The parties and pundits, presented with the reality that voters are leaving the duopoly in droves, try to downplay the defections. But they can't ignore the truth forever and still remain viable politically. And the truth is that Americans are fundamentally dissatisfied with their leadership.

Our ultimate goal should be to get to the point where credible

Independent candidates are running for every federal office in the United States. That's a tall order and will take years, even decades. Only by expanding the choices that voters have and challenging the status quo will we be able to get government working again. Without fundamental reforms and a shift in the people who represent us—from career, partisan politicians to true public servants—Washington will never be able to regain the trust of the American people.

In short, we need a battalion of Mr. Smiths and Ms. Smiths who are willing to go to Washington together to fix a system that no longer works for the American people. And we will need an army of empowered voters to send them there—voters like you.

If you're a disaffected voter and have stopped participating in the electoral process out of disgust or a belief that you can't make a difference, I hope you re-engage. I hope you realize how opting out of the process is precisely the response the political elites want you to make. If they can't control whom you vote for through partisan allegiance, they certainly don't want you voting unpredictably. As the founder of the Centrist Project, Charlie Wheelan, said to me, "We can't react to our broken politics the same way we respond to a bad restaurant." Not participating won't force bad politicians out of Washington the same way it can force a bad restaurant to close.

This is particularly important for millennials. As our country continues to neglect a whole range of strategic issues, from income inequality to stagnant wages to an unsustainable entitlement system to climate change, it's your generation that will ultimately be saddled with these issues. There's an old saying, "if you're not at the table, you're on the menu." Right now, given the low voter participation rates from millennials, your generation is not only on the menu—it is the menu!

If you're a disaffected Democrat or Republican, I'd love for you to join the ranks of political Independents. I realize that's a big ask. But my hope is that you realize you're not alone. Millions of Americans have come to the realization that their party left them, not the other way around. I've watched many lifelong Republicans and Democrats struggle to accept what their respective parties have become. It's like a family home that you've lived in for decades that is crumbling to the core from termite damage. While the home is replete with great memories and special moments, it's not a place where you can live.

If you're not yet ready to become an Independent, I'd encourage you to re-engage in your party's primary election process and exercise your Independent judgment within your party. In almost every congressional district, the primary is the election that matters the most. As independent-minded voters return to the voting booth in the primaries, candidates will be forced to consider their views and eschew the partisanship and extremism of those who choose their party's candidates.

If you're thinking about running for office as an Independent, I will cheer you on. My advice is to ignore the doubters. Pay no attention to those who tell you that your campaign will only spoil the race for one of the parties. Whoever said that only individuals who wear the label of one of two parties are entitled to serve? It certainly wasn't the nation's founders—they didn't like or trust political parties. While I believe there is a path to victory for Independents, spoiling the race for one party or the other isn't necessarily a bad thing, if it makes elected officials more responsive to the needs of voters.

In April of 2014, as I was considering my Senate run, I attended an event for a local Kansas City organization called Mind Drive. The program helped at-risk kids by coupling them with adult mentors as they worked together to build an electric vehicle. At this meeting, the organization's largest benefactor, a local businessman named Phil Kirk, got up to speak. Phil was terminally ill. In describing his commitment to Mind Drive, Phil said he didn't want to leave this world knowing that "when the challenge presented itself, I didn't show up." Phil showed up. I think we all need to show up.

Running for office is a daunting task. Many patriotic and competent Americans, who would make great elected leaders, find other ways to fulfill their need to show up, to give something back. They understand that politics can be ugly and that the price of participation includes repeated slurs against their reputation. As someone who went through that process, however, I can tell you a year after the fact that the damage is temporary and the payoff permanent. While some people chose to believe the drivel your opponents dish out, generally they aren't the people close to you or those you work with—or people you respect. Sybil and I still face an occasional voter who gives us a mean look or shouts "Democrat!" as if it's a racial slur, but there are far more people who approach us and thank us for running and trying to change Washington.

Theodore Roosevelt may have said it best. It is not the critic who counts the most, he said, not the person who carps how "the doer of deeds could have done them better." The credit, Roosevelt said, goes to the person "actually in the arena, whose face is marred by dust and sweat and blood; who strives valiantly; who errs, who comes short again and again, because there is no effort without error and shortcoming."[2]

If you're an independent-minded voter who is just waiting for others to join you, don't lose hope. There was a day in June of 1992 when Ross Perot led Bill Clinton and George Bush in the general election polls. A majority of Americans were dissatisfied with President Bush and viewed Clinton as an inadequate alternative. If the election were held that day, almost 40 percent of Americans polled said they would cast their ballot for an Independent. It was an unprecedented showing of support for a candidate who stood distinctly apart from the two major parties. While Perot ended up getting just under 19 percent of the popular vote on Election Day, as we've seen, his finishing third was more a product of his departure from the race during the summer of 1992 than a function of voters rejecting his message.

The conditions are riper today for Independents than they were in 1992. More Americans are dissatisfied with Washington, D.C., and more have come to understand that the real choice is not between Democrats and Republicans. The real choice is between preserving a broken political system that does not work for the people and that is allowing the greatness of America to slip away—or choosing a new kind of politics that says new leadership can rejuvenate both the people's sovereignty and our nation's future.

If you choose the latter, please go to my website, www.ideclare.us, and join the movement. The transformation of our nation's political life won't happen without the dedication of millions of Americans and the commitment of a small but purposeful group to lead the charge. How much you do is entirely up to you, but it starts with letting like-minded Independents know that you stand with each other.

Finally, regardless of whether or not you are a political Independent, I ask you to recommit to the power of the independent mind. I realize we've all developed a little bit of a shorthand to understand what candidates stand for based on their party label. As I've tried to show in this book, however, much of that is misleading at best. As we've explored in the previous chapters, you can hone your political thinking to reject the false choices of the two-party system, embrace common sense, and think through issues for yourself.

ACT WORTHY OF YOURSELVES

In his first inaugural speech, Ronald Reagan spoke of a man who might have become one of the most renowned of the Founding Fathers, Dr.

Joseph Warren, president of the Massachusetts Congress, whose greatness would be cut short in the Battle of Bunker Hill where he served as a simple soldier. On the eve of that battle, Warren said to his fellow Americans, "Our country is in danger, but not to be despaired of . . . On you depend the fortunes of America. You are to decide the important questions upon which rests the happiness and the liberty of millions yet unborn. Act worthy of yourselves."[3]

Will our children's and grandchildren's generations have the opportunities that are their rightful inheritance? This inheritance has been passed on by every generation, including our parents and grandparents. Now we are summoned to fulfill our obligation to the future.

Will America continue to provide leadership for the rest of the free world or will our dysfunction at home impair our ability to stand for progress globally? Will we move the world in a direction of growth, opportunity, and human rights for all, or will we allow the forces of human despair to prevail?

Our ability to live up to our potential as a nation is not merely a political issue—something to put on a bumper sticker. It is a moral issue, one we can no longer leave to the partisans and the politicians. It's an obligation that we, as citizens of our great nation, have to accept as our own, as the implicit price of the freedoms and opportunities that are essential to the American Idea that defines and empowers us. I genuinely believe we can rise up once again and demonstrate that our greatness comes from the unyielding spirit and endless capacity of our people to meet any challenge.

My belief begins with you.

ACKNOWLEDGMENTS

I'VE BEEN WRITING THIS book in my head for over fifteen years. In 2001, I started writing a book tentatively entitled *Good Politics Is Bad Policy*. My goal was to identify many of the issues that we would be facing as a nation in the twenty-first century that we were ill prepared to address because we were still focused on the problems of the twentieth century. I wanted to pull back the curtain on the forces that were preventing us from solving those 20th-century problems and lay them bare for everyone to see.

I suspect a number of the conclusions that I would have drawn in *Good Politics Is Bad Policy* would have been similar to the conclusions that I've drawn here. What would have been missing is the perspective that comes from having run for office in Kansas and being able to talk to my fellow citizens about issues that mattered to them. Without our campaign, there would be no book.

Running for the U.S. Senate was genuinely the honor of a lifetime. I thank the voters of Kansas who took my campaign seriously and allowed me to participate in our representative democracy. Without their willingness to look beyond Red and Blue and take the candidacy of an unknown Independent seriously, I wouldn't have gained the perspective and experience that shaped this book and will always guide my opinions on our country.

Our campaign also relied on hundreds of volunteers who took to the phones, gathered signatures, knocked on doors, delivered yard signs, made buttons, attended rallies, and went out of their way to make sure our message reached as many Kansans as possible. Many people opened their homes to Sybil and me, organized events, and put their reputations on the line to publically endorse me. Others spent hours every day volunteering their time to stand up for my candidacy on social media, in the comment sections of newspapers, and with their friends and neighbors. More than a handful endured angry criticism from people who weren't able to escape their partisan filters. For some, our campaign literally took over their lives. On election night, I declared that the greatest surprise of the campaign was the number of people who gave our campaign their time, talents, and treasure to help us change America. To them I will be forever grateful.

I also need to acknowledge everyone who worked so hard to lift our campaign beyond the traditional boundaries of an Independent candidacy. While I've only mentioned a few of them by name in the book, I am deeply appreciative for all the work done by my campaign staff. By September of 2014, as our campaign was entering its final phase, even though they were significantly outmanned by the other side, our team worked tirelessly in the service of giving Kansans a real option to the status quo in Washington, D.C.

I couldn't have written this book without the help and advice of Carl Cannon, who guided me through much of the process and expanded my view of recent events to put them into a broader, historical context. Carl's perspective on the motivations of the political class and his insight into their behaviors added an important dimension to this book.

I'm also grateful for the input and perspective that Pat Caddell lent to this effort. Pat's deep understanding of the political process was invaluable in explaining why the electorate is so dissatisfied with our government. More importantly, Pat helped me to find my voice during the campaign and put into words what was at stake during the election. Finally, I'm indebted to David Groff for his help in sharpening the arguments in the book to increase its impact.

I want to acknowledge and thank my family, who always believed in me and my campaign. My dad, Tim Orman, walked with me in almost every parade, drove our campaign bus, gathered signatures, and tried to persuade anyone who walked into his furniture store to vote for his son. My mother, Darlene Gates, made phone calls and knocked on doors, even though she was nervous during every encounter. My mother-in-law, Seana Niccum, drove her pick-up truck in every parade, fearlessly knocked on hundreds of doors and gathered hundreds of signatures, and installed yard signs regardless of the weather. My stepmother, Debbie, helped organize rallies and made sure my bus tour campaign finale was a success. My nine siblings, Mike, Lisa, Michelle, David, Jackie, McKenzie, Ben, Maddi, and Maureen, all participated in the campaign at varying points—gathering signatures, commenting on articles, organizing events, and calling voters from wherever they were. My uncle Gary, despite his strong Republican roots, supported me throughout the process and worked the phones during the last days of the campaign to encourage Kansans to vote for me. Mike Harrison, Sybil's surrogate father, who spent ten hours a day defending me on social media, shared bus driving duty with my father, and advocated for me at every turn.

Most importantly, I want to thank my wife, Sybil. Without her tireless support and encouragement, I never would have had the courage to step into the arena. I couldn't ask for a better partner on the campaign trail or in life.

APPENDIX: A RESOURCE GUIDE

IF YOU ARE LOOKING for further reading on the topics discussed in *A Declaration of Independents*, there are a number of books I recommend. Many of them I referred to throughout the book, and they clearly had an influence on my thinking and writing on issues ranging from being a political Independent to exploring centrism and consensus, and forging new and workable policies on health care and other issues. The books listed here that I have not mentioned in these pages are equally thought provoking.

The Big Sort: Why the Clustering of Like-Minded America is Tearing Us Apart, by Bill Bishop. Mariner Books, 2009.

The Centrist Manifesto, by Charles Wheelan. Norton, 2013.

Deadly Spin: An Insurance Company Insider Speaks Out on How Corporate PR is Killing Health Care and Deceiving Americans, by Wendell Potter. Bloomsbury, 2011.

Disconnect: The Breakdown of Representation in American Politics, by Morris Fiorina. University of Oklahoma Press, 2009.

Health Care Will Not Reform Itself: A User's Guide to Refocusing and Reforming American Health Care, by George C. Halvorson. Productivity Press, 2009.

How We Do Harm: A Doctor Breaks Ranks About Being Sick in America, by Otis Webb Brawley, M.D. St. Martin's Griffin, 2012.

Independent Nation: How Centrism Can Change American Politics, by John Avlon. Three Rivers Press, 2005.

Overtreated—Why Too Much Medicine is Making Us Sicker and Poorer, by Shannon Brownlee. Bloomsbury, 2008.

The Parties Versus the People: How to turn Republicans and Democrats into Americans, by Mickey Edwards. Yale University Press, 2013.

The Righteous Mind: Why Good People Are Divided By Religion and Politics, by Jonathan Haidt. Vintage, 2013.

Seeing Gray in a World of Black and White: Thoughts on Religion, Morality, and Politics, by Adam Hamilton. Abingdon Press, 2012.

In Chapter 2, I touched on my belief that the public sector could learn a great deal from the private sector's approach to solving problems. Over the course of my business career, I developed a framework for solving problems that was driven by my experience running companies. The stories of those experiences were cut from the text as we worked to focus the arguments in the book. One of the rules in my approach to problem solving is to focus on the root cause of a specific problem at hand.

As we look at the problems with our political environment, we can find a number of innovative organizations that are attacking the root causes of our political dysfunction. The first draft of *A Declaration of Independents* also contained significant references to these organizations that have taken creative approaches to reforming our political process. Most broadly, these organizations are addressing one of three root causes of our political dysfunction. They are focused on either: (i) encouraging more productive behavior from Democrats and Republicans, (ii) creating pathways to a new supply of leaders who are neither Democrats nor Republicans, or (iii) promoting more centrist policies. Interestingly, many of the organizations that are promoting more centrist policies have started to migrate towards creating pathways to a new supply of leaders as they have come to conclude that political reform is a necessary step towards policy reform.

Many of these organizations have had a profound effect on the evolution of my thinking. And while they are all approaching different aspects of the problem in our politics, they all fundamentally want the same thing—a Washington that works. I list and describe some of them here. The good news is this is by no means an exhaustive list. There are a lot of people working hard on solving our country's problems.

ENCOURAGING MORE PRODUCTIVE BEHAVIOR

No Labels

One of the groups focused on getting Democrats and Republicans to work together is an organization called No Labels. No Labels has been instrumental in putting the notion of problem solving front and center in the political reform movement. They have assembled an incredibly impressive leadership team, led by former Utah Governor Jon Huntsman and former U.S. Senator from Connecticut Joe Lieberman. As part of its work, No Labels has created a Problem Solving Caucus in Congress.

The organization's current strategy is to get Republicans and Democrats alike to focus on a shared set of goals for our country. In its National Strategic Agenda, No Labels has identified four broad shared objectives that can help focus our efforts in Washington, D.C. They include: creating 25 million new jobs over the next ten years, securing Social Security and Medicare for another 75 years, balancing the federal budget by 2030, and making America energy secure by 2024.

No Labels' National Strategic Agenda is an effort to get both politicians and citizens to understand that we share far more common ground than the divisive campaigning that we are exposed to would imply. Their goal of de-emphasizing partisanship in favor of genuine problem solving is a critical element of making fundamental change in Washington.

No Labels introduced their National Strategic Agenda into presidential politics in 2016, holding a very successful and well-attended convention in New Hampshire, which over 1,500 people from 37 states attended. Importantly, eight presidential candidates participated. For more information on No Labels, visit www.nolabels.org.

Independent Voter Project

The Independent Voter Project was instrumental in getting the top two primary reform instituted in California. The top two primary replaces party primaries with one primary where all candidates compete. The result has been the election of more moderate legislators, as the ability of extremists to control the primary process has been reduced. The Independent Voter Project is continuing its work to expand choices for voters and reduce the impact of political parties on our electoral process. It was deeply involved in a New Jersey lawsuit attacking the closed primary system and it has continued to support the litigation as it makes its way through the appeals process.

Currently, the Independent Voter Project is working to build infrastructure to support Independent candidates and various political reform movements. In that regard, I could have also included them among those organizations looking to create new sources of supply from which voters can choose. IVP's objective is to build the data infrastructure and lists of like-minded Americans, so that they can support Independent candidates the way Democratic and Republican Party organizations support their candidates. While they will have more hurdles to overcome than the major parties because campaign finance laws impede them from supporting Independent candidates to the same degree that major parties can, the Independent Voter Project believes that identifying, organizing, and mobilizing Independent voters and disaffected Rs and Ds is a prerequisite to the long-term success of Independent candidates. You can read more about the Independent Voter Project at www.independentvoterproject.org.

Govern for California

David Crane, a Northern California financial services company executive, has created an organization called Govern for California (www. governforcalifornia.org) to elect financially literate and courageous legislators to California's assembly and senate. They don't impose any requirements on them other than an ability to read financial statements and a willingness to remain independent of the special interests that dominate California politics. As they describe on their website:

> Upon closer inspection, Californians would learn that the missing ingredient is courage. In the case of Democrats, courage means the willingness to buck narrow special interests seeking ever-greater shares of government spending at the expense of programs, taxpayers and private-sector job growth.
>
> In the case of Republicans, courage means the willingness to buck no-tax groups who, even when presented with all the reforms they seek, refuse to acknowledge that sometimes more revenue for the government can produce better outcomes. And in the case of all legislators, courage means an unshakeable dedication to honest budgets, truthful accounting, open government and governing for the people rather than for personal gain or narrow interests.

Govern for California is a great example of citizens coming together to elect common sense candidates free from the influences of special interests. Given the top two primary system in California, Govern for California's candidates to date have all represented one of the major parties.

Open Primaries

Open Primaries is an organization that has been working to ensure access to the primary election process for all voters. Its fundamental belief is that no American should have to join a political party to vote in the primary election process. As we described in Chapter 5, in the vast majority of Congressional elections, the primary is the most important part of the electoral process—and to deny voters the right to participate at that stage of the process is akin to disenfranchisement. Open Primaries is fighting to rectify that injustice. The success of their approach should loosen the control of extremists on the primary election process, leading to more moderate elected officials. You can read more about them at: www.openprimaries.org.

CREATING PATHWAYS FOR NEW CANDIDATES

Level the Playing Field

Level the Playing Field (the successor to Americans Elect) is working to promote reforms that allow for greater competition and choice in elections. Today there is almost no way to mount a serious bid for the U.S. presidency outside of the two major parties. According to Level the Playing Field's chairman, Peter Ackerman, "this state of affairs is the product of collusion between operatives from the Democrat and Republican parties who—through the design of hidden rules—jealously guard the perpetuation of their duopoly."

One of these hidden rules involves access to the fall presidential debates. A person running as a Democrat or Republican knows that if they win the nomination they will be guaranteed a place in the fall Presidential debates. The Commission on Presidential Debates (CPD)—dominated by Republican and Democratic loyalists—requires every other candidate to meet a 15% polling hurdle in a three-way race decided just 7 weeks before the election. While 15% may seem reasonable the poll taken so late in the election cycle creates an insurmountable "Catch-22," and so that is why you haven't seen a third candidate on the debate stage since 1992.

I watched first-hand as Jesse Ventura's participation in the gubernatorial debates in Minnesota propelled him from 7 percent in the polls to victory in November. Ross Perot more than doubled his support in 1992 because of participation in the debates and had a fundamental impact on our policy for much of the ensuing decade. Their website www.changetherule.org contains a compelling argument for why the existing rules impede genuine competition.

Level the Playing Field has filed a federal lawsuit to change this rule and there is significant external support. The FEC received well over 1,200 comments in support of changing the debate rules for Independents and third party candidates. In fact, the only comment received by the FEC in support of the current rule was from the CPD itself. The good news is that this anti-competitive debate rule doesn't have the force of law and with good will and imagination can be either modified or eliminated.

This challenge to the rules will continue to play out in the courts, though it likely won't advance quickly enough to affect the 2016 election. One possible solution for 2020 is to let everyone who is not the Democratic or Republican nominee compete for a third spot in the debates based on a "Primary for Independents."

The Committee for Ranked Choice Voting

Ranked choice voting is an innovation that changes the way voters cast their ballots. The way it works is simple. Voters rank their candidates from favorite to least favorite. On Election Night, all the votes are counted and if one candidate receives over 50% of the vote in the first round, they win. But if no candidate receives 50% of the votes in the first round, the candidate with the fewest first choice rankings is eliminated. If your favorite candidate is eliminated, your vote is instantly counted for your second choice. This repeats until one candidate reaches a majority (the candidate who is most broadly supported) and wins.

In an election with more than two candidates, ranked choice voting eliminates the concerns from voters that they are wasting their vote or otherwise may be spoiling the race for one candidate or another. The Committee for Ranked Choice Voting is currently working to pass a statewide citizen's initiative in Maine and for good reason. Races with more than two candidates are common in Maine and often result in winners elected by fewer than half of voters. In 9 of the last 11 races for governor, candidates were elected by fewer than half of voters. In 5 of those races, candidates were elected by fewer than 40% of voters. None of Maine's governors have been elected to their first term by a majority of voters in the last 40 years.

The nonpartisan League of Women Voters of Maine has endorsed ranked choice voting as the most cost-effective solution to restore majority rule and to give voters more power. To learn more, you can visit the campaign's website at: http://www.rcvmaine.com/.

Action for America / New American Congress

Action for America is working to change the relationship between millennials and politics. They are trying to empower a next generation of leaders who are passionate about fixing our broken political system. As they state on their website www.actionforamerica.org,

> We are a community for those who believe effectiveness and pragmatism are the credentials for leadership, not party loyalty. We are the home and voice for the tens of millions of disaffected, independent, young, and moderate voters across the country who want to enact real change in our politics together.

In November of 2016, they plan to convene a New American Congress made up of one visionary leader from each Congressional District. Their objective is to identify 10 goals for our country to accomplish by the year 2026, when our nation is celebrating its 250th birthday.

PROMOTING CENTRIST POLICIES

The Centrist Project

The Centrist Project started out working to advance centrist policies based largely on the agenda laid out by Charlie Wheelan in *The Centrist Manifesto*. In that regard, their goals were very similar to No Labels' National Strategic Agenda. In 2014, they endorsed a slate of five candidates for the United States Senate who all advocated for a rational, problem solving agenda. The candidates they supported included a Democrat, a Republican, and three Independents (including me).

The Centrist Project is currently working to reinvigorate the Senate Fulcrum strategy. The Centrist Project's goal is to have credible Independent candidates running in a number of Senate races in every subsequent cycle with the eventual hope of preventing both parties from having a majority in the U.S. Senate. I believe if they achieve that goal it will have a powerful impact on how the chamber is run and ultimately the behavior of all elected officials in Washington.

This initiative requires the group to recruit candidates with a track record of success, assemble competent campaign staff and consultants, and raise money to support a slate of candidates. While most of the candidates the Centrist Project has supported are fiscally responsible and socially tolerant, it hasn't asked them to adhere to any specific litmus tests. The Centrist Project believes that if it recruits competent candidates with proven success in the private sector—men and women who want to be true public servants and who are not beholden to either political party or the special interests that bankroll them—it will get to the right answers from a policy perspective. Their website is www.centrist-project.org. While the Centrist Project's goals may seem overly hopeful, the same objectives had indeed worked at the state level.

Committee For a Responsible Federal Budget

The Committee For a Responsible Federal Budget was formed 35 years ago to educate the public about our country's financial situation. It is a bi-partisan organization made up of some of our nation's leading budget experts. Recently, they've started to focus on the issue of political reform as a catalyst for good governance and fiscal responsibility. They have brought together key participants in the political reform movement to share best practices and develop a more cohesive strategy for improving political incentives to ensure a more sustainable financial future for America. You can read more about them at www.crfb.org.

ENDNOTES

Opening Argument

1. Rep. Mike Simpson, speaking in the House Appropriations Committee, May 12, 2015.
2. Thomas B. Edsall, "The Value of Political Corruption," *The New York Times*, August 5, 2014.
3. "Millennials in Adulthood: Detached from Institutions, Networked with Friends," *Pew Research Center*, March 7, 2014.
4. Emily Elkins, "Millennials Favor Private Accounts for Social Security Even if Benefits Cuts to Current Seniors Required," *Reason* magazine, July 17, 2014.
5. H. Ross Perot, "Man Power," *Esquire* magazine, June 1988.
6. Robert Reich, January 2009 email to Michael Maiello, editor of *Forbes* magazine's Intelligence Investing section.
7. Josh Kraushaar, "The Most Divided Congress Ever, At Least Until Next Year," *National Journal*, February 6, 2014.
8. Gerald F. Seib, "From 1889 to 2014, Political Parallels Abound," *The Wall Street Journal*, July 7, 2014.
9. Gallup Poll, "Congress and the Public," June 2015.
10. Scott Canon, "John McCain Campaigns with Pat Roberts, Says Greg Orman Looks Like a Democrat," *The Kansas City Star*, September 24, 2014.
11. Philip Rucker, "In Kansas Rescue Mission, Palin Gives Roberts Tea Party Approval," *The Washington Post*, September 25, 2014.
12. George Will, "Staking the Senate on Kansas?" *The Washington Post*, September 24, 2014.
13. Jeffrey M. Jones, "In U.S., New Record 43% Are Political Independents," *Gallup Poll*, January 7, 2015.

Chapter One

1. Ronald Reagan, "Remarks and a Question-and-Answer Session with Members of the American Legion Boys Nation," *Public Papers of the Presidents*, July 25, 1986.
2. Alonzo L. Hamby, "1948 Democratic Convention: The South Secedes Again," *Smithsonian Magazine*, August 2008.
3. Robert Rector, "Marriage: America's Greatest Weapon Against Child Poverty," *Heritage Research Reports*, September 5, 2012.

Chapter Two

1. Sonni Efron and J. Michael Kennedy, "Angry Voters See Perot Riding in Like Cavalry: Campaign: Texas billionaire strikes a chord with petitioners weary of the usual political roundup," *Los Angeles Times*, March 22, 1992.
2. "The Daily History of the Debt Results," U.S. Treasury, http://www .treasurydirect.gov/NP/debt/current.
3. Philip Klein, "Learning from the Bush Legacy," *American Spectator*, November 2008.
4. Lloyd Grove, "Olympia Snowe on Her New Book, Overcoming Partisanship & More," *Daily Beast*, May 15, 2013.

Chapter Three

1. Jennie Chinn, *The Kansas Journey*, p. 163. (Gibbs Smith, 1999)
2. Andy Marso, "Independent Candidate Launches Bid for Roberts Seat," *Topeka Capital-Journal*, June 4, 2014.
3. Fred Mann, "Olathe Businessman Greg Orman Wants to Run for Pat Roberts' U.S. Senate Seat," *The Wichita Eagle*, June 5, 2014.
4. Kathy Ostrowski, "All Three Kansas Abortion Clinics Support Greg Orman Over Pro-Life Pat Roberts," *Life News*, October 31, 2014.
5. Andy Marso, "Dems Lure Moderates after GOP Primary Purge," *Topeka Capital-Journal*, August 8, 2012.
6. Annie Gowen, "In Kansas, Gov. Brownback Puts Tea Party Tenets into Action with Sharp Cuts," *The Washington Post*, December 21, 2011.
7. David A. Lieb, "In Many Statehouses, GOP Confronts Dissension," *Associated Press*, June 15, 2012.
8. Scott Rothschild, "Democrats Ask Moderate Republicans, Independents to Join Their Cause," *Lawrence Journal-World*, August 8, 2012.
9. Mark Peters, "Some in Kansas GOP Break with Gov. Brownback, Endorse Democratic Opponent," *The Wall Street Journal*, July 15, 2014.
10. Katrina Trinko, "Obama's Cousin to Primary Kansas Senator Pat Roberts," *National Review*, October 8, 2013.
11. Adam Wollner, "Obama Has a Tea Party Cousin—and He's Running for Senate," *National Public Radio*, October 9, 2013.
12. Katrina Trinko, "Another Tea-Party Senator?" *National Review*, October 9, 2013.
13. Scott Rothschild, "Americans for Prosperity Postcard Targets Group of GOP Senate Incumbents Who Claim AFP Assertion is False," *Lawrence Journal-World*, July 18, 2012.
14. Bryan Lowry, "Democrat Chad Taylor Drops Out of U.S. Senate Race," *The Wichita Eagle*, September 3, 2014.
15. Janet Hook and Mark Peters, "Kansas Democrat Withdraws from U.S. Senate Race, Upending Contest," *The Wall Street Journal*, September 3, 2014.

16. Kristina Peterson, "Chris LaCivita, the GOP's Hard-Charging 'Commando' Operative," *The Wall Street Journal*, October 21, 2014.
17. Roxana Hegeman and John Hanna, "'Alter-Ego' Replaced as Roberts' Campaign Manager," *Associated Press*, September 5, 2014.
18. Philip Rucker and Robert Costa, "Battle for the Senate: How the GOP Did It," *The Washington Post,* November 5, 2014.
19. Ibid.
20. Ibid.
21. Mary Clarkin, "Senate Debate Focuses on Reid," *Hutchinson News*, September 6, 2014.
22. Dave Helling, "Pat Roberts, Greg Orman Duel in Debate for U.S. Senate Seat from Kansas," *Kansas City Star*, October 8, 2014.
23. Philip Rucker and Robert Costa, "Battle for the Senate: How the GOP Did It," *The Washington Post*, November 5, 2014.
24. Dion Lefler, "Asked to Say Something Nice, Greg Orman and Pat Roberts Respond in Wichita Debate," *The Wichita Eagle*, October 16, 2014.
25. Ibid.
26. David Weigel, "Clownghazi and the Birth of the Transitive Property Gaffe," *Bloomberg News*, November 3, 2014.
27. Mark Liebovich, "The Socialist Senator," *The New York Times*, January 21, 2007.
28. Jonathan Topaz and Burgess Everett, "Biden: Orman Will Join with Dems," *Politico*, November 4, 2014.
29. Lindsay Wise, "If Greg Orman Should Win in Kansas, He Would Hold Leverage in Washington," *The Kansas City Star*, September 23, 2014.
30. Kelly O'Donnell and Frank Thorp V, "'Greg's Never Spoken to the VP in his Life': Team Orman Hits Back at Biden," November 4, 2014.

Chapter Four

1. Sir Winston Churchill, *The Grand Alliance*, p. 539 (Houghton Mifflin, 1950)
2. Frank Bruni, "Lost in America," *The New York Times*, August 25, 2014.
3. Patrick O'Connor, "Poll Finds Widespread Anxiety," *The Wall Street Journal*, August 5, 2014.
4. Andrew Ross Sorkin and Megan Thee-Brenan, "Many Feel the American Dream is Out of Reach, Poll Shows," *The New York Times*, December 10, 2014.
5. Peter Nicholas, "Donald Trump Walks Back His Praise of Hillary Clinton," *The Wall Street Journal*, July 29, 2015.
6. Fredreka Schouten, "Billionaires Crowd Out Bundlers in White House Race," *USA Today*, August 17, 2015.
7. Ale Eisele, "New Hampshire 1968: A Primary that Really Mattered," *Huffington Post*, May 25, 2011.

8. Tim Risen, "Protest Candidate Larry Lessig Wants to Do One Thing as President," *U.S. News & World Report*, August 13, 2015.

9. Eric Bradner, "Larry Lessig Drops 2016 Presidential Bid," *CNN*, November 2, 2015.

10. Representatives Sam Johnson and Xavier Becerra, letter to the U.S. Government Accountability Office, October 29, 2015.

11. GAO, "Report to the Subcommittee on Social Security, House Ways and Means Committee," October 2015.

12. Bruce Bartlett, "Medicare Part D: Republican Budget-Busting," *The New York Times*, November 19, 2013.

13. Alexander Bolton, "Lobbyists Try to Save Roberts," *The Hill*, October 7, 2014.

14. Ibid.

15. Bob Woodward, "Obama's Sequester Deal-Changer," *The Washington Post*, February 22, 2013.

Chapter Five

1. Franco Ordonez, "At World War II Memorial, Veterans Pay Tribute, But Question Closure," McClatchy New Service, October 2, 2013.

2. Letter from John Adams to Jonathan Jackson, October 2, 1780.

3. James Madison, Federalist Number 10, November 22, 1787.

4. Bill Bishop, *The Big Sort*, p. 6. (Houghton Mifflin, 2008)

5. Deborah Solomon, "Goodbye (Again) Norma Jean," *The New York Times*, September 19, 2004.

6. Bill Bishop, *The Big Sort*, p. 40.

7. Ibid. p. 298

8. Michelle Jamrisko, "Surging Childcare Costs are Hurting More and More Americans," *Bloomberg News*, August 12, 2015.

9. Dan Munro, "Annual Healthcare Costs for Family of Four Now at $24,671," *Forbes*, May 19, 2015.

10. Erik Eckholm, "A.C.L.U. in $50 Million Push to Reduce Jail Sentences," *The New York Times*, November 6, 2014.

11. Joseph J. Thorndike, "Can Debt Ceiling Debates Become Useful? History Says Maybe," *The Huffington Post*, August, 28, 2013.

12. Angie Drobnic Holan, "Obama Regrets 2006 Vote Against Raising the Debt Limit," *Politifact*, April 29, 2011.

13. Mike Memoli, "Obama Now Regrets 'Political' Debt Limit Vote," *Los Angeles Times*, April 14, 2011.

14. Jonathan Weisman, "In Congress, Gridlock and Harsh Consequences," *The New York Times*, July 7, 2013.

15. Carl M. Cannon, "Ten Years Later: Our Moment of Unity and Civility Was Toppled, Too," *RealClearPolitics*, September 11, 2011.

16. Mark DeMoss, "Why This Fear of a Civility Pledge?" *Politico*, November 25, 2010.

Chapter Six

1. Alan Fram, "U.S. Senate Changes Rule That Has Allowed GOP to Block Judicial Appointments," *Associated Press*, November 21, 2013.
2. Louis Jacobson, "Rep. Todd Says Social Security, Medicare, Medicaid Make Up 70 Percent of Federal Budget," *Politifact*, July 2, 2013.
3. Ace of Spades, "As Expected, John Boehner Sells Out the Conservatives in Yet Another Performance of 'Failure Theater,'" March 3, 2015.
4. Ted Cruz, "The Republican Party's Surrender Politics," *Politico*, September 23, 2015.
5. Ibid.
6. Olympia J. Snowe, *Tributes*, "Farewell to the Senate," Government Printing Office, December 13, 2012, p. ix
7. Robert D. Novak, "Dorgan's Poison Pill," *The Washington Post*, June 14, 2007.
8. Ted Cruz, "The Republican Party's Surrender Politics," *Politico*, September 23, 2015.
9. David M. Herszenhorn and Jonathan Martin, "John Boehner's Move Deepens a Republican Chasm," *The New York Times*, September 27, 2015.
10. Rebecca Kaplan, "John Boehner Warns of 'False Prophets' in D.C.," *CBS News*, September 27, 2015.
11. Philip Bump, "Democrats Who Voted for the CRomnibus Have Received Twice as Much Money From the Finance Industry as the 'No' Voters," *The Washington Post*, December 12, 2014.
12. Lou Cannon, *Ronnie & Jesse: A Political Odyssey*, p. 99. (Doubleday, 1969)

Chapter Seven

1. Mark S. Mellman, "Relationship of Parties and Policies," *The Hill*, March 13, 2013.
2. George Washington, letter to Arthur Fenner, June 4, 1790.
3. John Adams's letter to Jonathan Jackson, October 2, 1780.
4. James Madison, Federalist Number 10, November 22, 1787.
5. Aliyah Shahid, "Mitt Romney to Students Who Want to Start Their Own Business: Borrow Money From Your Parents," *New York Daily News*, April 28, 2012.
6. Krista Tippett interview with Jonathan Haidt, *On Being*, NPR, June 12, 2014.
7. Dan Kahan, "Why We Are Poles Apart on Climate Change," *Nature*, August 15, 2012.
8. Kevin Goebbert et al. "Weather, Climate, and Worldviews: The Sources and Consequences of Public Perceptions in Local Weather Patterns," *Journal of the American Meteorological Society*, April 2012.

9. Dan Kahan, "Why We Are Poles Apart on Climate Change," *Nature*, August 15, 2012.

10. Caroline May, "DeMint: Just Say No to Compromise," *Daily Caller*, February 1, 2012.

11. Daniel Yacavone, "A Covenant with Death and an Agreement with Hell," Massachusetts Historical Society newsletter, July 2005.

12. Carl M. Cannon interview with John Boehner, January 2011.

13. Jim DeMint, "Welcome, Senate Conservatives," *The Wall Street Journal*, November 3, 2010.

14. Daniel Patrick Moynihan, "Of 'Sons' and Their 'Grandsons,'" *The New York Times*, July 7, 1980.

15. Tamara Keith, "Heritage Foundation Rallies Support to Defund ObamaCare," *National Public Radio*, August 20, 2013.

16. Michael Dimock et al., "Political Polarization in the American Public," Pew Research Center, June 12, 2014.

17. Morris Fiorina, "Americans Have Not Become More Politically Polarized," *The Washington Post*, June 23, 2014.

18. James MacGregor Burns, *Roosevelt, the Soldier of Freedom: 1940-1945*, p. 511.

19. David Shribman, "The Culprits Behind Today's Polarized Politics," *Pittsburgh Post-Gazette*, November 20, 2011.

20. Lydia Saad, "Conservatives Remain the Largest Ideological Group in the U.S.," *Gallup Poll*, January 12, 2012.

21. Ezra Klein and Alvin Chang, "Political Identity is Fair Game for Hatred: How Republicans and Democrats Discriminate," *Vox*, December 7, 2015.

22 "Partisan Polarization Surges in Bush, Obama Years," *Pew Research Center*, June 4, 2012.

23. Pietro S. Nivola and David W. Brady, *Red and Blue Nation: Characteristics and Causes of America's Polarized Politics*, pgs. 168-169 (Brookings Institution Press, 2006).

24. Alan I. Abramowitz and Steven Webster, "The Only Thing We Have to Fear is the Other Party," *Center for Politics*, June 4, 2015.

25. Ezra Klein, "2 Political Scientists Have Found the Secret to Partisanship, and It's Deeply Depressing," *Vox*, October 27, 2015.

Chapter Eight

1. William Safire, "On Language: Government By Crony," *The New York Times*, February 1, 1988.

2. Lee Drutman and Alexander Furnas, "K Street Pays Top Dollar for Revolving Door Talent," Sunlight Foundation report, January 21, 2014.

3. Wendell Potter, "Big Pharma's Stranglehold on Washington," *Center for Public Integrity*, February 11, 2013.

4. Jason Meisner, "Ex-Speaker Hastert Charged with Lying to FBI About Hush Money Withdrawals," *Chicago Tribune*, May 28, 2015.

5. Katherine Skiba and Angela Caputo, "Dennis Hastert Had Multiple Sources of Income After Leaving Congress," *Chicago Tribune*, June 4, 2015.

6. Ana Marie Cox, "How 'Public Servant' Hastert Got His Riches," *The Daily Beast*, May 30, 2015.

7. Mike Dorning, James Kimberly, and Ray Gibson, "Hastert's Wealth is Grounded in Land," *Chicago Tribune*, July 6, 2006.

8. Tarini Parti, "How Dennis Hastert Made his Millions," *Politico*, May 29, 2015.

9. Wendell Potter and Nick Penniman, "Is America a Nation 'On the Take'? *NMPolitics*, March 11, 2016.

10. Joel Schoffstall, "427 Members of Congress Moved To Lobbying or Similar Work," *Free Beacon*, September 22, 2015.

11. Interview with Dennis Kucinich by Carl M. Cannon

12. Otis Brawley, "How Doctors Do Harm," *CNN*, January 30, 2012.

13. Shannon Brownlee, "Neutered," *Washington Monthly*, October 2007.

14. MJ Lee, "Why Hillary Clinton is Going After Hedge Funds," *CNN Politics*, April 16, 2015.

15. Andrew Ross Sorkin, "The Surprising Target of Jeb Bush's Tax Plan: Private Equity," *The New York Times*, September 14, 2015.

16. Jonathan Chew, "Here's What Donald Trump Had to Say About Hedge Fund Managers," *Fortune*, August 24, 2015.

17. Robert Reich, "Wall Street's Democrats," *Guernica*, December 9, 2014.

18. Lynn Forester de Rothschild, "A Costly and Unjust Perk for Financiers," *The New York Times*, February 24, 2013.

19. Daniel Gross, "The Golden Ass," *Slate*, June 19, 2007.

20. Stephen Schwarzman, "View from the Top," *Financial Times*, December 20, 2006.

21. Jessica Holzer, "Lott Expects to Whip GOP Against Blackstone Bill," *The Hill*, October 3, 2007.

22. Ibid.

23. Heidi Przybyla, "Schumer Wall Street Backers Target in Tax Fairness Debate," *Bloomberg News*, February 27, 2012.

24. Robert Reich, "Wall Street's Democrats," *Guernica*, December 9, 2014.

25. Alexander Bolton, "Lobbyists Try to Save Roberts," *The Hill*, October 7, 2014.

26. Steve Benen, "Meet the Tarpsters," *Washington Monthly*, October 6, 2010.

27. Zach Carter, "Crony Capitalism: Wall Street's Favorite Politicians," *The Huffington Post*, September 28, 2010.

28. Carrie Levine, "U.S. Chamber Doubling Down on Political Juggernaut," *Center for Public Integrity*, March 30, 2015.

29 "The Moral Crisis of Crony Capitalism," an interview with Peter Schweizer, *Religion & Liberty*, winter 2013.

30. Andrew Dugan, "Majority of Americans See Congress as Out of Touch, Corrupt," *Gallup Poll*, September 28, 2015.

31. John Cassidy, "Is America an Oligarchy?" *The New Yorker*, April 18, 2014.

32. Karen DeMasters, "Health-Care Costs Could Double in 20 Years, Study Says," *Financial Advisor*, December 9, 2015.

33. Jacob Goldstein, "$1 Trillion in Tax Loopholes," *National Public Radio*, April 3, 2012.

34. James McCartney and Molly Sinclair McCartney, *America's War Machine: Vested Interests, Endless Conflicts*, p. 45 (St. Martin's Press 2015)

35. Pete Yost and David Scott (Associated Press) "Edwards Ally Explains Payments to Mistress," *Los Angeles Times*, August 15, 2008.

36. Barry Gewen, "It Wasn't Such a Wonderful Life," *The New York Times*, May 3, 1992.

Chapter Nine

1. Jackson Connor, "TV News Does a Complete 180 on Ebola Coverage After Midterms," *The Huffington Post*, November 19, 2014.

2. Calvin Coolidge, "Address to the American Society of Newspapers Editors, Washington, D.C.," Public Papers of the Presidents, January 17, 1925.

3. Thomas Jefferson, "Establishing a Federal Republic," Online exhibit at the Library of Congress, https://www.loc.gov/exhibits/jefferson/jefffed.html

4. Julian Hattem, "Warren Turned Down Invite to See the Pope," *The Hill*, August 20, 2015.

5. Kristina Wong, "McCain Denies Trying to Freeze Out Cruz," *The Hill*, July 29, 2015.

6. Bill Bradley, "Did Sarah Palin Get Breast Implants," *Vanity Fair*, June 10, 2010.

7. Molly Ball, "The Mystery Candidate Shaking Up Kansas Politics," *The Atlantic*, September 27, 2014.

8. Carrie Dann and Kelly O'Donnell, "Orman: I Could 'Absolutely' Switch Parties After Picking Senate Side," *NBCNews.com*, October 6, 2014.

9. George F. Will, "Staking the Senate on Kansas," *The Washington Post*, September 24, 2014.

10. Jeremy W. Peters and Daniel Victor, "Megyn Kelly Says She Won't Be Cowed By Donald Trump," *The New York Times*, August 10, 2015.

11. Mark Binelli, "The Great Kansas Tea Party Disaster," *Rolling Stone*, October 23, 2014.

12. Bryan Lowry, "Greg Orman Once Sued Actress Debbie Reynolds Over $1 Million Loan to Museum," *Wichita Eagle*, September 9, 2014.

13. Michael Patrick Leahy, "Federal Judges Berates Kansas Senate Candidate Greg Orman in Boxing Equipment Lawsuit," *Breitbart News*, September 10, 2014

14. Jackie Calmes, "'They Don't Give a Damn About Governing': Conservative Media's Influence on the Republican Party," Shorenstein Center on Media, Politics, and Public Policy, July 27, 2015.
15. Jackie Calmes, "As the G.O.P. Base Clamors for Confrontation, Candidates Oblige," *The New York Times*, July 27, 2015.
16. Tom Fiedler and Carl M. Cannon, "Biden's Demise Leaves Egg on the Face of Image-Maker," *Philadelphia Inquirer*, September 27, 1987.
17. John Fund, "Bravo to Fox's Shepard Smith for Combatting Ebola Panic," *National Review*, October 16, 2014.

Chapter Ten

1. "America's Beer Duopoly," *The New York Times*, unsigned editorial, February 9, 2013.
2. Sasha Eisenberg, "Abolish the Secret Ballot," *The Atlantic Monthly*, July/August 2012.
3. Ibid.
4. Lawrence Goodwyn, *The Populist Moment*, p. 285
5. R. Alton Lee, "Anti-Fusion Laws in Populist Kansas," *Heritage of the Great Plains*, winter 2014.
6. Fair Vote for a More Perfect Union, http://www.fairvote.org/primaries#open_and_closed_primaries
7. Matt Zencey, "On Tuesday are You Paying for An Election You Can't Vote In?" *Patriot News*, May 15, 2014.
8. Chad Peace, "Political Parties Your Fundamental Right to Vote," *San Diego City Beat*, July 1, 2015.
9. Jack Nelson, "Bipartisan Group to Sponsor L.A. Debate After League of Women Voters Drops Out," *Los Angeles Times,* October 4, 1988.
10. Michael O'Connell, "Presidential Debate Hits 32-Year-Old Record in Gross Ratings," *The Hollywood Reporter*, October 4, 2012.
11. Brad Cooper, "Kansas' Secretary of State GOP Primary Race Heated Between Incumbent Kris Kobach, Scott Morgan," *The Kansas City Star*, July 27, 2014.
12. Dion Lefler, "Kris Kobach Proposes Bills to Return Straight-Ticket Voting, Change Election-Withdraw Procedure," *The Kansas City Star*, January 14, 2015.

Chapter Eleven

1. Morris P. Fiorina, "America's Missing Moderates: Hiding in Plain Sight," *The American Interest*, February 12, 2013.
2. Pew Research Center, "Partisan Polarization Surges in Bush, Obama Years," June 4, 2012.
3. Sabrina Tavernise, "Colorado's Effort Against Teenage Pregnancies Is a Startling Success," *The New York Times*, July 5, 2015.

4. Chris Edwards and Neal McCluskey, "Higher Education Subsidies," *Downsizing the Federal Government*, November 1, 2015.
5. Harold A. Pollack, "Saving SSDI," *The Atlantic Monthly*, August 31, 2015.
6. Rebecca Hiscott, "CEO Pay Has Increased by 937 Percent Since 1978," *The Huffington Post*, June 12, 2014.
7. Jason Fichtner and Jacob Feldman, "The High Cost of a Terrible Tax Code," *U.S. News & World Report*, May 28, 2013.
8. Adam Nagourney, "Bloomberg Quits G.O.P., Stirring Talk about '08 Race," *The New York Times*, June 19, 2007.

Chapter Twelve

1. Nicholas Carlson, "Google Co-Founder Sergey Brin is 'Dreading' Today's Elections," *Business Insider*, November 6, 2012.
2. Jonathan Haidt, *The Righteous Mind: Why Good People Are Divided By Politics and Religion*, p. 365 (Vintage Books, 2013)
3. Ronald Reagan, "Farewell Address to the Nation," Public Papers of the Presidents, January 11, 1989.
4. Theodore Roosevelt, "The Key to Success in Life," p. 5 (Federated Publishing Co., 1916).
5. Theodore Roosevelt, *The Roosevelt Policy*, (Current Literature Publishing Company, 1908)
6. Office of the Mayor, "Statement by Mayor Bloomberg on Party Affiliation," June 19, 2007.
7. Adam Nagourney, "Bloomberg Quits G.O.P., Stirring Talk about '08 Race," *The New York Times*, June 19, 2007.

Closing Argument

1. Roy P. Basler, editor, *Collected Works of Abraham Lincoln*, Volume 4, p 164. (Rutgers University Press, 1953)
2. Theodore Roosevelt, "Citizenship in a Republic," speech at the Sorbonne, in Paris, France, April 23, 1910.
3. Richard Frothingham, *Life and Times of Joseph Warren*, p. 435 (Little Brown, 1865)

ABOUT THE AUTHOR

GREG ORMAN IS A Kansas businessman who ran as an Independent candidate for the United States Senate in 2014. Orman's historic run for the Senate against a three-term Republican incumbent brought an unprecedented amount of attention not only to Kansas, but to the modern election process itself. Referred to by NBC News as "The Most Interesting Man in Politics," Orman had the Washington establishment on the run during his insurgent Independent campaign. The Republican Party was required to mobilize dozens of national political figures and spend a record amount of money to preserve a seat that had been held by a Republican since 1919.

Orman currently runs Exemplar Holdings, LLC, a private company that invests in and actively manages a portfolio of businesses throughout the United States. Orman has built numerous businesses over his twenty-five-year career in industries including energy-efficient technology, recycling, construction, sporting goods, business services, medical devices, specialty manufacturing, and real estate.

Orman lives in Olathe, Kansas with his wife, Sybil, and their daughter, Imogen.